KT-423-747

Visual
Methodologies

An Introduction to the
Interpretation of Visual Materials

Gillian Rose

SAGE Publications
London • Thousand Oaks • New Delhi

LRS: Somerset College

Dewey no.	Subject headings
302 .222 ROS	Visual communication Art Society
Location A—D	Abstract
3 Week 1 Week LUO Reference	Order details PO 20226 M1 20·05 63

© Gillian Rose 2001

First published 2001. Reprinted 2001, 2002, (twice). 2003, (twice).

Apart from any fair dealing for the purposes of research or private study, or criticism or review, as permitted under the Copyright, Designs and Patents Act 1988, this publication may be reproduced, stored or transmitted in any form, or by any means, only with the prior permission in writing of the publishers or, in the case of reprographic reproduction, in accordance with the terms of licences issued by the Copyright Licensing Agency. Inquiries concerning reproduction outside those terms should be sent to the publishers.

SAGE Publications Ltd
6 Bonhill Street
London EC2A 4PU

SAGE Publications Inc
2455 Teller Road
Thousand Oaks, California 91320

SAGE Publications India Pvt Ltd
32, M-Block Market
Greater Kailash – I
New Delhi 110 048

British Library Cataloguing in Publication data

A catalogue record for this book is available from the British Library

ISBN 0 7619 6664 1
ISBN 0 7619 6665 X (pbk)

Library of Congress catalog record available

Typeset by Mayhew Typesetting, Rhayader, Powys
Printed in Great Britain by The Cromwell Press Ltd, Trowbridge, Wiltshire

contents

list of figures

acknowledgements

This book is based on a course I taught at the
Graduate School for the Social Sciences, Edinburgh
University, in 1996, 1997 and 1998. Most thanks
must go to the students who took that course, for
their enthusiastic engagement with the images
I showed them and for their healthy scepticism
towards methods textbooks. The Human Geography
Reading Group at Edinburgh gave the first chapter a
thorough and very helpful going-over at an early
stage; Mike Crang and Don Slater were constructive
readers for Sage. Robert Rojek has been a very
supportive editor. And there were useful and, more
importantly, pleasurable conversations about
matters visual and interpretive with Sue Smith,
Charlie Withers and, especially, Mark Dorrian.
My thanks to them too. Finally, many thanks to
Anneliese Emmans for compiling the index.

The author and publishers wish to thank the following for permission to use copyright material:

Figure

1.2   *Ways of Seeing* by John Berger, 1972, Penguin Books. Reproduced by permission of Penguin Books.

1.3   Robert Doisneau, 'An Oblique Look', Rapho Paris.

2.1   *Self Portrait*, 1629 by Rembrandt Harmensz van Rijn (1606–69), Isabella Stewart Gardner Museum, Boston, Massachusetts, USA/Bridgeman Art Library. Oil on panel.

2.2   *Self Portrait*, 1657 by Rembrandt van Rijn (1606–69), The Collection of the Duke of Sutherland, on loan to the National Gallery of Scotland.

2.6   *Little Girl in a Blue Armchair*, 1878, Mary Cassat, Collection of Mr and Mrs Paul Mellon © 2000 Board of Trustees, National Gallery of Art, Washington. Oil on canvas.

3.1   *Adioukrou Woman* © Carol Beckwith/Agela Fisher.

3.2   *Reading National Geographic* by C.A. Lutz and J.L. Collins, 1993. By permission of Chicago University Press.

3.3   *Reading National Geographic* by C.A. Lutz and J.L Collins, 1993. By permission of Chicago University Press.

4.1, 4.6 *Decoding Advertisements: Ideology and Meaning in Advertising* by
4.7   Judith Williamson, 1978. Reproduced with permission of Marion Boyars.

4.5   *Reading Ads Socially* by R. Goldman, 1992. Reproduced by permission of Routledge.

5.2   Copyright © 2001 by Universal Studios, Inc. Courtesy of Universal Studios Publishing Rights. All Rights Reserved. The Stewart Family LLC and the Princess Grace Foundation, USA.

5.3   Courtesy of ABC Distributions and Joan Fontaine.

5.4   Copyright © 2001 by Universal Studios, Inc. Courtesy of Universal Studios Publishing Rights. All Rights Reserved. The Stewart Family LLC.

5.5   *The Ambassadors*, 1533, Hans Holbein the younger, Jean de Dinteville and Georges de Selve © National Gallery London.

6.1   Jan van Eyck, *The Arnolfini Wedding Portrait* © National Gallery, London.

6.2   Gustave Doré, illustration to *The Bridge of Sighs*. By permission of the British Library.

6.3, 6.4 W. Gray, *Lost* and *Found*. By permission of the British Library.

6.5   Hablot K. Browne, *The River*. By permission of the British Library.

6.6   *Found Drowned* (oil on canvas) by George Frederick Watts (1817–1904) Trustees of the Watts Gallery, Compton, Surrey, UK/Bridgeman Art Library.

6.7   *Charles Booth's descriptive map of London Poverty*, 1889. By permission of the London Topographical Society.

6.8   *Police Illustrated News*. By permission of the British Library.

Every effort has been made to trace all the copyright holders, but if any have been overlooked, or if any additional information can be given, the publishers will make the necessary amendments at the first opportunity.

introducing this book

There's an awful lot of hype around 'the visual' these days. We're often told that we now live in a world where knowledge as well as many forms of entertainment are visually constructed, and where what we see is as important, if not more so, than what we hear or read. So-called 'visual illiteracy' is berated, and there are calls to restructure school and college curricula so that visual grammar can be learnt alongside understandings of texts, numbers and molecules. Yet there's also a lot of confusion about what exactly all this might entail. Indeed, there's a lot of confusion about the visual itself. Is it like a language or not? How do visual images work? As W.J.T. Mitchell (1994: 13) says at the beginning of his book on *Picture Theory*, 'we still do not know exactly what pictures are, what their relation to language is, how they operate on observers and on the world, how their history is to be understood, and what is to be done with or about them'. So even if it was certain that the world, or at least some parts of it, is increasingly encountered visually (and this is itself a debatable claim), it isn't clear exactly what that might mean for what is seen and for what, how and who sees and doesn't. Nor is it clear what, practically, might be useful ways of examining these issues through empirical studies. Despite the huge amount of academic work currently being published on things visual, there are remarkably few guides to possible methods of interpretation and even fewer explanations of how to do those methods. This book aims to fill that gap. It is addressed to the undergraduate student who has found some intriguing visual materials to work with, knows that they raise some interesting issues, but isn't quite sure how to proceed from there.

This book offers a methodological guide to the production of empirically grounded responses to particular visual materials. As Stuart Hall says:

> It is worth emphasising that there is no single or 'correct' answer to the question, 'What does this image mean?' or 'What is this ad saying?' Since there is no law which can guarantee that things will have 'one, true meaning', or that meanings won't change over time, work in this area is bound to be interpretative – a debate between, not who is 'right' and who is 'wrong', but between equally plausible, though sometimes competing and contesting, meanings and interpretations. The best way to 'settle' such contested readings is to look again at the concrete example and try to justify one's 'reading' in detail in relation to the actual practices and forms of signification used, and what meanings they seem to you to be producing. (Hall, 1997a: 9)

Interpreting images is just that, interpretation, not the discovery of their 'truth' (although we will encounter the latter claim in some of the early chapters of this book). As Hall suggests, it is therefore important to justify your interpretation. To do that you will need to have an explicit methodology, and this book will help you develop one. It provides a basic introduction to a range of methods that can be used to interpret visual images, and it provides enough references for you to develop more detailed methods if you need to. It does not offer a neutral account of these different methods, though. Those debates on the visual, while often exaggerated, over-generalized, polarized and under-researched, also raise some key interpretative issues with which any research into visual materials must engage. So the first chapter of this book addresses some aspects of current, more theoretical, debates about the visual. In that first chapter, I agree with the participants in those debates who argue that the interpretation of visual images must address questions of cultural meaning and power, and that position has certain implications for the way in which I subsequently assess the various methods I discuss. For example, while quantitative methods can be deployed in relation to these sorts of issues (as Chapter 3 will suggest), nonetheless this emphasis on meaning and significance suggests that qualitative methods are more appropriate. Indeed, every chapter here except the third explores qualitative methodologies. More broadly, the first chapter also makes some specific suggestions about why it is important to consider visual images, why it is important to be critical about visual images, and why it is important to reflect on that critique. Answers to these three questions are developed in Chapter 1 into three criteria for what I term a 'critical visual methodology'. By 'critical' I mean an approach that thinks about the visual in terms of the cultural significance, social practices and power relations in which it is embedded; and that means thinking about the power relations that produce, are articulated through, and can be challenged by, ways of seeing and imaging. Those criteria then provide the means by which the various methods in this book are evaluated. For each method I ask: How useful is it in achieving a critical methodology for visual images?

Each chapter of this book focuses on one method, and most chapters also focus on just one kind of visual imagery. Individual chapters look at paintings, photographs, films, televised soaps and adverts. Clearly, this is a narrow selection of visual things; there's nothing on video, or the web, or medical imaging, or maps, for example. And what about buildings, built landscapes, sculpture? There is nothing to prevent the methods discussed here being applied to other sorts of visual images and objects, however. Each chapter focuses on one kind of visual thing and one method in order to offer a sustained and fairly detailed discussion of the issues each raises. In order to develop that detail, each chapter also has boxes which ask you to *focus* on specific parts of the method. However, there are *bibliographies* at the end of the book which will help you to find your way around other visual media and genres, if you plan to use one of the methods discussed here on a different sort of imagery. The book also highlights a number of *key terms*. *Visual Methodologies* explores both theoretical and methodological issues, each of which has their own, sometimes rather obscure, vocabularies. To help you recognize the key terms of these vocabularies, the first time they are discussed in the text they are **highlighted in bold and noted in the margin**. To check your understanding of them, the list of key terms on pages 216–17 tells you where these terms are explored in the book.

Finally, I'd like to comment on the limits of a book like this. The book offers some guidelines for investigating the meanings and effects of visual images. But the most exciting, startling and perceptive critics of visual images don't in the end depend entirely on a sound methodology, I think. They also depend on the pleasure, thrills, fascination, wonder, fear or revulsion of the person looking at the images and then writing about them. Successful interpretation depends on a passionate engagement with what you see. Use your methodology to discipline your passion, not to deaden it.

1

researching visual materials

towards a critical visual methodology

Choosing a particular research method depends on all sorts of factors. This chapter examines the factors related to the basic analytical approach you adopt in relation to visual images:

- It discusses some debates about the importance of the visual to contemporary Western societies.
- It offers a broad analytical framework for understanding how images become meaningful.
- It suggests some criteria for a critical approach to visual materials.
- It places different methodologies in that framework, to begin to suggest which methods might be best suited for which kinds of analysis.
- It offers some practical suggestions for referencing and reproducing images in your final work.

1   an introductory survey of 'the visual'

Over the last two or three decades, the way in which many social scientists understand social life has shifted. This shift is often described as the 'cultural turn'. That is, 'culture' has become a crucial means by which many social scientists understand social processes, social identities, and social change and conflict. **Culture** is a complex concept, but, in very broad terms, the result of its deployment has been that social scientists are now very often interested in the ways in which social life is constructed through the ideas that people have about it, and the practices that flow from those ideas. To quote one of the major contributors to this shift, Stuart Hall:

Culture

Culture, it is argued, is not so much a set of things – novels and paintings or TV programmes or comics – as a process, a set of practices. Primarily, culture is concerned with the production and exchange of meanings – the 'giving and taking of meaning' – between the members of a society or group . . . Thus culture depends on its participants interpreting meaningfully what is around them, and 'making sense' of the world, in broadly similar ways. (Hall, 1997a: 2)

Those meanings may be explicit or implicit, conscious or unconscious. They may be felt as truth or as fantasy, science or common sense; and they may be conveyed through everyday speech, elaborate rhetoric, high art, tv soap operas, dreams, movies or muzak; and different groups in a society will make sense of the world in different ways. Whatever form they take, these made meanings structure they way people behave – the way you and I behave – in our everyday lives.

This sort of argument can take very diverse forms. But recently, many writers addressing these issues have argued that the visual is central to the cultural construction of social life in contemporary Western societies. It is now often suggested that much meaning is conveyed by visual images. We are, of course, surrounded by different sorts of visual technologies – photography, film, video, digital graphics, television, acrylics, for example – and the images they show us – tv programmes, advertisements, snapshots, public sculpture, movies, surveillance video footage, newspaper pictures, paintings. All these different sorts of technologies and images offer views of the world; they render the world in visual terms. But this rendering, even by photographs, is never innocent. These images are never transparent windows on to the world. They interpret the world; they display it in very particular ways. Thus a distinction is sometimes made

Vision
Visuality
between **vision** and **visuality**. **Vision** is what the human eye is physiologically capable of seeing (although it must be noted that ideas about that capability have changed historically and will most likely continue to change: see Crary, 1992). **Visuality**, on the other hand, refers to way in which vision is constructed in various ways: 'how we see, how we are able, allowed, or made to see, and how we see this seeing and the unseeing therein' (Foster, 1988a: ix). Another phrase with very similar connotations

Scopic regime
to visuality is **scopic regime**. Both terms refer to the ways in which both what is seen and how it is seen are culturally constructed.

For some writers, the visual is the most fundamental of all senses. Gordon Fyfe and John Law (1988: 2), for example, claim that 'depiction, picturing and seeing are ubiquitous features of the process by which most human beings come to know the world as it really *is* for them', and John Berger (1972: 7) suggests that this is because 'seeing comes before words. The child looks and recognizes before it can speak'. (Clearly these writers pay little attention to those who are born blind.) Other writers, however, prefer to historicise the importance of the visual, tracing what they see as the increasing saturation of Western societies by visual images. Many claim that this process has reached unprecedented levels, so that Westerners now

Ocularcentrism

interact with the world mainly through how we see it. Martin Jay (1993) has used the term **ocularcentrism** to describe the apparent centrality of the visual to contemporary Western life.

This narrative of the increasing importance of the visual to contemporary Western societies is part of a wider analysis of the shift from premodernity to modernity, and from modernity to postmodernity (for example, see Mirzoeff, 1999: 1–33). It is often suggested – or assumed – that in premodern societies, visual images were not especially important, partly because there were so few of them in circulation. This began to change with the onset of modernity. In particular, it is suggested that modern forms of knowledge depend on a scopic regime that equates seeing with knowledge. Chris Jenks (1995), for example, makes this case in an essay entitled 'The centrality of the eye in western culture', arguing that 'looking, seeing and knowing have become perilously intertwined' so that 'the modern world is very much a "seen" phenomenon' (Jenks, 1995: 1, 2).

> We daily experience and perpetuate the conflation of the 'seen' with the 'known' in conversation through the commonplace linguistic appendage of 'do you see?' or 'see what I mean?' to utterances that seem to require confirmation, or, when seeking opinion, by inquiring after people's 'views'. (Jenks, 1995: 3)

Barbara Maria Stafford (1991), an historian of images used in the sciences, has argued that, in a process beginning in the eighteenth century, the construction of scientific knowledges about the world has become more and more based on images rather than on written texts; Jenks (1995) suggests that it is the valorization of science in Western cultures which has allowed everyday understandings to make the same connection between seeing and knowing. However, that connection was also made in other fields of modern practice. Richard Rorty (1980), for example, traces the development of this conflation of seeing with knowing to the intersection of several ideas central to eighteenth-century philosophy. Judith Adler (1989) examines tourism and argues that between 1600 and 1800 the travel of European elites was defined increasingly as a visual practice, based first on 'an overarching scientific ideology that cast even the most humble tourists as part of . . . the impartial survey of all creation' (Adler, 1989: 24), and later on a particular appreciation of spectacular visual and artistic beauty. John Urry (1990) has sketched the outline of a rather different 'tourist gaze' which he argues is typical of the mass tourism of the nineteenth and twentieth centuries (see also Pratt, 1992). Other writers have made other arguments for the importance of the visual to modern societies. The work of Michel Foucault (1977) explores the way in which many nineteenth-century institutions depended on various forms of surveillance (Chapters 6 and 7 here examine the methodological implications of his work); and in his study of nineteenth-century world fairs and exhibitions, Timothy Mitchell (1988) shows how European societies represented the whole world as an exhibition. In the twentieth century, Guy Debord (1983) claims that the world has turned into a 'society of the spectacle', and Paul Virilio (1994) argues that new visualizing technologies have created 'the vision machine' in which we are all caught.

Thus it has been argued that modernity is ocularcentric. It is argued too that the visual is equally central to postmodernity; Nicholas Mirzoeff (1998: 4), for example, has proclaimed that 'the postmodern is a visual culture'. However, in postmodernity, it is often argued, the modern relation between seeing and true knowing has been broken. Thus Mirzoeff (1998) suggests that postmodernity is ocularcentric not simply because visual images are more and more common, nor because knowledges about the world are increasingly articulated visually, but because we interact more and more with totally constructed visual experiences. Thus the modern connection between seeing and knowledge is stretched to breaking point in postmodernity:

> Seeing is a great deal more than believing these days. You can buy an image of your house taken from an orbiting satellite or have your internal organs magnetically imaged. If that special moment didn't come out quite right in your photography, you can digitally manipulate it on your computer. At New York's Empire State Building, the queues are longer for the virtual reality New York Ride than for the lifts to the observation platforms. Alternatively, you could save yourself the trouble by catching the entire New York skyline, rendered in attractive pastel colours, at the New York, New York resort in Las Vegas. This virtual city will shortly be joined by Paris Las Vegas, imitating the already carefully manipulated image of the city of light. (Mirzoeff, 1998: 1)

Simulacrum This is what Jean Baudrillard (1988) some time ago dubbed the **simulacrum**. Baudrillard argued that in postmodernity it was no longer possible to make a distinction between the real and the unreal; images had become detached from any certain relation to a real world with the result that we now live in a scopic regime dominated by simulations, or simulacra.

This story about the increasing extent and changing nature of the ocularcentrism in modernity and postmodernity is not without its critics, however. Two points of debate, for example, are the history and geography of this account: perhaps visual images of various kinds have always been important, and to all sorts of societies. Jeffrey Hamburger (1997), for example, argues that visual images were central to certain kinds of premodern, medieval spirituality, and Ella Shohat and Robert Stam (1998) have argued forcefully against the Eurocentrism that pervades many discussions of 'the visual'. The work of Hamburger (1997) and Shohat and Stam (1998), among others, makes it clear that if a narrative of increasing ocularcentrism in the West can be told, it must be much more nuanced, historically and geographically, than has so far been the case (see also Brennan and Jay, 1996). Moreover, there are also debates about the social relations within which these visualities are embedded, and particularly about the effects of simulacra. Baudrillard, for example, has often been accused of uncritically celebrating the simulacrum without regard for the often very unequal social relations that can be articulated through it, and the work of Donna Haraway (1991) is a salutary reminder of what is at stake in contemporary ocularcentrism. Like many others, Haraway (1991) notes the contemporary proliferation of visualizing technologies in scientific and everyday use, and she characterizes the scopic regime associated with these technologies thus: 'Vision in this technological feast becomes unregulated gluttony; all perspective gives way to infinitely mobile vision, which no longer seems just mythically about the god-trick of seeing everything from nowhere, but to have put the myth into ordinary practice' (Haraway, 1991: 189). Haraway is concerned to specify the social power relations that are articulated through this particular form of visuality, however. She argues that contemporary, unregulated visual gluttony is available to only a few people and institutions, in particular those that are part of the 'history of science tied to militarism, capitalism, colonialism, and male supremacy' (Haraway, 1991: 188). She argues that what this visuality does is to produce specific visions of social difference – of hierarchies of class, 'race', gender, sexuality, and so on – while itself claiming not to be part of that hierarchy and thus to be universal. It is because this ordering of difference depends on a distinction between those who claim to see with universal relevance, and those who are seen and categorized in particular ways, that Haraway claims it is intimately related to the oppressions and tyrannies of capitalism, colonialism, patriarchy and so on. Part of Haraway's critical project, then, is to examine in detail how certain institutions mobilize certain forms of visuality to see, and to order, the world. This dominant visuality denies the validity of other ways of visualizing social difference, but Haraway insists that there are indeed other ways of seeing the world, and she is especially interested in efforts to see social difference in non-hierarchical ways. For Haraway, as for many other writers, then, the dominant scopic regime of (post)modernity is neither an historical inevitability, nor is it uncontested. There are different ways of seeing the world, and the critical task is to differentiate between the social effects of those different visions.

The particular forms of representation produced by specific scopic regimes are important to understand, then, because they are intimately bound into social power relations. Haraway's (1991) argument makes clear the necessity of understanding what social relations produce, and are reproduced by, what forms of visuality, and the next section explores this argument more fully.

2 'visual culture': the social conditions and effects of visual objects

Paying attention to the effects of images is fundamental to a new field of study that has been emerging over the past few years, perhaps itself

Visual culture

another symptom of the importance of images in the contemporary period. The focus of this field is something called **visual culture**, although some writers whose work engages with the visual are highly sceptical that this is a useful term (see the debate in the journal *October* in 1996). Visual culture is not then a term to be used carelessly. There are, however, five aspects of the recent literature that engages with visual culture which I think are valuable for thinking about the social effects of images.

First, there is an insistence that images themselves do something. In the words of Carol Armstrong (1996: 28), for example, an image is 'at least potentially a site of resistance and recalcitrance, of the irreducibly particular, and of the subversively strange and pleasurable' (Armstrong, 1996: 28; see also Stafford, 1996). This kind of visual resistance, recalcitrance, particularity, strangeness or pleasure may be difficult to articulate; indeed, certain aspects of visual images – the colours of an oil painting, for example, or what Barthes (1982) called the *punctum* of a photograph (see Chapter 4, section 3.3) – may have to undergo a sort of translation when they are written about. This has led some writers to argue that the visual is not the same as language. This is a claim which could have important implications for some of the methods this book will discuss; semiology, examined in Chapter 4, and the sort of discourse analysis examined in Chapter 6, are both methods based on the analysis of language rather than imagery. However, it is important not to forget that knowledges are conveyed through all sorts of different media, including senses other than the visual, and that visual images very often work in conjunction with other kinds of representations. It is very unusual, for example, to encounter a visual image unaccompanied by any text at all, whether spoken or written (Armstrong, 1998; Wollen, 1970: 118). Even the most abstract painting in a gallery will have a written label on the wall giving certain information about its making, and in certain sorts of galleries there'll be a sheet of paper giving a price too, and these make a difference to how spectators will see that painting. So it's certainly correct, I think, that visual modes of conveying meaning are not the same as written modes; and thus that, as W.J.T. Mitchell (1994: 16) says, 'visual experience or "visual literacy" might not be fully explicable on the model of textuality'. However, because visual objects are always embedded into a range of other texts, some of which will be visual and some of which will be written and all of which intersect with each other, I find debates about the precise difference between words and images rather sterile. What is much more important, I think, is simply to acknowledge that visual images can be powerful and seductive in their own right.

The second point I take from the literature on (or against) 'visual culture' is its concern for the way in which images visualize (or render invisible) social difference. As Fyfe and Law (1988: 1) say, 'a depiction is never just an illustration . . . it is the site for the construction and depiction of social difference'. One of the central aims of 'the cultural turn' in the social sciences is to argue that social categories are not natural but instead

With the Conservatives, there are no 'blacks', no 'whites', just people.

Conservatives believe that treating minorities as equals encourages the majority to treat them as equals.

Yet the Labour Party aim to treat you as a 'special case', as a group all on your own.

Is setting you apart from the rest of society a sensible way to overcome racial prejudice and social inequality?

The question is, should we really divide the British people instead of uniting them?

WHOSE PROMISES ARE YOU TO BELIEVE?

When Labour were in government, they promised to repeal Immigration Acts passed in 1962 and 1971. Both promises were broken.

This time, they are promising to throw out the British Nationality Act, which gives full and equal citizenship to everyone permanently settled in Britain.

But how do the Conservatives' promises compare?

We said that we'd abolish the 'SUS' law.

We kept our promise.

We said we'd recruit more coloured policemen, get the police back into the community, and train them for a better understanding of your needs.

We kept our promise.

PUTTING THE ECONOMY BACK ON ITS FEET.

The Conservatives have always said that the only long term answer to our economic problems was to conquer inflation.

Inflation is now lower than it's been for over a decade, keeping all prices stable, with the price of food now hardly rising at all.

Meanwhile, many businesses throughout Britain are recovering, leading to thousands of new jobs.

Firstly, in our traditional industries, but just as importantly in new technology areas such as micro-electronics.

In other words, the medicine is working.

Yet Labour want to change everything, and put us back to square one.

They intend to increase taxation. They intend to increase the National Debt.

They promise import and export controls.

Cast your mind back to the last Labour government. Labour's methods didn't work then.

They won't work now.

A BETTER BRITAIN FOR ALL OF US.

The Conservatives believe that everyone wants to work hard and be rewarded for it.

Those rewards will only come about by creating a mood of equal opportunity for everyone in Britain, regardless of their race, creed or colour.

The difference you're voting for is this:

To the Labour Party, you're a black person.

To the Conservatives, you're a British Citizen.

Vote Conservative, and you vote for a more equal, more prosperous Britain.

LABOUR SAYS HE'S BLACK. TORIES SAY HE'S BRITISH.

CONSERVATIVE ☒

Figure 1.1

Conservative Party election poster

(Gilroy, 1987: 58)

are constructed. These constructions can take visual form. This point has been made most forcefully by feminist and postcolonial writers who have studied the ways femininity and blackness have been visualized. An example would be Paul Gilroy's (1987: 57–9) discussion of a poster used by the Conservative Party in Britain's 1983 General Election, reproduced in Figure 1.1.

The poster shows a young black man in a suit, with 'LABOUR SAYS HE'S BLACK. TORIES SAY HE'S BRITISH' as its headline text. Gilroy's discussion is detailed but his main point is that the poster offers a choice between being black and being British, not only in its text but also in its image. The fact that the black man is pictured wearing a suit suggests to Gilroy that 'blacks are being invited to forsake all that marks them out as culturally distinct before real Britishness can be guaranteed' (Gilroy, 1987: 59). Gilroy is thus suggesting that this poster asks its viewers not to see blackness. However, he also points out that the poster depends on other stereotyped images (which it does not show) of young black men, particularly as muggers, to make its point about the acceptability of this besuited man. This poster thus plays in complex ways with both visible and invisible signs of racial difference. Hence Fyfe and Law's general prescription for a critical approach to the ways images can picture social power relations:

> To understand a visualisation is thus to enquire into its provenance and into the social work that it does. It is to note its principles of inclusion and exclusion, to detect the roles that it makes available, to understand the way in which they are distributed, and to decode the hierarchies and differences that it naturalises. (Fyfe and Law, 1988: 1)

Looking carefully at images, then, entails, among other things, thinking about how they offer very particular visions of social categories such as class, gender, race, sexuality, able-bodiedness, and so on.

Third, writers on visual culture, among others, are concerned not only with how images look, but how they are looked at. That is, they argue that what is important about images is not simply the image itself, but how it is seen by particular spectators who look in particular ways. In 1972, John Berger wrote and illustrated a book to accompany a television series called **Ways of seeing** *Ways of Seeing*, and he elaborated that phrase **ways of seeing** in a manner very similar to the concerns of more recent writers. His argument is important because he makes clear that images of social difference work not simply by what they show but also by the kind of seeing that they invite. He uses the expression 'ways of seeing' to refer to the fact that 'we never look just at one thing; we are always looking at the relation between things and ourselves' (Berger, 1972: 9). His best known example is that of the genre of female nude painting in Western art. He reproduces many examples of that genre (see Figure 1.2), pointing out as he does so the particular ways they represent women: as unclothed, as vain, as passive, as sexually alluring, as a spectacle to be assessed.

Berger insists though on who it is that does the assessing, who this kind of image of woman was meant to allure:

> In the average European oil painting of the nude, the principal pro-tagonist is never painted. He is the spectator in front of the painting and he is presumed to be a man. Everything is addressed to him. Everything must appear to be the result of his being there. It is for him that the figures have assumed their nudity. (Berger, 1972: 54)

Thus for Berger, understanding this particular genre of painting means understanding not only its representation of femininity, but its construction of masculinity too. And these representations are in their turn understood as part of a wider cultural construction of gendered difference. To quote Berger again:

> One might simplify this by saying: *men act* and *women appear*. Men look at women. Women watch themselves being looked at. This determines not only most relations between women and men but also the relation of women to themselves. The surveyor of woman in herself is male: the surveyed female. Thus she turns herself into an object – and most particularly an object of vision: a sight. (Berger, 1972: 47)

While later critics would want to modify aspects of Berger's argument – most obviously by noting that he assumes heterosexuality in his discussion of masculinity and femininity – many critics would concur with his general understanding of the connection between image and spectator. Images work by producing effects every time they are looked at. Taking an image seriously, then, also involves thinking about how it positions you, its viewer, in relation to it.

Fourth, there is the emphasis in the very term 'visual culture' on the embeddedness of visual images in a wider culture (Mirzoeff, 1999: 22–6). Now, 'culture', as Raymond Williams (1976) famously noted, is one of the two or three most complicated words in the English language. It has many

She is not naked as she is.
She is naked as the spectator sees her.

Often – as with the favourite subject of Susannah and the Elders – this is the actual theme of the picture. We join the Elders to spy on Susannah taking her bath. She looks back at us looking at her.

In another version of the subject by Tintoretto, Susannah is looking at herself in a mirror. Thus she joins the spectators of herself.

50

The mirror was often used as a symbol of the vanity of woman. The moralizing, however, was mostly hypocritical.

You painted a naked woman because you enjoyed looking at her, you put a mirror in her hand and you called the painting *Vanity*, thus morally condemning the woman whose nakedness you had depicted for your own pleasure.

The real function of the mirror was otherwise. It was to make the woman connive in treating herself as, first and foremost, a sight.

The Judgement of Paris was another theme with the same inwritten idea of a man or men looking at naked women.

51

Figure 1.2

Double-page spread from John Berger's Ways of Seeing *(Berger, 1972: 50–1)*

connotations. Most pertinent to this discussion is the meaning it began to be given in various anthropological books written towards the end of the nineteenth century. In this usage, culture meant something like 'a whole way of life', and even from the brief discussion in this chapter so far you can see that some current writers are using the term visual culture in just this broad sense. Indeed, the term 'visual culture' was first used by Svetlana Alpers (1983: xxv) precisely to emphasize the importance of visual images of all kinds to seventeenth century Dutch society, and her example has been followed by, among others, Stafford (1996: 4) in her argument that new visualizing technologies have superseded written texts as 'the richest, most fascinating modality for conveying ideas', and by Karal Ann Marling (1994) in her book on the influence of television and its associated way of seeing in 1950s North America. In this sort of work, it is argued that a particular, historically specific visuality was central to a particular, ocular-centric culture. In using the notion of culture in this broad sense, however, certain analytical questions become difficult to ask. In particular, culture as whole way of life can slip rather easily into a notion of culture as simply a whole, and the issue of difference becomes obscured. Stafford's (1996) celebration of the visual in 'our' society has been criticized by Hal Foster (1996) in just these terms. Stafford never specifies who the 'we' to which she refers actually is, and she thus ignores this visuality's possible exclusions as well as the particularities of its inclusions.

In order to be able to deal with questions of social difference and the power relations that sustain them, then, a more nuanced notion of culture is required. But to understand culture through another one of its definitions, culture as artefacts, will not entirely do either. Some definitions of visual culture do claim that visual culture simply means visual objects: 'visual culture can be roughly defined as those material artefacts, buildings and images, plus time-based media and performances, produced by human labour and imagination, which serve aesthetic, symbolic, ritualistic or ideological-political ends, and/or practical functions, and which address the sense of sight to a significant extent' (Walker and Chaplin, 1997: 1–2). The difficulty with this definition is that it can neglect the important notion of ways of seeing. If Nancy Condee's (1995: x) definition – that 'visual culture is a process and not a thing, a particular way of perceiving the object and not the particular object perceived' – goes to the other extreme and dismisses the facticity of visual things entirely, her emphasis on visual culture as a visual relation between an object and a spectator is crucial. Visual objects mobilize certain ways of seeing.

Culture   If **culture** cannot be thought of as a singular whole, nor as constituted simply by objects, then, it is more helpful to think of it as the range of meaningful social practices in which visual images' effects are embedded, just as many social scientists are now doing (for an early example of this sort of approach, see Becker, 1982). I have already quoted Stuart Hall (1997a: 2) saying that culture is 'a process, a set of practices', and Ian Heywood and Barry Sandywell (1999: xi) make a similar claim in their account of visual culture as a 'socio-historical realm of interpretative practices'. Visual images are made, and may be moved, displayed, sold, censored, venerated, discarded, stared at, hidden, recycled, glanced at, damaged, destroyed, touched, reworked. Images are made and used in all sorts of ways by different people for different reasons, and these makings and uses are crucial to the meanings an image carries. An image may have its own effects, but these are always mediated by the many and various uses to which it is put. An image will depend for its effects on a certain way of seeing, as Berger assumed in relation to female nude painting. But this effect is always embedded in particular cultural practices that are far more specific than 'a way of life'. Berger, for example, talks about the ways in which nude paintings were commissioned and then displayed by their owners in his discussion of the way of seeing which they express. Describing a seventeenth-century English example of the genre, he writes:

> Nominally it might be a *Venus and Cupid*. In fact it is a portrait of one of the king's mistresses, Nell Gwynne . . . [Her] nakedness is not, however, an expression of her own feelings; it is a sign of her submission to the owner's feelings or demands. (The owner of both the woman and the painting.) The painting, when the king showed it to others, demonstrated this submission and his guests envied him. (Berger, 1972: 52)

It was through this kind of use, by those particular sorts of people interpreting it in that kind of way, that this kind of painting achieved its effects. The seeing of an image thus always takes place in a particular social context that mediates its impact. It also always takes place in a specific location with its own particular practices. That location may be a king's chamber, a Hollywood cinema studio, an avant-garde art gallery, an archive, a sitting-room, a street. These different locations all have their own economies, their own disciplines, their own rules for how their particular sort of spectator should behave, and all these affect how a particular image is seen too.

Finally, much of this work in visual culture argues that it is important to remember that, just as an image may be 'a site of resistance and recalcitrance', so too might a particular audience. Not all audiences will be able or willing to respond to the way of seeing invited by a particular images and its particular practices of display (Chapter 8 will discuss this in more detail).

Thus I take five major points from current debates about visual culture as important for understanding how images work: an image may have its *own visual effects* (so it is important to look very carefully at images); these effects, through the *ways of seeing* mobilized by the image, are crucial in the production and reproduction of visions of *social difference*; but these effects always intersect with the *social context of its viewing* and *the visualities its spectators bring* to their viewing.

3   towards a critical visual methodology

Given this general approach to understanding the importance of visual images, I can now elaborate on what I think is necessary for a 'critical approach' to interpreting visual images. A critical approach:

1   *takes images seriously.* While this might seem rather a paradoxical point to insist on, given all the work I've just mentioned that addresses visualities and visual objects, art historians of all sorts of interpretive hues continue to complain, often rightly, that social scientists don't look at images carefully enough. And often too, social scientists tend to assume that images are simply reflections of their social 'contexts' (for a critique of this approach, see Pollock, 1988: 25–30). In contrast, I argue that it is necessary to look very carefully at visual images, and it is necessary to do so because they are not entirely reducible to their context. Visual representations have their own effects.

2   *thinks about the social conditions and effects of visual objects.* As Griselda Pollock (1988: 7) says, 'cultural practices do a job which has major social significance in the articulation of meanings about the world, in the negotiation of social conflicts, in the production of social subjects'. Haraway's work is exemplary here. Cultural practices like

visual representations both depend on and produce social inclusions and exclusions, and a critical account needs to address both those practices and their cultural meanings.

3 *considers your own way of looking at images.* If ways of seeing are historically, geographically, culturally and socially specific, then how you or I look is not natural or innocent. So it is necessary to reflect on how you as a critic of visual images are looking. As Haraway (1991: 190) says, by thinking carefully about where we see from, 'we might become answerable for what we learn how to see'. Haraway also comments that this is not a straightforward task, however (see also Rogoff, 1998; Rose, 1997), and several of the chapters will return to this issue of reflexivity in order to examine its challenges further.

The aim of this book is to give you some practical guidance on how to do these things; but I hope it is already clear from this introduction that this is not simply a technical question of method. There are also important analytical debates going on about visualities. In this book, I use these particular criteria for a critical visual methodology to evaluate both theoretical arguments and methods.

Having very briefly sketched a critical approach to images that I find useful to work with and which will structure this book's accounts of various methods, the next section will continue to explore a number of different interpretations of visual objects, not all of which are compatible with each other. The next section also has another aim, though. It will begin to offer some more practical analytical tools.

4 towards some methodological tools: sites and modalities

As the editors of *The BLOCK Reader on Visual Culture* (Bird et al., 1996) make clear, the theoretical sources which have produced the recent interest in visual culture are diverse. This section will try to acknowledge some of that diversity, while also beginning to develop a methodological framework for interpreting visual images critically.

Sites Interpretations of visual images broadly concur that there are three sites at which the meanings of an image are made: the site(s) of the
Production production of an image, the site of the **image** itself, and the site(s) where it
Image is seen by various **audiences**. Many of the theoretical disagreements about
Audiences visual culture, visualities and visual objects can be understood as disputes over which of these is most important and why, and the following subsections will touch on some of these disagreements. I also want to suggest that these sites are complicated because there are different aspects to each
Modalities of their processes. These different aspects I will call **modalities**, and I'll suggest that there are three of these that can contribute to a critical understanding of images:

Technological 1 **technological.** Mirzoeff (1998: 1) defines a visual technology as 'any form of apparatus designed either to be looked at or to enhance natural vision, from oil paintings to television and the Internet'.

Compositional 2 **compositional.** When an image is made, it draws on a number of formal strategies: content, colour and spatial organization, for example. Often, particular forms of these strategies tend to occur together, so that, for example, Berger (1972) can define the Western art tradition painting of the nude in terms of its specific compositional qualities. Chapter 2 will elaborate the notion of composition.

Social 3 **social.** This is very much a shorthand term. What I mean it to refer to are the range of economic, social and political relations, institutions and practices that surround an image and through which it is seen and used.

These modalities, since they are found at all three sites, also suggest that the distinctions between sites are less clear than my subsections here might imply.

To focus the discussion, and to give you a chance to explore how these sites and modalities intersect, I'll often refer to the photograph reproduced in Figure 1.3. Take a good look at it now and note down your immediate reactions. Then see how your views of it alter as the following subsections discuss its sites and modalities.

4.1 site i: production

All visual representations are made in one way or another, and the circumstances of their production may contribute towards the effect they have.

Some writers argue this case very strongly. Some, for example, would argue that the *technologies* used in the making of an image determine its form, meaning and effect. Clearly, visual technologies do matter to how an image looks and therefore to what it might do and what might be done to it. Here is Berger describing the uniqueness of oil painting:

> What distinguishes oil painting from any other form of painting is its special ability to render the tangibility, the texture, the lustre, the solidity of what it depicts. It defines the real as that which you can put your hands on. (Berger, 1972: 88)

For a particular study it may be important to understand the technologies used in the making of particular images, and at the end of the book you will find some references which will help you do that.

In the case of the photograph here, it is perhaps important to understand what kind of camera, film and developing process the photographer was using, and what that made visually possible and what impossible. The

Figure 1.3

photograph was made in 1948, by which time cameras were relatively lightweight and film was highly sensitive to light. This meant that, unlike in earlier periods, a photographer did not have to find subjects which would stay still for seconds or even minutes in order to be pictured. By 1948, the photographer could have stumbled on this scene and 'snapped' it almost immediately. Thus part of the effect of the photograph – its apparent spontaneity, a snapshot – is enabled by the technology used.

However, another aspect of the photograph which we might be tempted to ascribe to its technology – its apparent truthfulness – has less to do with the technical capabilities of the camera and film and more to do with how photographs are understood. From its very invention, photography has been understood by some of its practitioners as a technology that simply records the way things really look. But also from the beginning, photographs have been seen as magical and strange (Slater, 1995). This debate should alert to us to the fact that notions of 'truthful' photographic representation have been constructed. Maybe we see this photograph as a snapshot of real life because we expect photos to show us snippets of truth. But this photo might have been posed: the photographer who took this one certainly posed others which nevertheless have the same 'real' look (Doisneau, 1991). Also, as Griselda Pollock (1988: 85–7) points out in her discussion of this photograph, its status as a snapshot of real life is also established in part by its content, especially the boys playing in the street, just out of focus; surely if it had been posed those boys would have been in focus? Thus the apparently technological effects on the production of a visual image need careful consideration, because some may not be straightforwardly technological at all.

The second modality of an image's production is to do with its *compositionality*. Some writers argue that it is the conditions of an image's production that govern its compositionality. This argument is perhaps **Genre** most effectively made in relation to the **genre** of images into which a particular image fits (perhaps rather uneasily). Genre is a way of classifying visual images into certain groups. Images that belong to the same genre share certain features. A particular genre will share a specific set of meaningful objects and locations and, in the case of movies for example, have a limited set of narrative problematics. Thus John Berger can define 'female nude painting' as a particular genre of Western painting because these are pictures which represent naked women as passive, available and desirable through various compositional devices. A certain kind of traditional art history would see the way that a particular artist makes reference to other paintings in the same genre (and perhaps in other genres) as he or she works at a canvas as a crucial aspect of understanding the final painting. It helps to make sense of the significance of elements of an individual image if you know that some of them recur repeatedly in other images. You may need to refer to other images of the same genre in order to explicate aspects of the one you're interested in. Many books on visual images focus on one particular genre.

The photograph under consideration here fits into one genre but has connections to some others, and knowing this allows us to make sense of various aspects of this rich visual document. The genre into which the photo fits most obviously, I think, is that of 'street photography'. This is a body of work with connections to another photography genre, that of the documentary (Hamilton, 1997; see also Pryce, 1997 for a discussion of documentary photography). Documentary photography originally tended to picture poor, oppressed or marginalized individuals, often as part of reformist projects to show the horror of their lives and thus inspire change. The aim was to be as objective and accurate as possible in these depictions. However, since the apparent horror was being shown to audiences who had the power to pressure for change, documentary photography usually pictures the relatively powerless to the relatively powerful. It has thus been accused of voyeurism and worse. Street photography shares with documentary photography the desire to picture life as it apparently is. But street photography does not want its viewers to say 'oh how terrible' and maybe 'we must do something about that'. Rather, its way of seeing invites a response that is more like, 'oh how extraordinary, isn't life richly marvellous'. This seems to me to be the response that this photograph, and many others taken by the same photographer, asks for. We are meant to smile wryly at a glimpse of a relationship, exposed to us for just a second. This photograph was almost certainly made to sell to a photo-magazine like *Vu*, *Life* or *Picture Post* for publication as a visual joke, funny and not too disturbing for the readers of these magazines. This constraint on its production thus affected its genre.

The third modality of production is what I have called the *social*. Here again, there is a body of work which argues that these are the most important factors in understanding visual images. Some argue that it is the economic processes in which cultural production is embedded that shape visual imagery. One of the most eloquent exponents of this argument is David Harvey. Certain photographs and films play a key role in his 1989 book *The Condition of Postmodernity*. He argues that these visual representations exemplify postmodernity. Like many other commentators, Harvey defines postmodernity in part through the importance of visual images to postmodern culture, commenting on 'the mobilization of fashion, pop art, television and other forms of media image, and the variety of urban life styles that have become part and parcel of daily life under capitalism' (Harvey, 1989: 63). He sees the qualities of this mobilization as ephemeral, fluid, fleeting and superficial: 'there has emerged an attachment to surface rather than roots, to collage rather than in-depth work, to superimposed quoted images rather than worked surfaces, to a collapsed sense of time and space rather than solidly achieved cultural artefact' (Harvey, 1989: 61). And Harvey has an explanation for this which focuses on the latter characteristics. He suggests that contemporary capitalism is organizing itself in ways that are indeed compressing time and collapsing space. He argues that capitalism is more and more 'flexible' in its organization of production techniques, labour markets and consumption niches, and that this has depended on the increased mobility of capital and information. Moreover, the importance of consumption niches has generated the increasing importance of advertising, style and spectacle in the selling of goods. In his Marxist account, both these characteristics are reflected in cultural objects – in their superficiality, their ephemerality – so that the latter are nothing but 'the cultural logic of late capitalism' (Harvey, 1989: 63; Jameson, 1984).

To analyse images through this lens you will need to understand contemporary economic processes in a synthetic manner. However, those writers who emphasize the importance of broad systems of production to the meaning of images sometimes deploy methodologies that pay rather little attention to the details of particular images. Harvey (1989), for example, has been accused of misunderstanding the photographs and films he interprets in his book – and of economic determinism (Deutsche, 1991).

Other accounts of the centrality of what I am calling the social to the production of images depend on rather more detailed analyses of particular industries which produce visual images. David Morley and Kevin Robins (1995), for example, focus on the audiovisual industries of Europe in their study of how those industries are implicated in contemporary constructions of 'Europeanness'. They point out that the European Union is keen to encourage a Europe-wide audiovisual industry partly on economic grounds, to compete with US and Japanese conglomerates. But they also argue that the EU has a cultural agenda too, which works at 'improving mutual knowledge among European peoples and increasing their consciousness of the life and destiny they have in common' (Morley and Robins, 1995: 3), and thus elides differences within Europe while producing certain kinds of differences between Europe and the rest of the world. Like Harvey, then, Morley and Robins pay attention to both the economic and the cultural aspects of contemporary cultural practices. Unlike Harvey, however, Morley and Robins do not reduce the latter to the former. And this is in part because they rely on a more fine-grained analytical method than Harvey, paying careful attention to particular companies and products, as well as understanding how the industry as a whole works.

Another aspect of the social production of an image is the social and/or political identities that are mobilized in its making. Peter Hamilton's (1997) discussion of the sort of photography of which Figure 1.3 is a part explores its dependence on certain postwar ideas about the French working class, for example. Here though I will focus on another social identity articulated through this particular photograph. Here is a passage from an introduction to a book on street photography that evokes the 'crazy, cockeyed' viewpoint of the street photographer:

> It's like going into the sea and letting the waves break over you. You feel the power of the sea. On the street each successive wave brings a whole new cast of characters. You take wave after wave, you bathe in it. There

is something exciting about being in the crowd, in all that chance and change. It's tough out there, but if you can keep paying attention something will reveal itself, just a split second, and then there's a crazy cockeyed picture! . . . 'Tough' meant it was an uncompromising image, something that came from your gut, out of instinct, raw, of the moment, something that couldn't be described in any other way. So it was TOUGH. Tough to like, tough to see, tough to make, tough to understand. The tougher they were the more beautiful they became. It was our language. (Westerbeck and Meyerowitz, 1994: 2–3)

This passage allows us to say a bit more about the importance of a certain kind of identity to the production of the photograph under discussion here. To do street photography, it says, the photographer has to be there, in the street, tough enough to survive, tough enough to overcome the threats posed by the street. There is a kind of macho power being celebrated in that account of street photography, in its reiteration of 'toughness'. This sort of photography also endows its viewer with a kind of toughness over the image because it allows the viewer to remain in control, positioned as somewhat distant from and superior to what the image shows us. We have more information than the people pictured, and we can therefore smile at them. This particular photograph even places a window between us and its subjects; we peer at them from the same hidden vantage point just like the photographer did. There is a kind of distance established between the photographer/audience and the people photographed, then, reminiscent of the patriarchal way of seeing that has been critiqued by Haraway (1991), among others (see section 1 of this chapter). But since this toughness is required only in order to record something that will reveal itself, this passage is also an example of the photograph being seen as a truthful instrument of simple observation, and of the erasure of the specificity of the photographer himself; the photographer is there but only to carry his camera and react quickly when the moment comes, just like our photographer snapping his subject. Again, this erasure of the particularity of a visuality is what Haraway (1991) critiques as, among other things, patriarchal. It is therefore significant that of the many photographers whose work is reproduced in that book on street photography, very few are women. You need to be a man, or at least masculine, to do street photography, apparently. However, this passage's evocation of 'gut' and 'instinct' is interesting in this respect, since these are qualities of embodiment and non-rationality that are often associated with femininity. Thus, if masculinity might be said to be central to the production of street photography, it is a particular, rather complicated, kind of masculinity.

Finally, it should be noted that there is one element active at the site of production to which many social scientists interested in the visual would pay very little attention: the individual often described as the author (or artist or director or sculptor or so on) of the visual image under consideration. The notion that the most important aspect in understanding a visual image is what its maker intended to show is sometimes called

Auteur theory auteur theory. However, most of the recent work on visual matters is uninterested in the intentionality of an image's maker. There are a number of reasons for this (Hall, 1997b: 25; see also the focus in Chapter 2, section 3). First, as we have seen, there are those who argue that other modalities of an image's production account for its effects. Second, there are those who argue that, since the image is always made and seen in relation to other images, this wider visual context is more significant for what the image means than what the artist thought they were doing. Roland Barthes (1977: 145–6) made this argument when he proclaimed 'the death of the author'. And third, there are those who insist that the most important site at which the meaning of an image is made is not its author, or indeed its production or itself, but its audiences, who bring their own ways of seeing and other knowledges to bear on an image and in the process make their own meanings from it. So I can tell you that the man who took this photograph in 1948 was Robert Doisneau, and that information will allow you, as it allowed me, to find out more information about his life and work. But the literature I am drawing on here would not suggest that an intimate, personal biography of Doisneau is necessary in order to interpret his photographs. Instead, it would read his life, as I did, in order to understand the modalites that shaped the production of his photographs.

4.2 site ii: the image

The second site at which an image's meanings are made is the image itself. Every image has a number of formal components. As the previous section suggested, some of these components will be caused by the *technologies* used to make, reproduce or display the image. For example, the black and white tonalities of the Doisneau photo are a result of his choice of film and processing techniques. Other components of an image will depend on *social* practices. The previous section also noted how the photograph under discussion might look the way it does in part because it was made to be sold to particular magazines. More generally, the economic circumstances under which Doisneau worked were such that all his photographs were affected by them. He began working as a photographer in the publicity department of a pharmacy, and then worked for the car manufacturer Renault in the 1930s (Doisneau, 1990). Later he worked for *Vogue* and for the Alliance press agency. That is, he very often pictured things in order to get them sold: cars, fashions. And all his life he had to make images to sell; he was a freelance photographer needing to make a living from his photographs. Thus his photography showed commodities and was itself a commodity (see Ramamurthy, 1997 for a discussion of photography and commodity culture). Perhaps this accounts for his fascination with objects, with emotion, and with the emotions objects can arouse. Just like an advertiser, he was investing objects with feelings through his images, and, again like an advertiser, could not afford to offend his potential buyers.

However, as section 2 here noted, many writers argue that an image may have its own effects which exceed the constraints of its production (and reception). Some would argue, for example, that it is the particular qualities of the photographic image that make us understand its technology in particular ways, rather than the reverse; or that it is those qualities that shape the social modality in which it is embedded rather than the other way round. The modality most important to an image's own effects, therefore, is often argued to be its *compositionality*. Pollock's (1988: 85) discussion of the Doisneau photograph is very clear about the way in which aspects of its compositionality contribute towards its way of seeing (she draws on an earlier essay by Mary Ann Doane (1982)). She stresses the spatial organization of looks in the photograph, and argues that 'the photograph almost uncannily delineates the sexual politics of looking'. These are the politics of looking that Berger explored in his discussion of the Western tradition of female nude painting. 'One might simplify this by saying: *men act* and *women appear*', says Berger (1972: 47). In this photograph, the man looks at an image of a woman, while another woman looks but at nothing, apparently. Moreover, as Pollock insists, the viewer of this photograph is pulled into complicity with these looks:

> It is [the man's] gaze which defines the problematic of the photograph and it erases that of the woman. She looks at nothing that has any meaning for the spectator. Spatially central, she is negated in the triangulation of looks between the man, the picture of the fetishized woman and the spectator, who is thus enthralled to a masculine viewing position. To get the joke, we must be complicit with his secret discovery of something better to look at. The joke, like all dirty jokes, is at the woman's expense. (Pollock, 1988: 47)

Pollock is discussing the organization of looks in the photograph and between the photograph and us, its viewers. She argues that this aspect of its formal qualities is the most important for its effect (although she has also mentioned the effect of spontaneity created by the out-of-focus boys playing in the street behind the couple, remember).

Such discussions of the compositional modality of the site of the image can produce persuasive accounts of a photograph's way of seeing. And such accounts would refuse to explain that way of seeing by referring to its conditions of production. Thus Pollock (1988) does not discuss the gendered production of street photography and its celebration of toughness. This is because she refuses to reduce the effect of the photograph to a mere reflection of social practices elsewhere.

4.3   site iii: audiencing

You might well not agree with Pollock's interpretation of the Doisneau photograph, and I'll discuss some of the other interpretations of the image made by students in some of my classes in this section. Your disagreement, though, is the final site at which the meanings and effects of an image are made, for you are an audience of that photograph and, like all audiences, you bring to it your own ways of seeing and other kinds of knowledges. John Fiske (1994) for one suggests that this is the most important site at **Audiencing** which an image's meanings are made, and uses the term **audiencing** to refer to the process by which a visual image has its meanings renegotiated, or even rejected, by particular audiences watching in specific circumstances. Once again, I would suggest that there are three aspects to that process.

The first is the *compositionality* of the image. Several of the methods that we will encounter in this book assume that the formal arrangement of the elements of a picture will dictate how an image is seen by its audiences. Pollock assumes just this when she claims that the Doisneau image is always seen as a joke against the woman, because the organization of looks by the photograph coincides with, and reiterates, a scopic regime that allows only men to look. It is important, I think, to consider very carefully the organization of the image, because that does have an effect on the spectator who sees it. There is no doubt, I think, that the Doisneau photograph pulls the viewer into a complicity with the man and his furtive look. But that does not necessarily mean the spectator sympathizes with that look. Indeed, many of my students often comment that the photograph shows the man (agreeing with Pollock, then, that the photograph is centred on the man) as a 'lech', a 'dirty old man', a 'voyeur'. That is, they see him as the point of the photograph, but that does not make the photograph an expression of a way of seeing that they approve of. Moreover, that man and his look might not be the only thing that a particular viewer sees in that photograph, as I'll suggest in a moment. Thus audiences make their own interpretations of an image.

Those theories that privilege the *technological* site at which an image's meanings are made similarly often imply that the technology used to make and display an image will control an audience's reaction. Again, this might be an important point to consider. How does seeing a particular movie on a television screen differ from seeing it on a large cinema screen with 3D glasses? How different is a reproduction in a book of an altarpiece from seeing the original in a church? Clearly at one level these are technological questions concerning the size, colour and texture, for example, of the image. At another level though they raise a number of other, more important questions about how an image is looked at differently in different contexts. You don't do the same things while you're flicking through a book of renaissance altarpieces as you do when you're in a church looking at one. While you're looking at a book you can be listening to music, eating, comparing one plate to another; in a church you may have to dress a certain way to get in, remain quiet, not get very close, not actually be able to see it at all well, let alone touch the image. Again, the audiencing of an image thus appears very important to its meanings and effects.

The *social* is thus perhaps the most important modality for understanding the audiencing of images. In part this is a question of the different social practices which structure the viewing of particular images in particular places. Visual images are always practised in particular ways, and different practices are often associated with different kinds of images in different kinds of spaces. A cinema, a television in a living-room and a canvas in a modern art gallery do not invite the same ways of seeing. This is both because, let's say, a Hollywood movie, a tv soap and an abstract expressionist canvas do not have the same compositionality or depend on the same technologies, but also because they are not done in the same way. Popcorn is not sold by or taken into galleries, generally, and usually soaps are not watched in contemplative, reverential isolation. Different ways of relating to visual images define the cinema and the gallery, for example, as different kinds of spaces. You don't applaud a sculpture the way you might do a film, but applauding might depend on the sort of film and the sort of cinema you see it in. This point about the spaces and practices of display is especially important to bear in mind given the increasing mobility of images now; images appear and reappear in all sorts of places, and those places, with their particular ways of spectating, mediate the visual effects of those images.

Thus, to return to our example, you are looking at the Doisneau photograph in a particular way because it is reproduced in this book and is being used here as a pedagogic device; you're looking at it often (I hope – although this work on audiences suggests you may well not be bothering to do that) and looking at in different ways depending on the issues I'm raising. You'd be doing this photograph very differently if you'd been sent it in the format of a postcard (and many of Doisneau's photographs have been reproduced as greetings cards, postcards and posters). Maybe you would merely have glanced at it before reading the message on its reverse far more avidly; if the card had been sent by a lover, maybe you'd see it as some sort of comment on your relationship . . . and so on.

There is actually very little discussion of these sorts of topics in the literature on visual culture; and most of the discussion that has taken place has explored the particular ways people watch television and videos in their homes. Chapter 8 will explore those studies. As we will see, they often rely on research methods that pay little attention to the images themselves and much more to the reactions and doings of their viewers. This is because many of those concerned with audiences argue that audiences are the most important aspect of an image's meaning. They thus tend, like those studies which privilege the social modality of the site of production of imagery, to use methods that don't address visual imagery directly.

The second and related aspect of the social modality of audiencing images concerns the social identities of those doing the watching. As Chapter 8 will discuss in more detail, there have been many studies which have explored how different audiences interpret the same visual images in very different ways, and these differences have been attributed to the different social identities of the viewers concerned.

In terms of the Doisneau photograph, it's seemed to me that as I've shown it to students over a number of years, their responses have changed in relation to some changes in ways of representing gender and sexuality in the wider visual culture of Britain from the late 1980s to the late 1990s. When I first showed it, students would often agree with Pollock's interpretation, although sometimes it would be suggested that the man looked rather henpecked and that this somehow justified his harmless fun. It would have been interesting to see if this opinion came significantly more often from male students than female, since the work cited above would assume that the gender of its audiences in particular would make a difference to how this photo was seen. More recently, though, another response has been made more often. And that is to wonder what the woman is looking at. For in a way, Pollock's argument replicates what she criticizes: the denial of vision to the woman. Instead, more and more of my students have started to speculate on what the woman in the photo is admiring. Women students now quite often suggest that of course what she is appreciating is a gorgeous semi-naked man, and sometimes they say, maybe it's a gorgeous woman. These responses depend on three things, I think. One is the increasing representation in the last few years of male bodies as objects of desire in advertising (especially, it seems to me, in perfume adverts); we are more used now to seeing men on display as well as women. Another development is what I would very cautiously describe as 'girlpower'; the apparently increasing ability of young women to say what they want, what they really really want. And a third development might be the recent fashionability in Britain of what has been called 'lesbian chic'. Now of course, it would take a serious study (using some of the methods I will explore in this book) to sustain any of these suggestions, but I offer them here, tentatively, as an example of how an image can be read differently by different audiences: in this case, by different genders and at different historical moments.

There are, then, two aspects of the social modality of audiencing: the social practices of spectating and the social identities of the spectators. Some work, however, has drawn these two aspects of audiencing together to argue that only certain sorts of people do certain sorts of images in particular ways. Sociologists Pierre Bourdieu and Alain Darbel (1991), for example, have undertaken large-scale surveys of the visitors to art galleries, and have argued that the dominant way of visiting art galleries – walking around quietly from painting to painting, appreciating the particular qualities of each one, contemplating them in quiet awe – is a practice associated with middle-class visitors to galleries. As they say, 'museum visiting increases very strongly with increasing level of education, and is almost exclusively the domain of the cultivated classes' (Bourdieu and Darbel, 1991: 14). They are quite clear that this is not because those who are not middle class are incapable of appreciating art. Bourdieu and Darbel (1991: 39) say that, 'considered as symbolic goods, works of art only exist for those who have the means of appropriating them, that is, of deciphering them'. To appreciate works of art you need to be able to understand, or to decipher, their style – otherwise they will mean little to you. And it is only the middle classes who have been educated to be competent in that deciphering. Thus they suggest, rather, that those who are not middle class are not taught to appreciate art; that although the curators of galleries and the 'cultivated classes' would deny it, they have learnt what to do in galleries and they are not sharing their lessons with anyone else. Art galleries therefore exclude certain groups of people. Indeed, in other work Bourdieu (1984) goes further and suggests that competence in such techniques of appreciation actually defines an individual as middle class. In order to be properly middle class, one must know how to appreciate art, and how to perform that appreciation appropriately (no popcorn please).

The Doisneau photograph is an interesting example here again. Many reproductions of his photographs were produced and could be bought in Britain from a chain of shops called Athena (which went out of business some time ago). Athena also sold posters of pop stars, cute animals, muscle-bound men holding babies, and so on. Students in my classes would be rather divided over whether buying such images from Athena was something they would do or not – whether it showed you had (a certain kind of) taste or not. I find Doisneau's photographs rather sentimental and tricksy, rather stereotyped – and I rarely bought anything from Athena to stick on the walls of the rooms I lived in when I was a student. Instead, I preferred postcards of modernist paintings picked up on my summer trips to European art galleries. This was a genuine preference but I also know that I wanted the people who visited my room to see that I was . . . well, cultured. And students I now teach tell me that they often think about the images with which they decorate their rooms in the same manner – they certainly look at the posters and postcards stuck up on their friends' walls in the same way. Our use of images, our appreciation of certain kinds of imagery, performs a social function as well as an aesthetic one. It says something about who we are and how we want to be seen.

These issues surrounding the audiencing of images are often researched using methods that are quite common in qualitative social science research: interviews, ethnography, and so on. This will be explored in Chapter 8. However, as I have noted above, it is possible and necessary to consider the viewing practices of one spectator without using such techniques because that spectator is you. It is important to consider how you are looking at a particular image and to write – or perhaps express visually – that into your interpretation. Exactly what this call to reflexivity means is a question that will recur throughout this book.

5   choosing a method

The previous section tried to translate the general concerns of the critical visual methodology outlined in sections 3 and 4 into some more empirically oriented areas of interest. This is an important step, because it allows subsequent chapters to evaluate the strengths and weaknesses of particular methods on the basis of their ability to access those areas of interest. Each of the following chapters discusses one method for analysing visual images in some detail. The method will be summarized and explored through a case study, and then its strengths and weaknesses will be discussed.

Before choosing your method and commencing your analysis, however, you need to do two sorts of preparatory reading. First, all of these methods require some sorts of contextual knowledge about the imagery you are interested in. It is always important to know something about all aspects of the image you want to research; even if the audience is your main analytical focus, it is often useful to know something about the production of the image too. So before you utilize any of the methods which the following chapters discuss, look at the bibliographies at the end of the book to help you find some background material, and use the other resources at your disposal too: libraries, databases, reading lists and so on. Search for what others have written on the medium in which you're interested – say, photography, in the Doisneau case – and on the genres which you think are relevant to the images you're concerned with – in this case, street photography. If you have an 'artist' of some kind as the producer of your images, look for what has been written on him or her.

Having said that you need some broad contextual knowledge, however, it is crucial to note that there are very few studies of visual culture which attempt to examine all the areas outlined in the previous section, and those that do suffer (I think) from a certain analytical incoherence. As I hope is clear, engaging with the debates in visual culture means deciding which site and which modalities you think are most important in explaining the effect of an image. Moreover, none of the methods discussed in this book claim to address all those areas either. Figure 1.4 is an attempt to suggest how the various methods this book will discuss – compositional interpretation, content analysis, semiology, psychoanalysis, discourse analysis and audience studies – each have their own analytical assumptions and thus their own empirical focus.

Both theoretically and methodologically, then, any interpretation of images must focus on just some of the issues raised in the previous section. As I hope this chapter has made clear, there are many ways of understanding visual imagery and different theoretical standpoints have quite different methodological implications. This means that you need to address some of the theoretical issues raised in this chapter before plunging into the analysis of visual material, and this is the second sort of preparatory reading you need to do. If, having done that, you think that the audience is the most important site at which the meaning of an image is made, and that the social is that site's most important modality (these are theoretical choices), then there is no point doing huge amounts of research on the production processes or the technologies of the image you're concerned with. Theoretical decisions will enable you to focus your methodological strategies.

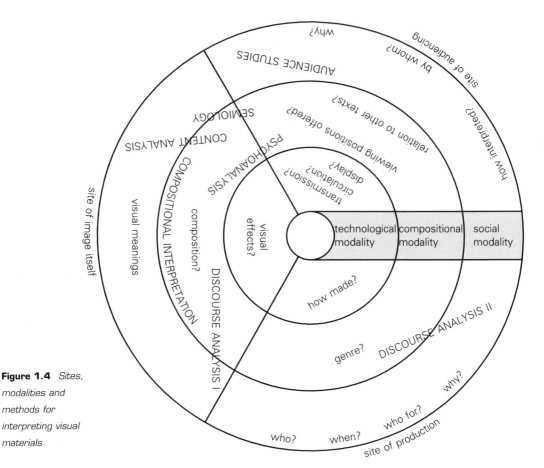

Figure 1.4 *Sites, modalities and methods for interpreting visual materials*

6 finding, referencing and reproducing your images

This book assumes that you have already found the images with which you want to research. If you haven't, the possible sources you might use are endless. There are contemporary exhibitions, galleries, magazines, cinemas, tv shows, videos and web pages; there are historical archives and museums. Lois Swan-Jones (1999) offers a useful guide to *Art Information on the Internet*, and there is also the *Picture Researcher's Handbook* (Evans and Evans, 1996; see also Eakins and Loving, 1985). The key texts listed in the bibliographies at the end of this book may also provide some ideas. If you find just one image that intrigues you, that's a start. You can find more related images by searching for published work on the artist who made that first image, or on the genre to which it belongs. If it's an historical image, contact its owners, and make use of archivists; they are almost always extremely helpful and knowledgeable.

Once you have found your images, there are a number of considerations to bear in mind in relation to their eventual use in your essay or dissertation. First, you need to be able to *reference* them in as clear a manner as you would reference any other source material. That is, you need to record as much of the following sort of information as possible. For a painting, for example, you'll need the name and date of the artist who made the image, the title of the piece, the date of its creation, the materials from which it is made, its dimensions, its condition, its current location and its accession number (if it is now in a collection). For an advertisement in a magazine, perhaps you'd need the name, date, volume number and place of publication of the magazine, plus the number of the page on which the advert appeared and its size; or, if you know about the whole campaign of which this advert is a part, you need to make systematic reference to the different parts of that campaign.

Second, you need to consider the precise *format* in which you will interpret your images. In particular, how much material beyond the image itself will you need? Surrounding text can make a big difference to a picture's interpretation. The Doisneau photograph, for example, has been give three different titles by the various books it has been reproduced in: 'A Sidelong Glance', 'Painting by Wagner in the window of the Galerie Romi, Rue de Seine, Paris 6e, 1948', 'An Oblique Look'. Each encourages a rather different interpretation. Other aspects of an image's format are important too. If you are studying a painting, is it important that you see the original, or is a reproduction good enough? Should you be concerned with its original site of display, or is seeing it in a gallery adequate? If it's an advertisement, how important is it to know what was printed next to it in a magazine? Some of these concerns depend, again, on what theoretical position you are adopting. Knowing where an advert appeared in a magazine would be more important if you were using discourse analysis (Chapter 6), for example, than if you were using compositional interpretation (Chapter 2) or content analysis (Chapter 3). However, they can be crucial regardless of your particular method. Cartoons, for example, are meaningless without their accompanying text.

Finally, it's always useful to bear in mind how you might *reproduce* the images you are researching. If you are writing something on visual images, it is important to show the reader what you are discussing. Don't crop or otherwise tamper with the reproduction without making your intervention clear to your reader (if you've cut an image down to show a small part of it, say it's a 'detail' of the work). In *Ways of Seeing*, John Berger (1972) goes even further and offers essays consisting entirely of images; you might feel that some of the things you want to say about your images are better shown visually, as a photo-essay perhaps, or by annotating your images with text and other images as Berger also does (see Figure 1.2). Colour photocopying is an excellent way to reproduce published images for essays (even black and white photographs are better copied this way because the various shades of grey are much better preserved). You can also download images from the web. If these sorts of reproductions are for private research purposes only, there is usually no problem with copyright. However, if you think you might publish your work, then you will often be legally obliged to obtain permission from the copyright holders to reproduce it; Rosemary Eakins and Elizabeth Loving (1985: 8–15) have a guide to pictures and the law. Reproduction for publication often entails paying a fee to the copyright holders too, and you will need your sources clearly recorded to do this.

7 summary

- visual imagery is never innocent; it is always constructed through various practices, technologies and knowledges.
- a critical approach to visual images is therefore needed: one that thinks about the agency of the image, considers the social practices and effects of its viewing, and reflects on the specificity of that viewing by various audiences including the academic critic.
- the meanings of an image or set of images are made at three sites: the sites of production, the image itself, and its audiencing.
- there are three modalities to each of these sites: technological, compositional, and social.
- theoretical debates about how to interpret images can be understood as debates over which of these sites and modalities is most important for understanding an image.
- these debates affect the methodology that is most appropriately brought to bear on particular images.
- consider your requirements for reproducing images as you choose which ones to discuss.

further reading

Stuart Hall in his essay 'The work of representation' (1997b) offers a very clear discussion of recent debates about culture, representation and power. A useful collection of some of the key texts that have contributed towards the field of visual culture has been put together by Jessica Evans and Stuart Hall as *Visual Culture: The Reader* (1999). Hal Foster's collection *Vision and Visuality* (1988b) contains essays by some leading theorists that nicely summarise their positions.

2

'The good eye'

looking at pictures using compositional interpretation

1　an introduction to compositional interpretation

The first criterion for a critical approach to visual imagery that the previous chapter outlined (in section 3) was the need to take images seriously.
That is, it is crucial to look very carefully at the image or images in which
you are interested, because the image itself has its own effects. These
effects are always embedded in social practices, of course, and may well be
negotiated by the image's audiences; nevertheless, it seems to me that there
is no point in researching any aspect of the visual unless the power of the
visual is acknowledged. As Norman Bryson (1991: 71) says of paintings,
'the power of the painting is there, in the thousands of gazes caught by its
surface, and the resultant turning, and the shifting, the redirecting of the
discursive flow'. Paintings, like other visual images, catch the gazes of
spectators and affect them in some way, and they do so through how they
look.

　　But how can you describe how an image looks? This chapter explores
one approach which offers a detailed vocabulary for expressing the
appearance of an image. I have chosen to call this approach 'compositional
interpretation'. This is a term I have invented for describing an approach to
imagery which has developed through certain kinds of art history. I need to
invent a term because the method has tended to be conveyed by example
rather than by explication (some exceptions to this generalization include
Acton, 1997; Gilbert, 1995; O'Toole, 1994; Taylor, 1957). This method
depends on what Irit Rogoff (1998: 17) calls 'the good eye'; that is, a way
of looking at paintings that is not methodologically explicit but which
nevertheless produces a specific way of describing paintings. The 'good eye'
pays attention to what it sees as high Art, and refuses to be either
methodologically or theoretically explicit. It thus functions as a kind of

Connoisseurship　visual **connoisseurship**.

> Connoisseurship involves the acquisition of extensive first-hand experience of works of art with the aim, first, of attributing works to artists and schools, identifying styles and establishing sources and influences, and second, of judging their quality and hence their place in a canon. (Fernie, 1995: 330)

Developing a 'good eye' requires a lot of a certain kind of what the previous chapter described as 'contextual information'. Specifically, you need a lot of knowledge about particular painters, about the kinds of painting they did, about the sorts of visual imagery they were looking at and being inspired by. All this is then used by the 'good eye' to assess paintings for their 'quality'. Thus compositional interpretation claims to look at images for 'what they are', rather than for, say, what they do or how they were or are used. The 'good eye' therefore looks mostly at the site of an *image itself* in order to understand its significance, and pays most (although not exclusive) attention to its *compositional* modality.

As this is an approach long established in art history, it is usually used in relation to one of the sorts of objects that art historians have traditionally studied: paintings. This chapter will mostly follow that practice, although section 4 will introduce some terms for describing the compositional modality of moving images. Its case study of compositional interpretation is a review written by Adrian Searle in 1999 for *The Guardian* newspaper of an exhibition of self-portraits by Rembrandt van Rijn, a Dutch painter who was born in 1606 and died in 1669. Most of this review is reprinted, with two of its five illustrations, below.

'I can think of no room of paintings in the world so moving'.

Adrian Searle is astounded by Rembrandt's self-portraits.

It is night in the National Gallery. The lights are off. The machines that sniff the humidity and check the temperature are quietly ticking over, the alarm system is primed. The guards make their rounds, and outside in Trafalgar Square the clubbers are waiting for the night bus home. From tomorrow morning the queues will be forming for the exhibition 'Rembrandt By Himself', which brings together almost all of Rembrandt's self-portraits, the paintings, etchings and drawings he made of himself over the entirety of his artistic career. But for now I imagine Rembrandt's self-portraits, looking out into the twilit empty rooms in the Sainsbury Wing. I know they're there.

I think of his ghost, with what Picasso called 'that elephant's eye of his', that bulbous nose and the head with its curls spilling from under a mob cap, a turban, a plumed beret, a helmet. Rembrandt young, porcine and adenoidal; Rembrandt old as the painter-king. Rembrandt grimacing open-mouthed into a mirror as he draws on an etching-plate.

Rembrandt dressed as an Oriental Potentate, Rembrandt in a cloak and Rembrandt as a beggar. I think of his multiple selves looking out into the dark, painting himself as though he were already a figure from history . . .

Looking at late Rembrandt, we think we can tell how it is to be old, to have been old then, in 1669, prematurely aged at 63. What we are looking at is an old man with old skin in an old painting with a cracked and sallow surface, Rembrandt in the soft yellowing light, the last bright highlights in his eyes. It is almost impossible to look at Rembrandt's paintings of himself without regarding them as the artist's meditations on mortality, as a dialogue with himself conducted with a heart-breaking truthfulness and candour. That is how we are accustomed to read these self-portraits, we look into their painted space, now three-and-a-half centuries old. We think we are looking at the painter as much as the paintings, seeing the man himself in his own self-image, and in the brushwork that created it. The paint molten, distressed, frank, concentrated, cursory, darkened, yellowed, translucent and papery. The painted surface at times as worn and slovenly as an old man's table, as though the painting itself were evidence of human fortitude and endurance. The catalogue essays can't dispel this view, but they set Rembrandt's self-portraiture within a context that tempers our projected existential feelings about it. It is odd, isn't it, that Rembrandt painted himself so often in clothing from the dressing-up box of the previous century – a rag-bag property-box of costumes, outlandish headgear, brocades and cloaks – and yet that he should also be a painter whose timelessness and contemporaneity continues to strike us so forcibly . . .

But what scholarship cannot do, finally, is to dispel the disquiet Rembrandt's paintings arouse, the sense that Rembrandt was both unrepeatable and inescapable as a painter of himself. He painted and drew with a candour – at least, we suppose it was candour – about what was happening to his appearance as he got older. Perhaps he saw himself as a 'type', no less than his paintings were 'types', and saw his own face as a vessel of universal characteristics – melancholia and black bile marking his like a map . . .

Later, he tries on all manner of costumes, and grows in stature and solidity with every one. He paints the spots on this cheek and that inescapable great nose. He goes on to paint himself in all his guises, but he ends up painting himself, both with a sort of grandeur, and with what we can only see as humility.

'Rembrandt By Himself' is undoubtedly going to be a block-buster, although it is a much smaller show than Monet at the Royal Academy, with only 30 painted self-portraits by the artist – over some of which, the question of attribution still hangs – as well as his numerous etchings of himself, in numerous states, and works by Rembrandt's pupils, and paintings which might be seen as precursors to the artist's works, such as the National's *Portrait of a Man*, by Titian, assumed by some to be Titian himself.

Apart from the two self-portraits by Carel Fabritius, Rembrandt's most talented pupil (who was accidentally blown up when a gunpowder factory exploded in Delft), most of these works are unnecessary to the show. They are makeweights. But there's nothing to truly argue with here. I can think of no other room of paintings in the world at this moment (apart from the room of Goya's black paintings in the Prado) so moving and disquieting as the central gallery of the Rembrandt show, containing the self-portraits of the last half of his career. Standing in this room I realised that you can't review Rembrandt. Rembrandt reviews you.

extracted from *The Guardian*, 8 June 1999,
page 12 of arts supplement

Figure 2.1
Rembrandt van Rijn,
Self-portrait, *1629*
(Isabella Stewart
Gardner Museum,
Boston)

Figure 2.2
Rembrandt van Rijn,
Self-portrait, *1657*
(Duke of Sutherland
collection, on loan to
the National Gallery
of Scotland)

I will return to this review in sections 2 and 3 of this chapter.

As a method for developing a critical visual methodology along the lines sketched in the previous chapter, compositional interpretation has its limitations. Visual images do not exist in a vacuum, and looking at them for 'what they are' neglects the ways in which they are produced and interpreted through particular social practices. Bryson makes this clear when he adds two qualifications to his comments quoted above about the power of the painting. First, he says, 'my ability to recognise an image . . . is . . . an ability which presupposes competence within the social, that is socially constructed, codes of recognition' (Bryson, 1991: 65). Second, 'the social formation isn't . . . something which supervenes or appropriates or utilizes the image so to speak *after* it has been made; rather, painting . . . unfolds from within the social formation from the beginning' (Bryson, 1991: 66). Moreover, compositional interpretation does not reflect on its own practices. This chapter will therefore be able to pay little attention to these two aspects of a critical visual methodology.

Despite these absences, compositional interpretation remains a useful method because it does offer a way of looking very carefully at the content and form of images. The successful deployment of many of the other methods discussed in this book – methods which I think are more appropriate for a critical visual methodology – nonetheless rely, initially, on the detailed scrutiny of the image itself. Nigel Whitely (1999) complains that too often in the social sciences, this initial stage is neglected and the power of the image is subordinated to the theoretical debates in which its interpretation is embedded. Whitely (1999: 107) insists that compositional interpretation should be undertaken seriously, and that it should then be 'conjoined to other types of analysis so that the visual scrutiny of what can literally be seen can be studied in relation to reception, meaning and content'. This chapter will offer some suggestions about how to achieve that 'visual scrutiny' adequately; and in order to be helpfully explicit, I will occasionally draw on writers whose work has in many ways distanced itself from more traditional art history approaches, but who still offer useful methodological pointers. So this chapter will:

- explore the key terms used by compositional interpretation to describe the compositional modality of an image itself;
- discuss the method's reliance on certain implicit ideas about high Art;
- assess the usefulness of compositional interpretation for a critical visual methodology.

2 the production of the image: technologies

Despite its lack of methodological explicitness, then, compositional interpretation is a very particular way of looking at images. It focuses most strongly on the image itself, and although it pays most attention to its compositionality, it also pays some attention to its *production*. Usually a note is made of aspects of the *social* modality of its production: who commissioned it, why, who painted it, and what then happened to it before it ended up in its current location (the various owners and locations of a **Provenance** painting are known as its **provenance**). And connoisseurship also involves exploring the *compositional* modality of its production.

But attention is usually focused mostly on the *technological* modality of the making of an image. As the discussion of technologies in the previous chapter noted, it can be important to know with what material and technique an image is made because that can affect the impact an image has. Joshua Taylor (1957) provides some very useful discussions of the various technologies that have been used to produce pictorial images. He explores the particular qualities of both certain media – drawing, painting, graphic arts, sculpture and architecture – and the various ways in which these can be deployed. His discussion of painting, for example, examines the different techniques of fresco, watercolour, tempera, oil, encaustic and collage. James Monaco (2000) examines the technologies of moving images in similar detail. However, as Taylor (1957: 70) notes, the only reason for paying much attention to the technologies of an image's production is 'when a knowledge of the technique helps in describing the particular characteristics of the work'.

focus

Where does Searle's essay refer to the effect of their use of oil paints on Rembrandt's portraits? What effects does his description of the oils have?

3   the image itself: its compositionality

Compositional interpretation pays most attention to the compositionality of the image itself. This section breaks down the compositionality seen by the 'good eye' into a number of components. This is a schematic device, however, since in practice few of these components are completely distinct **Composition** from each other. Indeed, the notion of **composition** refers to all these elements in combination.

3.1   content

When looking at an image for itself, a starting point could be its content. What does the image actually show? This might seem a very obvious question not worth spending much time on. And for some images it will indeed be a very simple question. For others, though, it will not. For example, some viewers of the Doisneau photograph reproduced as Figure 1.3 need a bit of time to work out that the photographer is inside the gallery looking out into the street. Moreover, some images picture particular religious, historical, mythological, moral or literary themes or events, as Acton (1997) discusses (and section 3.2 in Chapter 6 will explore a method whose aim is to decode the conventionalized visual symbols used to refer to such themes and events: iconography). Take some time to be sure you are sure about what you think an image is showing.

3.2 colour

Colour is another crucial component of an image's compositionality. Taylor (1957) offers three ways of describing the colours of a painting:

Hue

1 **hue.** This refers to the actual colours in a painting. Thus the dominant hues used in the Rembrandt portraits reproduced for Searle's review are browns, blues and flesh.

Saturation

2 **saturation.** Saturation refers to the purity of a colour in relation to its appearance in the colour spectrum. Thus saturation is high if a colour is used in a vivid form of its hue, and low if it is nearly neutral. The blues and flesh colours in the review's illustrations are low, but the browns are high: rich and intense.

Value

3 **value.** This refers to the lightness or darkness of a colour. If a colour is in its near-white form, then its value is high; if in its near-black form, its value is low. The browns, blacks and some of the blues in the illustrations have low value: they are all dark. But other blues, and flesh colours, seem to have quite high value.

These terms can describe the colours used in a painting. But it is also necessary to describe the effects of the colours in an image. Colour can be used to *stress* certain elements of an image, for example. The flesh colours in particular in the illustrations to Searle's essay seem to have quite high value, because they are often where the light falls in the painting; but of course since these are portraits, the high value of the face colours serves to draw our attention to the point of portrait paintings, the face.

There is also the question of how *harmonious* the colour combination of a painting is. There have been many theories about what colours combine most harmoniously with each other, and John Gage (1993) offers a very full account of the different ways in which colour has been understood 'from antiquity to abstraction', as the subtitle of this book says. For our purposes here, however, it is sufficient to consider whether the colours of a painting rely on contrasts or on the blending of similar value or saturation hues. The Rembrandt illustrations appear very harmonious since they have a limited range of colours which blend into each other; even the blue is a muted contrast to the brown since, like the browns, it is mostly of low saturation. Gunther Kress and Theo van Leeuwen (1996: 163–5) also suggest that the combination of hues, values and saturations of an image affect how realistic audiences will imagine that image to be. If the colours look the same as a colour photograph of the same subject would, then our sense of its realism is heightened, they suggest.

Atmospheric perspective

Colour can also work to suggest an effect of distance in a painting, especially in landscape paintings. In that genre, the hues used often become more bluish as a means of suggesting the way a landscape recedes. This is known as **atmospheric perspective**.

3.3 spatial organization

All images have their space organized in some way, and there are two related aspects of this organization to consider: the organization of space 'within' an image, and the way the spatial organization of an image offers a particular viewing position to its spectator. This offer is part of an image's way of seeing.

First, the spatial organization within the image (Acton, 1997: 1–24 has a useful discussion of this). Take a look at the *volumes* of an image. How are these arranged in relation to each other? Are some volumes connected in some way to others, while others are left isolated? How? What about the *lines* of the volumes and their connections? Which directions do they follow? Are they fluid curves or jagged fragments? What sort of *rhythm* do they have: static or dynamic? What are the effects of these things? Kress and van Leeuwen (1996: 79–118) have an interesting discussion of images such as diagrams, flow charts and maps that explores how their elements are conventionally structured in relation to each other.

Then consider the space in which these volumes are placed. Acton (1997: 25–50) suggests thinking about width, depth, interval and distance. Is this space simple, or complicated? In answering this question, it is important to understand something about perspective, which is the method used in Western art to make a two-dimensional image look as if it shows three-dimensional space. Perspective, like colour, has a long history in Western discourse, and there is more than one kind of system of perspective (Andrews, 1995; Edgerton, 1975; Elkins, 1994; Kress and van Leeuwen, 1996). Section 3.2 has already mentioned that colour can be used to convey distance in landscape painting. This section considers **geometrical perspective**, and even this has its variations. However, there are some basic principles which provide starting points for thinking about the space represented by an image. Perspective depends on a geometry of rays of vision, and your eye is central to this geometry (several perspective systems assume that the viewer of a scene is a single point and thus that you have only one eye). The level of your eye is always the same as the horizon of a painting. It is also the level at which the rays of vision converge at what is called the vanishing point. Figure 2.3 shows what

Geometrical perspective

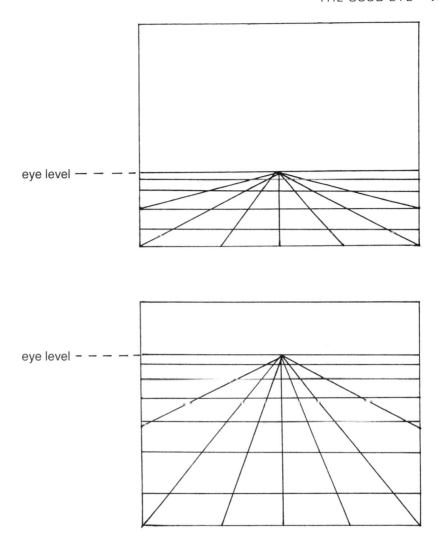

eye level — — — —

eye level — — — —

Figure 2.3

difference your eye level makes to the representation of a paved area, if you were sitting first on the ground and then on a high wall, according to this kind of perspective.

Now let's see what happens if some basic building blocks appear in this scene, one close to us and one further apart (Figure 2.4).

Finally, Figure 2.5 shows what happens if there are two different eye levels and two different vanishing points in an image of blocks.

Paintings can have different effects depending on their manipulation of this kind of perspective. In relation to Figure 2.5, for example, since one eye is assumed to be normal in this geometrical system, the space constructed with two eye levels seems strange and incoherent. Other paintings try to shift the spectator's point of view through their use of perspective. For example, using a very low eye level might represent the way a child

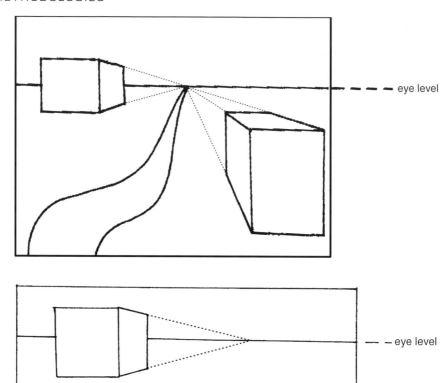

Figure 2.4

Figure 2.5

sees the world, and Pollock (1988: 65) suggests that Mary Cassatt painted some of her canvases with this effect in mind (see Figure 2.6).

Or a low eye level might suggest that the painting was made to be seen from below, and this is the case with, for example, Masaccio's crucifixion, painted in about 1427 as a fresco on the wall of the church of Santa Maria Novella in Firenze, where the congregation would sit beneath it (Edgerton, 1975). Perspective thus provides a means of representing three-dimensional space on a two-dimensional surface. It dominated Western painting for centuries, from its first explication in the fifteenth century to its rejection by some painters in the early twentieth. Although now it is only one means among many of organizing its space, it can provide a benchmark for thinking about the representation of space in any particular image.

Figure 2.6 *Mary
Cassatt*, Little Girl
in a Blue
Armchair, *1878*
(National Gallery
of Art,
Washington,
Mellon collection)

focus

How do the Rembrandt portraits use geometrical perspective? Do we look down on
the painted figure, or up to him?

A useful way to explore these aspects of the spatial organization within an image is
to try to draw a summary diagram of the image you're looking at (see Taylor, 1957
and Kress and van Leeuwen, 1996: 47 for some examples). Look for lines that
show the edges of things; extend them, and see where and how they intersect. The
Rembrandt illustrations reproduced here are perhaps too simple in terms of their
spatial organization to make this a worthwhile exercise; but you might try making
a simplified version of the painting reproduced as Figure 6.1 which is a marriage
portrait of Giovanni Arnolfini and Giovanna Cenami and was painted in 1434 by
Jan van Eyck. Try extending the lines of the floorboards, the windowsill and the
bedstead, for example. James Elkins (1991) has explored the use of perspective in
this painting through just such a diagram of its converging and diverging lines.
Compare his to yours.

This discussion of perspective brings us to the second aspect of the
spatial organization of an image which is necessary to consider. This is the
way in which the picture also offers a particular position to its viewers. We
have already seen this process at work in our discussion of the Doisneau

photograph in Chapter 1. The elements 'inside' that photo are arranged in such a way that they construct a particular viewing position 'outside' the photo (and this makes the distinction between 'inside' and 'outside' difficult to sustain). The Doisneau photograph aligns the spectator with the look of the man. Michael Ann Holly (1996) has argued that it is this positioning of the viewer that is most important when thinking about how visual images have their own effects. (This is not an uncontroversial claim; Chapter 8 in particular will emphasize that particular spectators may not take up the position offered to them by an image.) In asking 'what the work of art does for us' (Holly, 1996: xiv), Holly argues that it is the spatial and temporal organization of a painting which structures its effects

Logic of figuration most profoundly. This organization she calls the **logic of figuration** of an image. She says, 'legislated and predicted by the spatial and temporal organisation of the visual field: we stand where the works tell us to stand and we see what they choose to reveal' (Holly, 1996: 9). Kress and van Leeuwen (1996: 119) talk in similar terms about the ways images can be seen as 'designing the position of the viewer' through, in part at least, their spatial organization. Holly examines this effect through a discussion of early renaissance paintings and 'a few classic cultural histories from the nineteenth and twentieth centuries' (Holly, 1996: xiii), suggesting that the histories, in their panoramic sweep, reflect the rules of perspective through which the paintings were constructed.

Kress and van Leeuwen (1996: 119–58) also explore the effects of the spatial organization of visual images on the position of the viewer. Like Holly, they examine the effects of geometrical perspective in some detail. They suggest, for example, that the *angle* between the spectator and what is pictured produces particular effects, with frontal angles engaging the viewer more with what is pictured than oblique angles (Kress and van Leeuwen, 1996: 140–6). They also explore the effects of apparent differences in *height* between the spectator of an image and what is pictured: if the viewer is positioned by the image's perspective to look down on it, Kress and van Leeuwen (1996: 146–8) argue, they are given some sort of power over its subject matter; if they look up to it, then they are positioned as in some way inferior to it; and if they look at it on the same level, then a relationship of equality between spectator and pictured is suggested. They also look at other aspects of the spatial organization of images: *distance*, for example, suggesting that pictures of people in close-up usually offer a relation of intimacy between the person pictured and the spectator (Kress and van Leeuwen, 1996: 130–5). Searle assumes this in his discussion of the Rembrandt portraits. However, an exception to this latter claim suggests that these sorts of generalization must always be carefully examined in relation to specific images: think, for example, of the use of police mugshots in newspaper reports of crimes, where the close-up format of the mugshot suggests precisely a big difference between the person pictured – the criminal – and the person looking – the innocent newspaper reader. In this case, too, though, the spatial organization of the composition is a crucial element of the relationship between an image and its audiences.

Mieke Bal (1991: 158–60), on the other hand, advocates concentrating on the visual organization of looks and gazes in her notion of the **Focalizers** **focalizers** of an image. She points out that all paintings have a range of viewers: addressed, implied and represented. Each focalizes in their own way (see also Kress and van Leeuwen, 1996: 121–35). The relations of looks between them – who can see what and how – can tell us much about how the image works to catch our looks. For if an external focalizer – a spectator – can look in the same way at the same things as a focalizer in the picture, then the spectator's identification with the image will be strong, says Bal. An example of this sort of analysis is Pollock's (1988) account of the Doisneau photograph that was discussed in the previous chapter. Pollock examined the structure of the looks in the photograph and the way in which the look of the spectator was incorporated into these.

Thus the spatial organization of an image is not innocent. It has effects. It produces a specific relation between image and spectator.

---

focus

What position are we offered by the logic of figuration and the focalizers of the Rembrandt portraits? What account does Searle give of this position?

Through their use of geometrical perspective, the Rembrandt portraits position us as looking at the same level as the painter; we neither look down on to his image nor up at it. In that spatial sense we are at the same level as him. And we look at him in the way that he seems to be looking at us: directly.

Searle develops this sense of directness and equality between the artist's self-image and our view of it in particular ways. Searle says that these are paintings done by a man in dialogue with himself; we as spectators are now in the place of the mirror that Rembrandt must have used to make these pictures of himself. But he also suggests that Rembrandt's face is 'a vessel of universal characteristics' that he painted with 'candour'; the artist's honesty, his directness in confronting his own image and now us, mean that his portraits touch us now in 'moving and disquieting' ways. Indeed, such is the strength of Rembrandt's gaze, Searle eventually claims that he is reviewing us, not the other way round. Thus Searle glosses aspects of the spatial organization and focalization of these portraits in specific ways. He gives a particular meaning to them.

3.4 light

The light shown in an image is clearly related to both its colours and its spaces. What *type* of light a painting represents – candlelight, daylight, electric light – will clearly affect the saturation and value of its hues. And the illusion that geometrical perspective realistically represents three-dimensional space can be enhanced or called into question by the use of light *sources*. The apparent realism of the Arnolfini portrait (Figure 6.1) is increased, for example, by the dominant source of light coming from the window and the way all the shadows in the painting are consistent with this. Light can also be used to *highlight* certain elements of a painting, as we have seen in the case of the Rembrandt portraits.

3.5 expressive content

Expressive content

Finally in this section, I want to mention a more elusive aspect of this approach to images because, despite its rather uncertain methodological status, it is crucial to this mode of interpretation and to many others. That is the evocation in writing of the 'feel' of an image, or what, after Taylor, I will call its **expressive content**. Taylor (1957: 43–4) describes an image's expressive content as 'the combined effect of subject matter and visual form'. Separate consideration of expressive content is necessary because breaking an image into its component parts – spatial organization, colour, content, light – does not necessarily capture the look of an image. Instead, what may be needed is some imaginative writing that tries to evoke its affective characteristics. As an example, here is the art historian Erwin Panofsky writing about the Arnolfini portrait reproduced as Figure 6.1:

> In a comfortably furnished interior, suffused with a warm, dim light, Giovanni Arnolfini and his wife are standing represented in full-length . . . The husband gingerly holds the lady's right hand in his left while raising his right in a gesture of solemn affirmation. Rather stiffly posed and standing as far apart as the action permits, they do not look at each other yet seem to be united by a mysterious bond. (Panofsky, 1953: 201–2)

Panofsky uses terms like 'comfortably', 'gingerly' and 'solemn' which would be difficult to produce relying solely on the list of concerns this chapter has offered, yet they seem necessary elements in any account of this painting.

The expressive content of an image is always crucial to consider. However, it is important that your reaction to it does not obscure other issues concerning the meaning of the image.

focus

Return to Searle's review one more time. The expressive content of the Rembrandt portraits is central to his discussion of them. Pick out the moments in his text when he evokes it.

Searle's efforts to articulate the expressive content of the Rembrandt self-portraits are particularly interesting because they explicitly reject (or marginalize) other ways of relating to the paintings. What does Searle imply are unimportant in understanding the portraits, compared to the impact of their expressive content?

Searle suggests that both the gallery and the catalogue become somewhat irrelevant next to the extraordinary effects of the portraits. This tactic is typical of the connoisseurship central to the 'good eye'. Only the 'quality' of the paintings matter; everything else – all the other sorts of interpretive apparatus brought to bear on them – is insignificant.

But of course Searle too is bringing an interpretive apparatus to bear on the portraits; the 'good eye' is itself an interpretive technique. This apparatus assumes that only the paintings are important, to begin with. But his discussion of them also draws on at least two other assumptions regarding great art. One is that it is

Genius produced by something called **genius**: a marvellously gifted individual who can rise above the specificities of his circumstances to touch what are apparently the fundamental concerns of human life (see Battersby, 1994 for a critique of the notion of genius, particularly the way it is a masculinized category). And the other

Art is that art – **Art** – can speak directly to this humanity in everyone.

Victor Burgin summarizes these definitions of Art and genius thus:

> *Art* is an activity characteristic of humanity since the dawn of civilisation. It any epoch the *Artist*, by virtue of special gifts, expresses that which is finest in humanity . . . the visual artist achieves this through modes of understanding and expression which are 'purely visual' . . . This special characteristic of art necessarily makes it an autonomous sphere of activity, completely separate from the everyday world of social and political life. The autonomous nature of visual art means that questions asked of it may only be properly put, and answered, in its own terms – all other forms of interrogation are irrelevant. (Burgin, 1986: 30)

Hence Searle's assertion that galleries and catalogues are irrelevant in relation to the Rembrandt portraits; because these portraits are Art, only his, and our, humanity matters. In this view, art is seen as cross-cultural, with universal appeal. In the introduction to their book on *Visual Culture*, Norman Bryson, Michael Ann Holly and Keith Moxey make clear the difference between approaches to visual images that depend on this notion of Art, and the approach to visual images that the contributors to their book adopt:

> Instead of seeking to promote and sustain the value of 'great' art by limiting discussion to the circumstances of the work's production and to speculation about the extraordinary impulses that may have characterized the intentions of its makers, these contributors examine the work performed by the image in the life of culture . . . Instead of applying a Kantian aesthetic, according to which value is an intrinsic characteristic of the work of art, one capable of being perceived by all human beings regardless of their location in time and place – a recognition that depends only on one's status as a human being – these writers betray an awareness that the aesthetic value of a work depends on the prevailing cultural conditions. They invest the work with value by mean of their appreciation of its meaning both in the cultural horizon of its production and its reception. (Bryson, Holly and Moxey, 1994: xvi)

Thus, while the connoisseurship usually accompanying the exercise of 'the good eye' denies the cultural specificity of Art, the notion of visual culture addresses that specificity directly.

A question remains, though. Is it possible to retain a sense of the power of (some) images, of their often visceral impact, if it is assumed that 'the aesthetic value of a work depends on the prevailing cultural conditions'?

4 the compositional interpretation of moving images

Thus far, compositional interpretation has been described as a method for describing paintings, but the same terms could be used to describe other sorts of still images too: photographs, for example. Some aspects of moving images – film, television and video, for example – can also be described using the terminology of compositional interpretation. Some of the terms used in the previous sections are conventionally given other names when used in relation to moving images, however, and moving images also require a further set of terms to describe their dynamic qualities. Monaco offers a detailed vocabulary for describing the spatial and temporal organization of moving images, and this section will draw on his very useful discussion (Monaco, 2000: 152–225).

Mise-en-scène

Montage

Monaco's discussion begins with a basic distinction between the spatial organization of a film, which is called its **mise-en-scène**, and its temporal organization, or its **montage**. Monaco (2000: 179) suggests that mise-en-scène is a result of decisions about what to shoot and how to shoot it, while montage is how the shots are presented. His descriptive vocabulary is divided between each of these. Two further considerations in interpreting many moving images is the sound that accompanies them, and, in the case of films that tell a story, their narrative structure.

4.1 mise-en-scène

Monaco (2000) suggests that what is shot involves looking at how the film frame is used, and that how it is shot concerns the structure of the shots themselves.

Screen ratio

There are three aspects of the framing of scenes to which Monaco (2000) calls attention. The first of these is the **screen ratio**. The screen ratio is the ratio between the height of the projected image and its width: that is, the screen ratio describes the shape of the screen. In classic Hollywood movies – those made in the Hollywood studio system of the 1930s, 1940s and 1950s – the screen ratio was 1.33. Monaco (2000: 184) suggests that this proportion facilitated directors and audiences focusing on faces and dialogue. In the 1950s, the arrival of widescreen with screen ratios 2.33 or more was parallelled by more landscape shots, location shooting and action movies. The second aspect of framing, according to Monaco (2000) is how the **screen frame** works. If the action is filmed in such a way that the space

Screen frame

beyond the screen frame is important, then the screen frame is *open*. If, on the other hand, the scene makes no reference to the space beyond its own frame, the screen frame is *closed*. Finally, Monaco (2000: 186–7, 192) discusses the **screen planes**. There are three of these, and they intersect. The *frame plane* is how forms are distributed across the screen; the *geographical plane* is how forms are distributed in three-dimensional space; and the *depth plane* is how the apparent depth of the images is perceived.

Also in relation to the frame, Monaco (2000) points out that a frame can contain **multiple images** if it is split, or images can shown as **superimpositions**, through techniques such as double exposure.

The second aspect of moving images' mise-en-scène is their shots. **Shot distance** refers to how much of a figure is shown by a particular shot, and a shot can be an *extreme long shot* (where the figure is in the far distance), a *long shot*, or a *full, three-quarters, medium, head and shoulders* or *close-up* shot. Monaco (2000) tentatively suggests some of the effects that the frequent use of one or other of these sorts of shots might produce in a particular film. The repeated use of close-ups, for example, may produce a sense of claustrophobic intensity, while long shots may imply alienation and emptiness. However, as was noted in section 3.3 of this chapter and as Monaco comments, these sorts of generalizations about the effects of the spatial organization of images always need to be assessed carefully in relation to specific images.

The **focus** of shots is also important. *Deep focus* is when the foreground, middle ground and background of a shot – all of the frame's geographical plane – are in focus. *Shallow focus* is when one of these grounds is more in focus than others. Focus can also be *sharp* or *soft*. Again, Monaco comments that certain kinds of focusing may have particular effects. Soft focus may be used to create a romantic or nostalgic feel to a scene, for example. But again, the precise effects of a particular kind of focus may not correspond to these sorts of generalizations.

The **angle** of shots also needs to be considered. The angle of *approach*, for example: is it square or oblique? The angle of *elevation* matters too: it can be overhead (looking right down on to the scene), high-angle, eye-level or low-angle (looking up at the scene). The shot may also *roll*, which is when the horizon of the image tilts, although Monaco notes that this is rare since it disrupts the union between camera and audience that cinema especially very often tries to maintain.

The **point of view** adopted by shots is also crucial to a film's effects. The camera may adopt the point of view of a particular character, for example, and in Chapter 6 we will see what use Hitchcock made of this device in his film *Vertigo*. The *reverse-angle* shot is a particular case of the camera adopting characters' points of view. It is very often used to show a conversation between two people: one is seen talking or listening from approximately the other's viewpoint as the other listens or talks. A recent celebrated example of this technique was the conversation between villain Robert de Niro and cop Al Pacino in Michael Mann's *Heat*: their

Screen planes

Multiple images
Superimpositions
Shot distance

Focus

Angle

Point of view

conversational confrontation in the movie was shot entirely with reverse angles so the viewer never saw the two men in the same frame together, an indication of the divisions between them perhaps. The camera may also adopt what Monaco (2000: 211) calls the '*third person*' shot, in which 'the camera often seems to take on a character of its own, separate from those of the characters'. In classic Hollywood movies, the opening point of view is very often a particular sort of this third-person shot. It is an *establishing* shot, which works to give the audience the information they need about place, time and character before the narrative begins.

Finally, Monaco offers a number of terms that refer to the way that the camera itself moves in film images. The camera can revolve while remaining stationary, or it can physically move. There are three kinds of

Pan shots possible when the camera revolves (Monaco, 2000: 97): the **pan**, when the camera moves along a horizontal axis, perhaps along the horizon

Tilt of a landscape; the **tilt**, when it moves along a vertical axis, perhaps

Roll moving from the head to the feet of a character; and the **roll**, which has

Tracking already been noted. When the camera itself moves, the shot is a **tracking**

Crane shot if the line it follows is horizontal, and a **crane** shot if the line it follows is vertical. An example of a tracking shot mentioned by Monaco (2000: 219) is the opening shot of Robert Altman's film *The Player*. This is a very long tracking shot which is also an establishing shot, as it moves through the lot of a Hollywood studio introducing location and characters to the

Zoom audience. Finally, there is the **zoom** shot, which is similar to a tracking shot but is made by a stationary camera. In a zoom shot, the figure in a scene remains the same size while the surroundings they are moving through changes in size.

4.2 montage

Montage refers to how the shots of a film are put together; that is, how

Editing they are presented. Another term for montage is **editing**. As Monaco (2000) comments, the vocabulary for describing different montage techniques is much less well developed than that which can be used to describe frames and shots.

In classic Hollywood cinema, and in many of its commercial products today, the principle behind montage is the maintenance of an impression of both narrative flow and spatial coherence. The kind of editing used to

Continuity cutting achieve this is known as **continuity cutting**. Shots are edited in order to allow the clear development of the story and to maintain a realistic representation of the spaces which the narrative occupies. There are many ways in which this is done, and as audiences of films we take many of them for granted. Establishing shots and reverse angles, for example, are seen as realistic ways of showing place and characters. Editing techiques like *jump cuts*, for example, when two completely unrelated images are spliced together, were rare in classic Hollywood cinema, because we do not perceive the world like that (although as Monaco, 2000 comments, many of the techniques we see as representing realistically how we see the world bear little resemblance to how we do actually look).

Cut   The jump cut is one sort of connection, or **cut**, that can be made between shots. It is an example of an *unmarked cut*, where one image ends and another starts. Other sorts of connections are the *fade*, where an image fades to black, the *dissolve*, which superimposes a fade in over a fade out, the *iris*, in which the image is reduced in size by an encroaching border circle, and the *wipe*, where one image removes another. The *rhythm* of cuts, determined by how long each shot is held, may also be important in considering a film's effects. For example, a series of progressively shorter scenes may contribute to the accumulation of tension as a narrative climax develops. Monaco (2000: 220–4) also spends some time on the complicated schema for describing montage developed by Christian Metz, a rare example of an attempt to formulate a typology for all montage possibilities and rather elaborate as a result.

4.3 sound

Sound is crucial to many moving images, especially movies. Monaco (2000) suggests that there are three types of sound: *environmental*, *speech* and *music*. Environmental sounds are noise effects, whether 'real' or artificial, and Monaco (2000: 213) comments that they can be crucial to a movie's expressive content. The music soundtrack of a movie is also fundamental to its effect. Monaco (2000: 214–15) also suggests three overlapping ways in which the relation between the sound and the image of a film can be considered. The *source* of the sound can be in or out of the frame. *Parallell* sound is sound which is actual, synchronous with and related to the image. In contrast, *contrapuntal* sound is commentative, asynchronous and opposes the image.

4.4 a summary of Monaco's schema

To summarize Monaco's descriptive vocabulary, the mise-en-scène can be understood in terms of:

1 *frame*:
   - *screen ratio*;
   - *screen frame*: open or closed;
   - *screen planes*: frame plane, geographical plane and depth plane;
   - *multiple images*;
   - *superimpositions*.
2 *shots*:
   - *shot distance*: extreme long shot, long shot, full, three-quarters, medium, head and shoulders, close-up shot;

- *shot focus*: deep or shallow, sharp or soft;
- *shot angle*: angle of approach, angle of elevation, angle of roll;
- *point of view*: character, third person, establishing, reverse angle;
- *pans*, *tilts*, *zooms* and *rolls*, when the camera remains in one position;
- *tracking* and *crane* shots, when the camera itself moves.

The montage of a moving image can be described with reference to:

3   *cuts*:
- *type of cut*: unmarked, fade, dissolve, iris, jump;
- *rhythm*.

The sounds of moving images can be described by considering:

4   *type*: music, environmental sound, speech;
5   *relation to the image*: source, parallel, contrapuntal.

Narrative structure

Finally, one thing to which Monaco (2000) pays little attention but which is central to some kinds of film and to criticism of those films: **narrative structure**. What is the story that a movie tells? What happens to its characters? Section 6 in Chapter 5 will discuss an interpretation of a film that pays close attention to the structure of its story as well as to its visual representation.

5   compositional interpretation: an assessment

Compositional interpretation thus offers ways of describing the content, colour, spatial organization, light and expressive content of a still image, and the mise-en-scène, montage, sound and narrative structure of a moving image. This is very useful as a first stage of getting to grips with an image that is new to you, and it remains useful as a way of describing the visual impact of an image. In its concern for the spatial organization of an image, moreover, compositional interpretation may also begin to say something about an image's possible effects on a spectator.

However, in relation to the criteria for a critical visual methodology spelled out in Chapter 1, compositional interpretation has many short-comings. It does not encourage discussion of the production of an image (other than of its technological or compositional modalities), nor of how it might be used and interpreted by various viewers. And with its unprob-lematized concern for visual images 'as they are', it does not allow for a reflexivity that considers the particularity of any intepretation. Thus compositional interpretation can end up relying on notions of connoisseur-ship, or genius, or Art, for example, as Searle's essay does, which simply cannot get to grips with the concerns of the previous chapter about the specificities of particular visualities. It thus needs to be combined with other methodologies in order to address these latter sorts of issues. In his discussion of film, for example, Monaco (2000) uses terms drawn from semiology (see Chapter 4) to explore how films carry meanings.

6 summary

- compositional interpretation pays some attention to the production of images, especially their technologies, but is mostly concerned with the image itself in its compositional modality.
- according to compositional analysis, some of the key components of a still image are its content, colour, spatial organization, light and expressive content. Moving images can be described in terms of their mise-en-scène, montage, sound and narrative structure.
- this method demands careful attention to the image.
- a disadvantage of this method is its uninterest in the social practices of visual imagery.

further reading

Joshua Taylor's *Learning to Look* (1957) is very useful for still art images, while James Monaco's *How to Read a Film* (2000) is excellent for approaching film, television and video images (and also covers far more ground than just compositional interpretation). For an account of the inadequacies of this approach, and for an elaboration by an art historian of some of the issues raised in the previous chapter, see Michael Baxandall's *Painting and Experience in Fifteenth Century Italy* (1972). This book was one of the earliest efforts to show that 'social history and art history are continuous, each offering necessary insights into the other' (Baxandall, 1972: v).

content analysis

counting what you (think you) see

1 an introduction to content analysis

This chapter discusses a method of analysing visual images that was originally developed to interpret written and spoken texts: content analysis. In one way, content analysis stands in sharp contrast to the method examined in the previous chapter. Whereas compositional interpretation is methodologically silent, relying instead on that elusive thing called 'the good eye', content analysis is methodologically explicit. Indeed, it is based on a number of rules and procedures that must be rigorously followed for the analysis of images or texts to be reliable (on its terms). Don Slater puts the contrast between these two methods into the broader context of social science and humanities research more generally. Speaking of the post-World War II period, he says:

> The main line of development of (particularly Anglo-Saxon) social science was structured by the ideals of quantification and natural science methodology. In this context, social research which relied on cultural meanings as data was seen as shaky and subjective, incapable of rigorous control. Moreover, whereas interpretive, qualitative approaches to social *action* secured footholds in social science, cultural *texts* seemed to belong in the domain of literary or art criticism, which were irredeemably woolly and had more to do with refined 'cultural appreciation' than with any tradition of sustained analysis and investigation. (Slater, 1998: 233–4)

Content analysis was concerned to analyse cultural texts in accordance with 'the ideals of quantification and natural science methodology'. It was first developed in the interwar period by social scientists wanting to measure the 'accuracy' of the new mass media, and was given a further boost during World War II, when its methods were elaborated in order to detect implicit messages from German domestic radio broadcasts (Krippendorf, 1980).

Hence its explicit methodology, through which, it was claimed, analysis would not be woolly but rigorous, reliable and objective.

Some critics of content analysis argue that its definition of 'reliable' equates reliability with quantitative methods of analysis (Ball and Smith, 1992; Slater, 1998). However, as Krippendorf (1980) makes clear in his helpful discussion of content analysis, it also involves various qualitative procedures (see also Weber, 1990). Instead of focusing on the question of quantification, Krippendorf's definition of content analysis emphasizes two different aspects of what might be called 'natural science methodology': replicability and validity (these terms will be defined in sections 2.2 and 2.3 of this chapter respectively). 'Content analysis', he says, 'is a research technique for making replicable and valid inferences from data to their context' (Krippendorf, 1980: 21). In line with the broad approach to visual images outlined in Chapter 1, he insists that content analysis is a way of understanding the symbolic qualities of texts, by which he means the way that elements of a text always refer to the wider cultural context of which they are a part. Content analysis aims to analyse those references in any one group of texts in a replicable and valid manner.

Nonetheless, studies using content analysis do tend to use lots of numbers to make their points. This is because, in its concern for replicability and validity, content analysis offers a number of techniques for handling large numbers of images with some degree of consistency. In their study of nearly 600 of the photographs used in the magazine *National Geographic* over nearly three decades, for example, Catherine Lutz and Jane Collins decided to use content analysis for just this reason. Their defence of content analysis suggests that it can be useful for the visual critical methodology outlined in Chapter 1 of this book:

> Although at first blush it might appear counterproductive to reduce the rich material in any photograph to a small number of codes, quantification does not preclude or substitute for qualitative analysis of the pictures. It does allow, however, discovery of patterns that are too subtle to be visible on casual inspection and protection against an unconscious search through the magazine for only those which confirm one's initial sense of what the photos say or do. (Lutz and Collins, 1993: 89)

This passage is worth expanding on. First, like Krippendorf, these authors are insisting that content analysis can include qualitative interpretation. Content analysis and qualitative methods are not mutually exclusive. Second, Lutz and Collins are suggesting that content analysis can reveal empirical results that might otherwise be overwhelmed by the sheer bulk of material under analysis, and their own study seems to provide evidence for this. Finally, they suggest that content analysis prevents a certain sort of 'bias'. Clearly they are not referring to the sort of bias that worried some of the early proponents of content analysis; they are not concerned that their work is subjective, 'woolly' or theory driven, for example. Rather, they are referring to a sort of bias produced by a refusal to be reflexive about your research procedures. They are suggesting that using the rules of content analysis forces a researcher to be methodologically explicit (rather than relying on 'unconscious' strategies). This coincides with the third criterion for a critical visual methodology that Chapter 1 outlined: the need to be as methodologically explicit as possible in order to make your own way of seeing as evident as possible. This chapter will assess these claims by using Lutz and Collins's (1993) book as its case study of a content analysis.

Content analysis would appear to have some other disadvantages in relation to visual images, however. There are aspects of visual imagery which it is not well equipped to address. It focuses almost exclusively on the *compositional* modality of the site of the *image* itself. It therefore has very little to say about the production or the audiencing of images. In this sense, it is paradoxically very much like compositional interpretation, which also has little to say about those two sites of meaning-making. Its uninterest in audiencing feeds into its proponents' faith in the replicability of content analysis, as we will see in section 2.3. Critics like Michael Ball and Gregory Smith (1992) and Don Slater (1998) suggest that the different ways different people interpret the same text has to be ignored if replicability is to be achieved. Finally, some of its critics also argue that content analysis cannot satisfactorily deal with the cultural significance of images either. This latter criticism, it seems to me, depends on how successfully the links between the content of the images undergoing content analysis and their broader cultural context are made. If those links are tenuous, then this final criticism is valid.

This chapter examines content analysis by:

- exploring its claims to replicability and validity;
- describing its procedural rules;
- assessing the usefulness of the kinds of evidence it produces, using the criteria for a critical visual methodology outlined in Chapter 1.

2 four steps to content analysis

The method of content analysis is based on counting the frequency of certain visual elements in a clearly defined sample of images, and then analysing those frequencies. Each aspect of this process has certain requirements in order to achieve replicable and valid results.

2.1 finding your images

As with any other method, the images chosen for a content analysis must be appropriate to the question being asked. Lutz and Collins describe their research question thus:

> Our interest was, and is, in the making and consuming of images of the
> non-Western world, a topic raising volatile issues of power, race, and
> history. We wanted to know what popular education tells Americans
> about who 'non-Westerners' are, what they want, and what our rela-
> tionship is to them. (Lutz and Collins, 1993: xii)

Given that research question, they then explain why they chose *National
Geographic* as an appropriate source of images:

> After much consideration, we turned to the examination of *National
> Geographic* photographs as one of the most culturally valued and potent
> media vehicles shaping American understandings of, and responses to,
> the world outside the United States. (Lutz and Collins, 1993: xii)

They point out that *National Geographic* is the third most popular magazine subscribed to in the USA, that each issue is read by an estimated
37 million people worldwide, and that in its reliance on photography it
reflects the importance of the visual construction of social difference in
contemporary Western societies (see Figure 3.1).

Unlike many other of the methods this book will discuss, however,
content analysis places further strictures on the use of images. To begin
with, content analysis must address all the images relevant to the research
question. This raises questions for content analysts about the *representativeness* of the available data. If, for example, you are interested in tracing
the increasing acceptability of facial hair on bourgeois men in the nineteenth century, you may decide that the most appropriate source of images
for assessing this acceptability are the popular magazines that those men
would have been reading. If however you find that a twenty-year run of the
best-selling of those magazines is missing from the archive to which you
have access, you face a serious problem in using content analysis: your
analysis cannot be representative since your set of relevant images is
incomplete.

Ensuring that the images you use are representative does not necessarily entail examining every single relevant image however. Almost all
content analyses rely on some sort of sampling procedure. This is because
most content analyses work with large data sets; this chapter has already
noted that this is one of the strengths of content analysis. Sampling in
content analysis is subject to the same concerns it would be in any
quantitative study. It should be both *representative* and *significant*. There
are a number of sampling strategies described in Krippendorf (1980) and
Weber (1990). They include:

1 *random*. Number each image from 1 onwards, and use a random
   number table to pick out a significant number of images to analyse.
2 *stratified*. Sample from subgroups that already exist in the data set,
   choosing your image from within each subgroup and again using a
   clear sampling strategy.

Figure 3.1

Adioukrou

woman, an image

from National

Geographic

magazine (© Carol

Beckwith/Angela

Fisher)

3 *systematic*. Select every third or tenth or nth image. Be careful that the interval you are using between images does not coincide with a cyclical pattern in your source material, otherwise your sample will not be representative. For example, in a study of weekday newspaper advertisements, choosing every sixth paper might mean that every paper in your sample contains the weekly motoring page, which might mean that your sample will contain a disproportionate number of adverts for cars.

4 *cluster*. Choose groups at random and sample from them only.

Which sampling method you choose – or which combination of methods – will depend on the implications of your research question. If you wanted to sample the full range of television programmes in order to explore how often people with disabilities were given airtime, you might use a stratified sampling procedure as described by Krippendorf (1980: 67): this involves 'stratifying a whole year's programming into weekdays and time slots and then randomly selecting for each time slot 1 out of the 52 possibilities'.

focus

If you were interested in the representation of Edinburgh in contemporary picture postcards, a random sample would be an appropriate sampling strategy. But this raises some interesting questions about how you access a representative random sample of that sort of imagery. How would you do that?

Would you go into every shop in Edinburgh's main tourist street – the Royal Mile – and buy five cards at random? Would you contact all the postcard manufacturers and ask them to send you copies or catalogues of their current postcards, and select from there?

Think about what you want your postcards to be representative of. While the latter method would be more representative of current postcard production, the former would be more representative of the cards most often on sale.

There are no hard and fast rules for deciding what size your sample should be. Sample size depends on the amount of variation among all the relevant images. If there is absolutely no variation, a sample of one will be representative. However, if there is a whole range of extreme variations, the sample size must be large enough to contain examples of those extremes. There are also practical considerations, though, in considering sample size. The sample should not be so large that it overwhelms the resources you have available for analysing it. In their study of *National Geographic*, Lutz and Collins chose one photo at random from each of the 594 articles on non-Western people published between 1950 and 1986 (Lutz and Collins, 1993: 88). This was a stratified sampling procedure, since they were choosing an image from subgroups, in this case the groups of photos contained in each article; and they had two research assistants to help them analyse the large number of images that resulted from this procedure.

2.2 devising your categories for coding

Having selected a sample of images to work with, the next stage is to devise a set of categories for coding the images. 'Coding' means attaching a set of descriptive labels (or 'categories') to the images. This is a crucial stage. As Slater (1998: 236) notes, much of the rigour of classic content analysis relies on the structure of categories used in the coding process, because the categories should be apparently objective in a number of ways and therefore describe only what is 'really' there in the text or image. More recent users of content analysis like Lutz and Collins (1993) develop their categories in relation to their theoretical concerns so that their categories are immediately more obviously interpretive. This is one of their tactics that allows them to make their claim that content analysis and qualitative analysis are not mutually exclusive.

The coding categories used must have a number of characteristics regardless of their putative status as descriptive or interpretive, however. They must be:

1 *exhaustive*. Every aspect of the images with which the research is concerned must be covered by one category.
2 *exclusive*. Categories must not overlap.
3 *enlightening*. As Slater (1998: 236) says, the categories must produce 'a breakdown of imagery that will be analytically interesting and coherent'.

Achieving a list of coding categories that satisfies these criteria is extremely difficult. When faced with a large number of images, their sheer richness is likely to be overwhelming. For advertisements or tv programmes, the written or spoken text will also need coding, and so too may background music. As Lutz and Collins (1993: 89) say, the process of reducing the rich material in any photograph to a series of codes is just that: a reduction in which much will be lost. The key point to remember, though, is that the images must be reduced to a number of component parts which can be labelled in a way that has some analytical significance. That is, the codes used must depend on a theorized connection between the image and the broader cultural context in which its meaning is made; 'theorized', because making this connection entails drawing on a theoretical and empirical understanding of the images under consideration. Thus the connection between text, context and code requires careful thought, and it is on the

Valid   integrity of this link that the codes can be judged **valid** (Krippendorf, 1980: 129). A starting point is the research question driving the content analysis. What coding categories does that suggest? Some may be obvious. For more, though, it is necessary to return to the wider theoretical and empirical literature from which the research question has been formulated. Are there arguments there that suggest other codes? This return to the broader context of the research question will hopefully ensure that the categories eventually decided upon are 'enlightening'. Further codes might suggest themselves from the familiarity you already have with this particular set of images. Does anything strike you as interesting, unusual or unexpected about them that might bear further analysis?

The coding categories developed by Lutz and Collins (1993: 285) depend on a particular theoretical literature about 'power, race, and history'. Each of the 598 photographs in their sample was coded for:

1 world location
2 unit of article organization (region, nation-state, ethnic group, other)
3 number of photographs including Westerners in an article
4 smiling in a photograph
5 gender of adults depicted
6 age of those depicted
7 aggressive activity or military personnel or weapons shown
8 activity level of main foreground figures
9 activity type of main foreground figures
10 camera gaze of main person photographed
11 surroundings of people photographed

12 ritual focus
13 group size
14 Westerners in photograph
15 urban versus rural setting
16 wealth indicators in photograph
17 skin colour
18 dress style ('Western' or local)
19 male nudity
20 female nudity
21 technological type present (simple handmade tools, machinery)
22 vantage (point from which camera perceives main figures)

focus

Think about these categories. Are they exhaustive? Are they exclusive?

Lutz and Collins (1993) are fairly clear about the connection between these coding categories and their initial research question. Their question is formulated by drawing on a large body of work that examines how the West has seen and pictured people in the non-Western world. Some of the key texts they cite include Sarah Graham-Brown's (1988) book on photographs of women taken by European travellers in the Near East, Sander Gilman's (1985) study of racial stereotypes, Elizabeth Edward's (1992) edited collection on anthropologists' uses of photography in the nineteenth century and Christopher Lyman's (1982) work on photographs of native American peoples. Drawing on this body of work, they argue that in very broad terms, Westerners have represented non-Western peoples as everything that the West is not (hence their use of the term 'non-Western'). This structure of representation is complex; it draws on a wide range of discourses and varies both historically and geographically, and Lutz and Collins address various aspects of this complexity in their book.

However, to take one example of how their codes connect to this understanding of certain parts and peoples of the world as the opposite of the West, much of the literature they draw on suggests that, historically, non-Western peoples have been represented by Westerners as 'natural'. The West sees itself as technologically advanced but therefore also alienated from nature; thus non-Westerners are represented as technologically less advanced and as closer to nature. Non-Westerners are thus often pictured as using little or so-called primitive technologies, for example, being more spiritual, more in tune with the environment and their bodies, wearing fewer clothes. These analyses inform a number of Lutz and Collins's codes: 12 (ritual focus), 15 (urban versus rural setting), 19 and 20 (male and female nudity) and 21 (technological type present). Given the way their codes flow from a wider set of ideas about power and representation, it is clear that many of their codes are likely to be enlightening, and so it proves. For example, they point out that *National Geographic* represents non-Western people as either natural or as modern, but very rarely as both. It is as if non-Westerners can only be the opposite of, or the same as, the West.

As well as being enlightening, though, exhaustiveness and exclusivity must also be considered when coding categories are being formulated. The only way to ensure that the categories fulfil these latter two requirements is to try them out on the images. Putting the initial categories to use in a trial run on a few of your sample images will almost certainly reveal overlaps between categories and relevant elements of images not covered by categories. The categories must be revised and tried again until they are exhaustive and exclusive. Oddly, the list of codes used by Lutz and Collins (1993), at least as it is reproduced in their book, does not seem to fulfil these other requirements of content analysis coding. There seem to me to be some examples of overlap, for example. Thus 'surroundings of people photographed' seems to overlap with 'urban versus rural setting'; and perhaps 'ritual focus' overlaps with 'dress style', since ritual would be seen as such (on the theoretical arguments that Lutz and Collins draw on) only if it was in local dress.

2.3 coding the images

Now, Lutz and Collins offer only the list of categories as I have reproduced it. Presumably the list they actually worked with had its categories defined much more fully. One would hope so, otherwise there are more ambiguities in their list; if 'world location' is taken to imply which country the article was picturing, then there is a potential overlap with 'unit of article organization'. My queries about the Lutz and Collins categories raise the issue that content analysis tries to obviate, which is that different coders might interpret what seem to be the same codes in different ways.

In order to avoid this possibility, according to content analysis, the coding categories must be completely unambiguous. They must be so clearly defined that different researchers at different times using the same categories would code the images in exactly the same way. This, it is **Replicable** claimed, makes the coding process **replicable**. A content analysis should take various steps to ensure this replicability. Codes must be defined as fully as possible and a pilot study should ensure that two different coders using the same codes produce the same results from the same set of images. If they do not, the codes must be refined so that they do. Further tests of coder reliability may also take place during the research process. Lutz and Collins (1993: 88) say that the photographs in their study were coded independently by two coders, with 86 per cent agreement between them after the final codes had been agreed. The disagreements were resolved by discussion, they say. Their categories must therefore have been defined much more fully than the list they reproduce in their book.

Then the coding proper begins. The application of any set of coding categories must be careful and systematic. Each image must be carefully examined and all the relevant codes attached to it. This process is both tedious and extremely important. It needs a great deal of attention, otherwise the danger of 'unconscious' lapses looms, but it can also be rather boring.

Practically, there are different ways to record your coding. You might do it manually, with an index card for each image on which you note the codes you think are relevant to it (perhaps in some abbreviated form). Or you might be able to set up a computer spreadsheet to record this information. The advantage of the latter is that it might make subsequent quantitative analysis easier, especially if you want to do more than just count up totals (see section 2.4).

2.4 analysing the results

The sample of images is now coded. Each image has a number of codes attached to it. The next stage is to count them, in order to produce a quantitative account of their content.

The simplest way to count the codes is to produce frequency counts, which can be absolute or relative (the latter expressed as a percentage of the total number of images, for example). If you are using a spreadsheet, producing frequency counts is very easy; make sure that you don't count everything simply for the sake of it, though. Choose the important frequencies only, deciding which are important by referring to the broader theoretical and empirical framework with which you are working.

A common use of frequencies is to compare them with some other value. A comparison can be made across time, for example. Lutz and Collins (1993: 40) do this for their code 3 (number of photographs including Westerners in an article). (This code too seems rather odd: their codes were apparently applied to one photograph randomly chosen per article, but this code refers not to a photograph but to the article.) This shows a striking decrease in the number of times Westerners were shown in *National Geographic* photographs after the mid-1960s (see Figure 3.2).

In making sense of this drop, Lutz and Collins again turn to their contextual understanding of the *National Geographic*. They suggest that, unlike some other photo-magazines, *National Geographic* consistently avoids presenting images of conflict. Yet the 1960s were a period of conflict both in the USA and elsewhere, and of conflict moreover focusing on precisely the issues of 'race, power, and history'. Both the civil rights movement in the USA and anti-colonial struggles elsewhere in the world, particularly in Vietnam, made the relations between West and non-West, black and white, especially troubled. The *National Geographic* responded by removing pictures which showed West and non-West, black and white, in contact. Thus the illusion of social harmony could be preserved. Lutz and

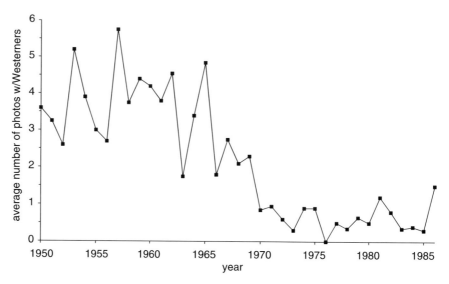

Figure 3.2

Average number

per article of

National

Geographic

photographs with

Westerners in

non-Western

settings, 1950–

86 (Lutz and

Collins, 1993: 40)

Collins (1993: 120) also compare frequency counts across space, pointing out that the distribution of *National Geographic* articles does not follow the distribution of world population, but rather the geopolitical interests of the USA (see Figure 3.3).

focus

Figures 3.2 and 3.3 reproduce some of Lutz and Collins's (1993) results. Representing these forms of analysis visually, as they do, is often more striking for a reader than a list of numbers. But there are standard ways of designing graphs and charts in order to show quantitative results (Edward Tufte, 1983 provides a useful discussion and assessment of these). These visual ways of presenting quantitative data themselves have a certain effect.

How do Figures 3.2 and 3.3 strike you? Are they particularly persuasive because they seem to be 'scientific'?

A more sophisticated analysis can be developed by exploring the relations between different coding categories. This can be done qualitatively and quantitatively. Quantitative measures of possible relationships between categories include associations, cross-tabulations and correlations between two variables, and multivariate analyses between more. Krippendorf (1980) offers guidance here. Lutz and Collins use quantitative correlations at certain points in their book. They note, for example, that 'ritual tends to be depicted in color (x^2 = 3.008, df = 1, p = .083)' (Lutz and Collins, 1993: 94). The correlation between colour and ritual suggests that these are exotic people living spectacular lives; as they say, 'color is the vehicle of spectacle' (Lutz and Collins, 1993: 94).

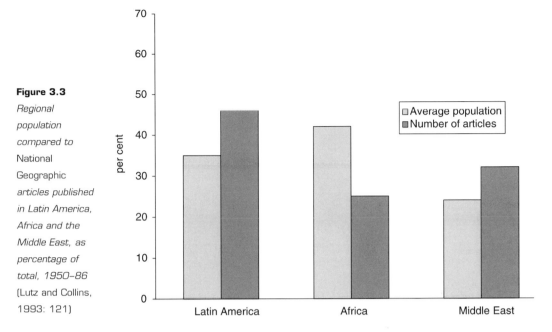

Figure 3.3

Regional
population
compared to
National
Geographic
articles published
in Latin America,
Africa and the
Middle East, as
percentage of
total, 1950–86
(Lutz and Collins,
1993: 121)

But Lutz and Collins (1993) mostly seem to rely on qualitative interpretations of the relations between their categories. They say that from their content analysis of *National Geographic*, four overarching themes emerged. These were the depiction of third world people as exotic, idealized, naturalized, and sexualized. Now, none of these themes appear directly in the list of coding categories deployed by Lutz and Collins. Instead, they were reached by amalgamating some of those codes on the basis of the theoretical and empirical literature upon which their study was drawing. Thus 'idealized' was formed from a number of codes: 'smiling in a photo', 'group size', 'aggressive activity' and 'wealth indicators'. Given the number of smiling portraits, the prevalence of pictures of small groups, the rarity of pictures of aggression, and the dominance of pictures of work and middle-class social groups, Lutz and Collins conclude that third world people are presented as 'idealized': 'gentle natives and wars without brutalized bodies' (Lutz and Collins, 1993: 98). Non-Westerners are not shown as ill or very poor or hungry or deformed: instead they are given the qualities that the North American *National Geographic* would like to see: happy, not too badly off, hard-working, content. In this way, Lutz and Collins elaborate the symbolic meanings carried by *National Geographic*.

Thus content analysis is a technique the results of which need interpreting through an understanding of how the codes in an image connect to the wider context within which that image makes sense. To do that requires not just quantitative skills but also qualitative ones. Even an advocate of quantitative, computerized content analysis like Robert Weber (1990: 69) has to acknowledge that 'time, effort, skill, and art are required to produce results, interpretations, and explanations that are valid and theoretically interesting'.

3   is content analysis a critical visual methodology?

Clearly, every stage of content analysis, from formulating the research question, to developing coding categories, to interpreting the results, entails decisions about meaning and significance. While Ball and Smith (1992) suggest that content analysis is pretty much useless for understanding the cultural meaning of the visual components it analyses, the case study explored in this chapter seems to dispute this claim. Lutz and Collins (1993) suggest that, especially if the coding of images is carefully formulated, content analysis can be used to interpret the cultural meaning of images. Thus Lutz and Collins (1993) are clear that content analysis is on the borderline between quantitative and qualitative methods. But Lutz and Collins (1993) also advocate content analysis as a method that can lend rigour and consistency to large-scale qualitative projects like theirs. Here perhaps there are some more difficult questions about the relevance of content analysis to a critical visual methodology.

First, numbers do not translate easily into significance. There is a tendency in content analysis to assume that if something occurs very often, it is more important than something that occurs rarely. As Weber (1990: 72) and Ball and Smith (1992) note, this is not necessarily the case. Something that is kept out of the picture may nonetheless be extremely significant to its meaning. An example here would be the election poster analysed by Gilroy (1987: 57–9) (see section 2 in Chapter 1). I am not making the point here that there is a single reality which visual images only selectively represent. Rather, I mean to suggest that certain representations of what is visible depend on other things being constructed as their invisible opposite; and content analysis is incapable of addressing these invisibilized others.

Moreover, content analysis does not discriminate between occurrences of a code: that is, it cannot discriminate between an aspect of an image that exemplifies a code perfectly, and one that is only a weak example of it. Thus simple frequencies may be problematic to interpret. A further problem arises when the difficulty content analysis has in handling the context of its coded image components is considered. Content analysis breaks an image into parts and has no way of handling any interconnections that may exist between its parts, other than by statistical correlation. This is probably not the best way to understand how an image works. Lutz and Collins (1993) demonstrate this when they turn, not to statistical tests, but to theoretical accounts, to pull together some of their codes into overarching themes that form the basis of their analysis of the *National Geographic* photographs.

There is also another problem produced by the fragmentation of an image when it undergoes content analysis, which is the inability of content analysis to articulate what compositional interpretation would call the expressive content of an image. It is very hard to evoke the mood of an image through codes.

Finally, there are the broader issues in analysing visual images that content analysis cannot address. Content analysis focuses on the image itself. But there are the two other sites at which an image's meanings are made: the site of its production, and the site of its audiencing. Content analysis simply ignores both of these. Indeed, as section 3.1 pointed out, in its concern for coder replicability, content analysis assumes that different viewers can see the same image in the same way, and as a method it therefore has no interest in audience creativity. Lutz and Collins (1993) try to overcome these absences by using other research methods to access the way meaning is made at these other sites. At the site of *National Geographic* production, they conducted interviews with the magazine's photographers and editors, to gain an understanding of the social and compositional modalities of production. And at the site of *National Geographic* audiencing, they conducted group interviews with *National Geographic* readers in which they discussed particular photographs. What they found was that at each site the meanings given to the photographs varied. However, what they do not discuss is the relationship between these three sites. Moreover, further issues are raised if we recall their description of their own content analysis. They gave it the status of the 'discovery of patterns that are too subtle to be visible on casual inspection' and suggested that it gave 'protection against an unconscious search through the magazine for only those which confirm one's initial sense of what the photos say or do' (Lutz and Collins, 1993: 89). Lutz and Collins have apparently 'discovered' patterns (which implies that they have uncovered a pre-existing and therefore, perhaps, more real *National Geographic* way of seeing) and have removed any unconscious interpretive predilections. This removes any need on their part to be reflexive. Reflexivity is not part of content analysis because content analysis assumes it is an objective method. But what does that suggest about the other meaning makers whom Lutz and Collins interviewed? That their interpretations are more unconscious? Less valid? More 'woolly', perhaps? Lutz and Collins (1993) deny that they are implying this. But their defence of content analysis leaves that lingering impression nonetheless. Maybe the natural science legacy of content analysis is harder to leave behind than Lutz and Collins hope.

4 summary

- content analysis was developed as a social science research method that would be scientific by being replicable and valid.
- it offers clear methodological guidelines for achieving those qualities.

- these guidelines can be useful in approaching a large number of images in a consistent manner.
- there are a number of problems in approaching the issue of visual meaning through quantitative techniques. Various issues of relative significance and context are difficult to address.
- content analysis has no way of dealing with those sites at which the meanings of images are made other than that of the image itself.
- content analysis does not demand reflexivity on the part of the researcher.

further reading

For a clear discussion of content analysis as it can be applied to written texts, consult Krippendorf's *Content Analysis: An Introduction to its Methodologies* (1980).

semiology

laying bare the prejudices beneath the smooth
surface of the beautiful

1 an introduction to the semiological analysis of visual images

This chapter examines an approach to visual images which has been much more prominent than either compositional interpretation or content analysis in the development of the debates about the visual that were briefly reviewed in Chapter 1. This method is semiology (sometimes also called semiotics). Its prominence is due in part to the fact that semiology confronts the question of how images make meanings head on. It is not simply descriptive, as compositional interpretation appears to be; nor does it rely on quantitative estimations of significance, as content analysis at some level has to. Instead, semiology offers a very full box of analytical tools for taking an image apart and tracing how it works in relation to broader systems of meaning. As a method, semiology draws upon the work of several major social theorists. Judith Williamson (1978), for example, in her classic semiological study *Decoding Advertisements*, cites only Althusser, Barthes, Benjamin, Berger, Brecht, Foucault, Freud, Gramsci, Lacan, Lévi-Strauss, Marx and Sassure at the end of her book, but this is a roll-call of many of the twentieth century's most important critical writers. Semiology is thus embedded in a rich and complex series of ideas whose implications are still actively debated; hence there are different analytical emphases within semiology, which this chapter will briefly touch on. The most important tool in the semiological box, though, is the 'sign': semiology means 'the study of signs'. As Mieke Bal and Norman Bryson (1991: 174) say in their defence of semiology, 'human culture is made up of signs, each of which stands for something other than itself, and the people inhabiting culture busy themselves making sense of those signs'. Semiology has an elaborate analytical vocabulary for describing how signs make sense, and this is one of its major strengths. A semiological analysis entails the deployment of a highly refined set of concepts which produce detailed accounts of the exact ways the meanings of an image are produced through that image.

Semiology offers a certain kind of analytical precision, then. As was noted in the previous chapter, so too does content analysis. And, again like content analysis, a certain sort of semiology claims to be a scientific approach to the analysis of meaning. Content analysis is said to be a science because it is quantitative, replicable and valid. These are not the grounds on which the advocates of semiology as a science claim semiology as a science, however. Semiologists depend on a definition of science that **Ideology** contrasts scientific knowledge with **ideology** (this distinction is usually elaborated with reference to the Marxist theorist Louis Althusser). Ideology is knowledge that is constructed in such a way as to legitimate unequal social power relations; science, instead, is knowledge that reveals those inequalities. This use of the term ideology is evidence of the formative influence of Marxism on semiology. Marx and Engels famously claimed in *The German Ideology* that 'the ideas of the ruling class are in every age the ruling ideas', and here are Robert Hodge and Gunther Kress defining ideology in the introduction to their book *Social Semiotics*:

> In contemporary capitalist societies as in most other social formations there are inequalities in the distribution of power and other goods. As a result there are divisions in the social fabric between rulers and ruled, exploiters and exploited: such societies exhibit characteristic structures of domination. In order to sustain these structures of domination the dominant groups attempt to represent the world in forms that reflect their own interests, the interests of their power. (Hodge and Kress, 1988: 3)

Ideology is those representations that reflect the interests of power. In particular, ideology works to legitimate social inequalities, and it works at the level of our subjectivity:

> Ideology is the meaning made necessary by the conditions of society while helping to perpetuate those conditions. We feel a need to belong, to have a social 'place'; it can be hard to find. Instead we may be given an imaginary one. (Williamson, 1978: 13)

Williamson's use of the term 'imaginary' is complex, but for the moment we can understand it as contrasting the imaginary with the real: she is contrasting the imaginary social positions produced by ideology with the actual social relations produced by capitalism as revealed by scientific knowledge. Semiology, then, is centrally concerned with the social effects of meaning.

Williamson (1978) argues that one of the most influential ideological forms in contemporary capitalist societies is advertising. She claims that advertisements are ubiquitous and thus appear autonomous, so that they have 'a sort of independent reality that links them to our own lives' (Williamson, 1978: 11). Robert Goldman agrees. 'Ads saturate our lives,' he says, and goes on, 'yet, because ads are so pervasive and our reading of them so routine, we tend to take for granted the deep social assumptions embedded in advertisements: we do not ordinarily recognise them as a sphere of ideology' (Goldman, 1992: 1). Both Williamson and Goldman choose to use semiology as a method that can help them penetrate the apparent autonomy and reality of adverts, in order to reveal their ideological status. Williamson describes her understanding of adverts thus:

> In our society, while the real distinctions between people are created by their role in the *process* of production, as workers, it is the *products* of their own work that are used, in the false categories invoked by advertising, to obscure the real structure of society by replacing class with the distinctions made by the consumption of particular goods. Thus instead of being identified by what they produce, people are made to identify themselves with what they consume . . . we are made to feel that we can rise or fall in society through what we are able to buy, and this obscures the actual class basis that still underlies social position. The fundamental differences in society are still class differences, but use of manufactured goods as a means of *creating* classes or groups form an overlay on them. This overlay is ideology. (Williamson, 1978: 13)

It is evident in this passage that Williamson is happy to make a clear distinction between the 'real' structures of society – class relations – and the 'false' knowledge of social differences offered by adverts. And that false knowledge is, for Williamson, ideological. She uses semiology, described as a science (Williamson, 1978: 9), to dissect the workings of ideology. Hence Margaret Iversen's (1986: 84) description of semiology as 'laying bare the prejudices beneath the smooth surface of the beautiful'. Williamson's book will be this chapter's case study.

Some semiologists writing more recently, however, are much more circumspect than Williamson in claiming that their knowledges are scientifically true. Hodge and Kress (1988) suggest that any knowledge which sanctions a particular form of social organization must be described as ideological. Thus knowledge that legitimates the social position of dominant groups is ideological; but so too are those knowledges of other possibilities for social organization that are held by dominated groups. To capture this 'double and contradictory' notion of ideology, they prefer to use the term 'ideological complex': 'a functionally related set of contradictory versions of the world, coercively imposed by one social group on another on behalf of its own distinctive interests or subversively offered by another social group in attempts at resistance in its own interests' (Hodge and Kress, 1988: 3). The implication of this argument is that the critical goals of semiology are just as ideological as the adverts or whatever that are being critiqued; the difference between them is in the social effects of the knowledges each depends on, not its truth status.

Bal and Bryson (1991) offer another version of this argument, simply pointing out that since all knowledge depends on signs, all knowledge is vulnerable to semiological reinterpretation, including that of the semiologists themselves. Elsewhere Bal (1996) has described this as a process of 'double exposure'. When a critic writes about, let's say, a video, not only is the video interpreted and exposed to interpretation; the interpretation is also on display, exposing the critic's ideas to interpretation by others. As she says, there are 'intricacies between . . . academic subjectivity and the subject matter it purports to analyse' (Bal, 1996: 7). Bal therefore acknowledges the importance of the third criterion outlined in Chapter 1 for a critical visual methodology, and tries to be reflexive about her own viewing practices.

Williamson's (1978) account of ideology focuses on class relations in both their 'real' and 'false' forms. In her book though she also recognizes the centrality of gender to how adverts are constructed, and another development in more recent semiological studies is the way in which the signs of many forms of social difference are explored: class, gender, race, able-bodiedness and so on. Semiology assumes that these constructions of social difference are articulated through images themselves. Section 1 of Chapter 2 has already quoted Norman Bryson making this point, and it's now possible to see the theoretical inspiration for his remarks:

> The social formation isn't, then, something which supervenes or appropriates or utilizes the image so to speak *after* it has been made; rather painting, as an activity of the sign, unfolds within the social formation from the beginning. And from the inside – the social formation is inherently and immanently present in the image and not a fate or an external which clamps down on an image that might prefer to be left alone. (Bryson, 1991: 66)

Many semiological studies therefore tend to concentrate on the *image itself* as the most important site of its meaning. Its focus on signs means that semiology always pays very careful attention to the *compositional* modality of that site; but its concern for the social effects of an image's meaning mean that some attention is also paid to the *social* modality of that site. However, and again more recently, there have been some efforts to emphasize what this book is calling the social modality at other sites. Bal and Bryson (1991: 184), for example, emphasize above all the site of an image's *audiencing*, arguing that semiology 'is centrally concerned with reception', and Hodge and Kress (1988) have developed what they call 'social semiotics' as a way of emphasizing what this book is calling the social modality at all sites of meaning making. This chapter will consider their arguments in section 4.

This introduction is suggesting, then, that semiology can fulfil the criteria for a critical visual methodology that were outlined in the first chapter of this book. It offers a range of tools for looking at images carefully; it is centrally concerned with the ways in which social difference is created; and at least some of its practitioners advocate a reflexivity in its deployment. However, as a method it also has its drawbacks. Semiology is conceptually elaborate. Each semiological term carries substantial theoretical baggage with it, and there is a tendency for each semiological study to invent its own analytical terms. This terminological precision accounts for the analytical precision of semiology. It also accounts, however, for a certain density of terminology which is not always easy for the novice to grasp; Michael Ball and Gregory Smith (1992) are not the only ones to see this as one of the disadvantages of this method. Don Slater (1998) offers another criticism: that for all its analytical richness, semiology does not offer a clear method for its application. This chapter therefore focuses more on suggesting some ways to do semiology than on elaborating its theoretical implications. This chapter will:

- examine the central importance of 'the sign' to semiology;
- explore the connections made by semiology between signs and broader structures of meaning;
- look at some work which attempts to consider the social modalities of the production and audiencing of images;
- offer an assessment of the strengths and weaknesses of semiology as a method for a critical visual methodology.

2 choosing images for a semiological study

Semiological studies require extensive knowledge of the type of image which the case studies will examine. Judith Williamson (1978: 9) tells her readers that she arrived at the University of California at Berkeley to take a course on popular culture in the mid-1970s with 'a bulging file of advertisements collected over many years' that eventually provided the illustrations for her book, and Goldman (1992: 2) says he was 'watching ads for over decade' before writing his book. However, neither suggest they had a rigorous sampling procedure, as a content analyst would; nor do either say how they chose which of these many adverts to discuss in detail as examples in their books. This is because semiologists choose their images on the basis of how conceptually interesting they are, it seems. There is no concern among semiologists to find images that are statistically representative of a wider set of images, for example, as there is in content analysis. Images are interpreted in close relation to semiological theory, and the discussion of particular images is often directed at exemplifying analytical points. Thus semiology very often takes the form of detailed case studies of relatively few images, and the case study stands or falls on its analytical integrity and interest rather than on its applicability to a wide range of material.

3 the sign and its meaning-making processes

The 'sign' is the most fundamental unit of semiology. The sign is a unit of meaning, and semiologists argue that anything which has meaning – an advert, a painting, a conversation, a poem – can be understood in terms of its signs and the work they do. Signs make meaning in complex ways, and much of the technical vocabulary of semiology describes the precise ways in which signs make sense.

3.1 what is a sign?

Semiological understanding of the sign depends in part on the work of Ferdinand de Saussure, and in particular on his *Course on General Linguistics*. Saussure wanted to develop a systematic understanding of how **Sign** language works, and he argued that the **sign** was the basic unit of language. The sign consists of two parts, which are only distinguishable at the analytical level; in practice they are always integrated into each other. The **Signified** first part of the sign is the **signified**. The signified is a concept or an object, let's say 'a very young human unable to walk or talk'. The second part of **Signifier** the sign is the **signifier**. The signifier is a sound or an image that is attached to a signified; in this case, the word 'baby'. The point that Saussure made with this distinction between signifier and signified, and which semiological analysis depends upon, is that there is no necessary relationship between a particular signifier and its signified. We can see this if we think of the way in which different languages use different words for the same signified: 'baby' in English is 'bimbo' or 'bimba' in Italian, for example. Moreover, the same signifier can have different meanings; 'baby' can also be a term of endearment between adults, for example, and in English 'bimbo' does not refer to babies at all but is rather a term that stereotypes certain kinds of adult women. Whatever stability attaches to a particular relationship between a signifier and signified does not depend on an inherent connection between them, then. Instead, Saussure argued that it depends upon the difference between that particular sign and many others. Thus one meaning of 'baby' in English depends for its significance not on a necessary relation between the word 'baby' and 'very young humans unable to walk or talk', but rather on the difference between the sign 'baby' and other signs such as 'toddler', 'child', 'kid', 'teenager', 'adolescent', 'adult' and so on. The actual object in the world to which the sign is related is called the **Referent** sign's **referent**.

The distinction between signifier and signified is crucial to semiology, because it means that the relation between meanings (signifieds) and signifiers is not inherent, but rather is conventional and can therefore be problematized. While 'a sign is always thing-plus-meaning' (Williamson, 1978: 17), the connection between a certain signifier and a certain signified can be questioned; and the relations between signs can also be explored.

The elaborate vocabulary of semiology is aimed at clarifying the different ways in which signifiers and signifieds are attached to (and detached from) each other. The first stage of a semiological analysis, though, is to identify the basic building blocks of an image: its signs. Bal and Bryson (1991: 193–4) point out that it is often quite difficult to differentiate between visual signs, because often there are no clear boundaries between different parts of an image. However, once certain elements of an image have been at least tentatively identified as its signs, their meanings can be explored.

Gillian Dyer's *Advertising as Communication* (1982) points out that the photographs of many adverts depend on signs of humans which symbolize particular qualities to their audience. These qualities – these signifieds – are shifted in the ad from the human signifiers and on to the product the ad is trying to sell. Here is Judith Williamson analysing an advert for the Halifax Building Society (see Figure 4.1), which offers mortgages for house purchase. Her focus is the way hands are signs.

> The ring . . . stand[s] for marriage, and in [the] picture the strong male hand stands for 'Promise, Confidence, and Security'. The pictures are clichéd illustrations of three words. But the point of the ad is to undermine the 'Confidence and Security' offered by the man . . . The cliché of masculine security and promise is exposed, to show the need for the Halifax. Yet simultaneously, the image of the ad, the hand and the ring, etc., undermined in its literal sense of marriage-as-security, is used in all its clichédness to represent the promise, security and confidence offered in reparation by the Halifax . . . In other words, Security, signified by the hand, becomes a signifier, in its possible absence, of the need for Halifax; it is then returned to its original status of signified through the conduit of the product. (Williamson, 1978: 34)

Dyer (1982: 96–104) has a useful checklist for exploring what signs of humans might symbolize:

1 *representations of bodies*:
   - *age*. What is the age of the figures in the photograph meant to convey? Innocence? Wisdom? Senility?
   - *gender*. Adverts very often rely on stereotyped images of masculinity and femininity. Men are active and rational, women are passive and emotional; men go out into the world, women are more associated with the domestic.
   - *race*. Again, adverts often depend on stereotypes. To what extent does an advert do this? Or does it normalize whiteness by making it invisible (see Dyer, 1997)?
   - *hair*. Women's hair is often used to signify seductive beauty or narcissism.

Figure 4.1

Advertisement

(Williamson,

1978: 34)

- *body*. Which bodies are fat (and therefore often represented as undesirable and unattractive) and which are thin? Are we shown whole bodies, or does the photo show only parts of bodies (women's bodies are often treated in this way in cosmetic ads)?
- *size*. Adverts often indicate what is more important by making it big.
- *looks*. Again, adverts often trade on conventional notions of male and female beauty. Susan Bordo's book *Unbearable Weight* (1993) is an excellent discussion of, among other things, how adverts picture bodies in ways that depend on cultural constructions of race, gender and beauty.

2 *representations of manner*
- *expression*. Who is shown as happy, haughty, sad and so on? What facial and other expressions are used to convey this?
- *eye contact*. Who is looking at whom (including you) and how? Are those looks submissive, coy, confrontational?
- *pose*. Who is standing and who is prone?

3 *representations of activity*
- *touch*. Who is touching what, with what effects?
- *body movement*. Who is active and who is passive?
- *positional communication*. What is the spatial arrangement of the figures? Who is positioned as superior and who inferior? Who is intimate with whom and how? Hodge and Kress (1988: 52–63) have a useful discussion of positional communication.

4 *props and settings*
- *props*. Objects in adverts can be used in a way unique to a particular advert, but many ads rely on objects that have particular cultural significance. For example, spectacles often connote intelligence, golden light indicates tranquillity, and so on.
- *settings*. Settings range from the apparently 'normal' to the supposedly 'exotic', and can also seem to be fantasies. What effects does its setting have on an advert?

Dyer's list provides a good way of specifiying in some detail how a visual image of humans produces certain signifieds. However, this kind of interpretation clearly requires the kind of extensive knowledge of images of culturally specific social difference and social relations.

focus

Look at the adverts reproduced in Figures 4.2, 4.3 and 4.4. What do the various human figures signify?

3.2 ways of describing signs

There is some debate about how useful Saussure's legacy is to semiology beyond this fundamental understanding of the structure of signs. Bal and Bryson (1991) and Hodge and Kress (1988) both argue that Saussure had rather a static notion of how signs work and was uninterested in how meanings change and are changed in use. Other writers wonder whether a theory based on language can deal with the particularities of the visual. Iversen, for example, suggests that the relation between signifier and signified is different in many visual images from that in written or spoken signs:

> Linguistic signs are arbitrary in the sense that there is no relation between the sound of a word and its meaning other than convention, a 'contract' or rule. It is clear that visual signs are not arbitrary, but 'motivated' – there is some rationale for the choice of signifier. The word 'dog' and a

picture of one do not signify in the same way, so it is safe to assumed that a theory of semiotics based on linguistics will fall far short of offering a complete account of visual signification. (Iversen, 1986: 85; see also Armstrong, 1996; Hall, 1980: 132)

Both Bal and Bryson (1991) and Iversen (1986), therefore, while acknowledging the importance of Saussure's discussion of the sign, prefer to turn to the work of the American philosopher Charles Sanders Pierce (see also Wollen, 1970: 120). This is because 'Pierce's richer typology of signs enables us to consider how different modes of signification work, while Saussure's model can only tell us how systems of arbitrary signs operate' (Iversen, 1986: 85).

Pierce suggested that there were three kinds of signs, differentiated by the way in which the relation between the signifier and signified is understood:

Icon   1   **icon.** In iconic signs, the signifier represents the signified by apparently having a likeness to it. This type of sign is often very important in visual images, especially photographic ones. Thus a photograph of a baby is an iconic sign of that baby. Diagrams are also iconic signs, since they show the relations between the parts of their object.

Index   2   **index.** In indexical signs, there is an inherent relationship between the signified and signifier. 'Inherent' is often culturally specific, so a current example familiar to Western readers might be the way that a schematic picture of a baby soother is often used to denote a room in public places where there are baby-changing facilities.

Symbol   3   **symbol.** Symbolic signs have a conventionalized but clearly arbitrary relation between signifier and signified. Thus pictures of babies are often used to represent notions of 'the future', as in a postcard produced by the Italian communist newspaper *Il Manifesto* (see Figure 4.2). This shows a sleeping baby with a raised fist, and the text 'la rivoluzione non russa' ('the revolution isn't snoring/sleeping' but also 'not the Russian revolution').

Paradigmatic
Syntagmatic

Since signs work in relation to other signs, it might also be useful to distinguish between two further kinds of signs, **paradigmatic** and **syntagmatic**. **Syntagmatic** signs gain their meaning from the signs that surround them in a still image, or come before or after them in sequence in a moving image. Syntagmatic signs are often very important for semiologies of film, since film is a sequence of signs. Thus certain signs in a film may gain extra meaning because they have occurred in a previous scene (for a discussion of semiology in relation to film specifically, see Monaco, 2000: 151–225). Paradigmatic signs gain their meaning from a contrast with all other possible signs; thus the baby in the postcard is a paradigmatic sign because we understand that sign as a baby by deciding that it is not a toddler, an adolescent or an adult.

La rivoluzione non russa.

il manifesto

Figure 4.2

Advertisement for the Italian newspaper Il Manifesto, *circa 1994*

Signs are complex and can be doing several things at once; so you may have to describe the same sign using several of the terms discussed in this section.

focus

Study the adverts reproduced in Figures 4.3 and 4.4, using the terms introduced so far in this section.

What are the photographs' signs? What do each of the photograph's signs signify? In doing this, are they indexical, iconic, or symbolic? Are there syntagmatic signs? What about the text? What signifieds does it evoke? Given the signifieds attached to the visual signifiers, what qualities are viewers of these ads meant to associate with the product?

Denotive

Diegesis

There are other ways of describing signs. Signs can be distinguished depending on how symbolic they are. Signs can be **denotive**, that is, describing something: a baby, a soother. Roland Barthes (1977) suggests that signs which work at the denotive level are fairly easy to decode. We can look at a picture of a baby and see that it is a baby and not a toddler or an adult, for example. A related term is **diegesis**. Diegesis is the sum of the denotive meanings of an image. My description of the postcard reproduced as Figure 4.2 as showing 'a sleeping baby with a raised fist, and the text 'la rivoluzione non russa'' is a diegesis of that image. The term is often used in film studies to offer a relatively straightforward account of a film, before a more complex analysis begins. However, although denotive signs at one level may be easy to understand, at another they may have so many potential meanings that a viewer may be confused. A postcard showing a baby, for example, could be a birth announcement, or an advert for baby

Figure 4.3

Silver Cross advertisement, 1998

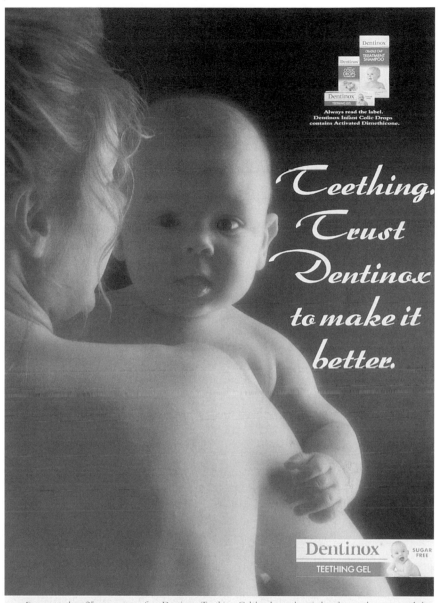

Always read the label.
Dentinox Infant Colic Drops
contains Activated Dimethicone.

*Teething.
Trust
Dentinox
to make it
better.*

Dentinox
TEETHING GEL
SUGAR FREE

For more than 25 years, sugar-free Dentinox Teething Gel has been the tried and trusted answer to baby teething. Dentinox quickly relieves pain and soothes sore gums and can be confidently used from birth onwards. When you want to make it better, trust Dentinox.

Figure 4.4

Dentinox teething gel advertisement, 1998

Anchorage

Relay-function

cream or cot blankets, or a cute card. In the case of the postcard discussed here, the text provides what Barthes (1977: 38–41) called **anchorage**. It allows the reader to choose between what could be a confusing number of possible denotive meanings of a postcard showing a baby. Text in adverts often works as anchorage. In other media, however (television is an example), the text is much more important in relation to the image; they are complementary, and in this case Barthes (1977: 38–41) described the written or spoken text as having a **relay-function**.

Connotive
But signs can also be **connotive**. Connotive signs carry a range of higher-level meanings. For example, that postcard uses a picture of a baby as a connotive sign, because that baby connotes the future when the revolution will happen. Connotive signs themselves can be divided into two kinds:

Metonymic
1 **metonymic**. This kind of sign is something associated with something else, which then represents that something else. Thus in the postcard example, babies are associated with notions of the future, and the baby is thus a metonymic sign.

Synecdochal
2 **synecdochal**. This sign is either a part of something standing in for a whole, or a whole representing a part. Thus the city of Paris is often represented by a picture of one part of it, the Eiffel Tower: the image of the tower is a synecdochal sign of Paris as a whole.

Again, it is important to stress that any one sign may be working in one or more of these ways.

Thus semiology offers a detailed vocabulary for specifying what particular signs are doing.

> focus

At this point, it is appropriate to mention an interpretive debate among semiologists over the status of signs in photographic images. It is relevant first because it has implications for interpreting (some sorts of) photographic images; it suggests that the vocabulary developed in this section may not fully address the impact of photographic imagery on its viewers. Second, it is relevant because semiologists sometimes get overwhelmed by their formidable analytical arsenal and forget that there may be other ways to respond to visual images which are no less important.

Photography is often thought of as picturing reality. Unlike any other visual technology, there is a sense in which the camera is an instrument that records what was in front of its lens when the shutter snapped; and although photographic images can be framed and filtered and cropped, and can subsequently be manipulated in all sorts of ways and put to all sorts of uses, they nevertheless always retain a visual trace of what was there when the picture was made. Paradoxically, the writer who has made this claim most persuasively – and most movingly – is Roland Barthes, who has also contributed hugely to semiological studies. In his book *Camera Lucida*, which is prompted by Barthes's search for a photograph of his mother, Barthes suggests that:

> It is as if the Photograph always carries its referent with itself, both affected by the same amorous or funereal immobility, at the very heart of the moving world; they are glued

together, limb by limb, like the condemned man and the corpse in certain tortures. (Barthes, 1982: 5–6)

Studium

Punctum

The referent is there in photographic images in ways that it is not in other sorts of visual imagery, Barthes argues. As a result, he suggests that photographs can be interpreted in two ways. First, there is the level of the **studium**, which is a culturally informed reading of the image, one that interprets the signs of the photographs. But he says that some photographs produce a different response, which is a second kind of reading, by containing what he called a **punctum**. A punctum is unintentional and ungeneralizable; it is a sensitive point in an image which pricks, bruises, disturbs a particular viewer out of their usual viewing habits. He went so far as to suggest that 'while the *studium* is ultimately always coded, the *punctum* is not' (Barthes, 1982: 51). That is, there are points in some photographs that escape signifiers and shock the viewer with their 'intractable reality' (Barthes, 1982: 119).

Other semiologists disagree with Barthes's claim that parts of some photographs are beyond signification (see for example Hall, 1980: 131–2). They argue that photographs are always understood through the meanings which are articulated through them and no photograph can escape that process even partially. John Tagg (1988), for example, insists that the signifieds of photographic signs always have signifiers, and section 1 of Chapter 7 will return to his argument. Even in iconic signs, where the signifier represents the signified by having a likeness to it, these semiologists insist that that likeness is culturally established, not inherent. As Iversen (1986: 92) says, iconic signs have 'a reception as a reflection of the real'. That is, they are seen like that; they are not actually like that.

Photography thus raises some specific questions in relation to semiology, and these have methodological implications. Is the analytical language of signs adequate to the task of elucidating the impact of photographs? Or is some notion, like the *punctum*, of disruptive possibilities beyond the field of meaning necessary?

3.3 signs in relation to each other

To reiterate a point already made in passing, the distinction between signifier and signified can help us understand the structure of advertisements. Goldman (1992) and Williamson (1978) argue that adverts work by transferring (or trying to transfer) visual and textual signifieds on to their product. Thus the signs in an ad's image and writing usually signify notions of taste, luxury, health, happiness and so on, and adverts attempt to shift the signifiers from the signs in the image and text to their own product. This section explores this process of meaning transference in advertising images more fully.

One of the most productive aspects of Williamson's (1978) analysis of images is precisely the way she shows how adverts work by shifting signifieds from one signifier to another. Indeed, she suggests that this is crucial to how adverts work. The signifieds attached to certain signs in ads get transferred to other signifiers. This process is at work in both adverts in Figures 4.3 and 4.4. Williamson suggests that the transfers are often made **Objective correlates** so persuasively that certain objects become the **objective correlates** of certain qualities: certain objects become taken for granted as having certain qualities. Thus by the 1990s it seems quite comprehensible to have a muscled, naked, youngish man represented as 'strong, dependable, irresistible'. That image can be the objective correlate of strength, dependability and irresistibility, and ads can transfer those qualities from a sign of a man to, in this case, the brand name of a pram and pushchair company.

Williamson (1978: 20–4) discusses some of the formal mechanisms used by adverts that facilitate this transfer of meaning between objects, humans and qualities in an image. She suggests that the spatial composition of the advert is important: what is put next to what, how certain elements are framed. Goldman (1992) concurs, and he notes that most adverts have the same basic visual structure (1992: 39–40). First, they have a photographic image; second, they have what Goldman (1992: 61–84) **Mortise** calls a **mortise**, which is an image of the product framed in some way; third, they have text in the form of headlines, captions and copy; and finally, they use graphic framing devices to make certain visual links between these components. (However, as Goldman, 1992: 70 notes, the mortise box may not literally appear in the advert; and indeed, in Figure 4.3 the product is not pictured at all.) Williamson (1978) suggests that one of the most subtle ways in which signifieds are transferred by images is in their use of colour. The use of similar colours in different signs in an advert work to connect those signs and to effect a transfer of their signifieds. These transfers can be between the product and an object, the product and the world, the product and a person, or the whole world might be retinted in the product's colours (as in the adverts for the *Financial Times* newspaper. The paper is printed on pink paper, and its adverts use black and the same pink photography. With their slogan 'No *FT*, no comment', these ads suggest the world is unknowable, or certainly unsayable, without looking through the pink filter of the *FT*'s journalism).

The transfers of meaning within an image – which operate between and within both text and image – can be very complex. Goldman (1992: 77) suggests that one way to begin to unravel that complexity is to map the transfers. He offers an example of this technique in which he reduces an advert to its basic spatial organization by sketching its compositional structure (see section 3.3 of Chapter 2 for another example of this technique). As Figure 4.5 shows, he then labels the signs in the ad and draws arrows between them to show a transferred signified.

Goldman suggests this is rather a schematic and crude way to represent a process as complex and fluid as the advert's meaning-making, and in this he is correct. But it is also a useful way to begin to think carefully about the relationships between signs in an advert.

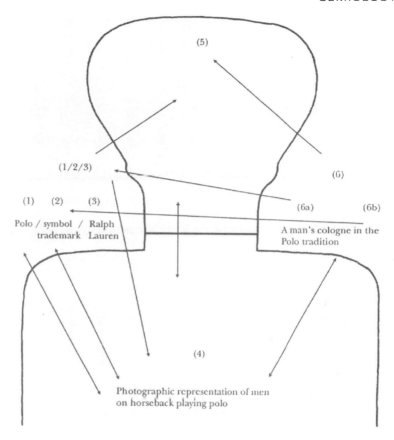

(5)

(1/2/3)

(6)

(1)   (2)   (3)

(6a)   (6b)

Polo / symbol / Ralph
trademark Lauren

A man's cologne in the
Polo tradition

(4)

Photographic representation of men
on horseback playing polo

Figure 4.5

Basic spatial

organization of an

advertisement

(Goldman, 1992: 77)

focus

How do the adverts in Figures 4.3 and 4.4 work to transfer signifieds between
signifiers? Try mapping these exchanges of meaning using Goldman's suggestions:
sketch the structure of the adverts, label each sign and draw links to show the
transfers of meaning between signs.

Williamson (1978) also shows how the relationship between the signs
in different adverts have meaningful effects. Her example is two perfume
ads, one for Chanel and one for Babe (Williamson 1978: 25–6). Figure 4.6
reproduces them.

Williamson quickly notes how the signifieds attached to the two women
are transferred within the adverts from the women to the perfumes they are
advertising. Thus Chanel is given connotations of French chic and sophistication by the juxtaposition of Catherine Deneuve's face and the bottle,
while Babe is made energetic and young by the leaping figure of Margaux
Hemingway. But Williamson also argues that the meanings generated by the
adverts depend not only on these slippages within each advert. They also

Figure 4.6
Chanel and Babe
advertisements,
1978
(Williamson,
1978: 25, 26)

depend on the contrast between the two adverts. Thus the quiet sophistication of Chanel is constructed through Deneuve and in opposition to Babe/Hemingway, whereas Babe's youth is constructed through Hemingway and in opposition to Chanel/Deneuve. As Williamson notes, this must be the case, not only because signs work in relation to each other, but also because of the ideological purpose of advertising. As she points out, actually (scientifically) there's very little difference between the products that advertisers aim to sell, so advertisers have to create difference. Thus two bottles of perfume are sold not only in terms of what they apparently are (sophisticated or youthful) but also in terms of what they apparently are not (youthful or sophisticated).

focus

Williamson (1978: 29) uses this diagram to represent her analysis of the Chanel and Babe adverts (Figure 4.7).

Figure 4.7 *Analysis of Chanel and Babe advertisements,* (Williamson, 1978: 29)

$$C.D. \; (\not=) \; M.H.$$
$$\| \qquad \qquad \|$$
$$No. \; 5 \, (\not=) \; Babe$$

Semiological studies often use diagrams to represent structures of meaning spatially: diagrams like Williamson's here, or Goldman's mapping technique. Barthes (1973) notes that this spatialization is only a metaphor: in other words, a metonymic sign. Compare this to Pierce's definition of diagrams as iconic.

In relation to the connections between adverts, Williamson's argument has some methodological implications which she does not spell out. It suggests that in order to analyse one image, or a few, it is necessary to look at the images they are constructed in contrast to, or in relation to. But how are these other images to be identified? Williamson offers no guidance on this point, other than implying that, since adverts have to create difference between basically the same products, it is to other ads for the same sort of product that the semiologist should look. Hence her example comparing two perfume adverts. However, there are a number of other issues to bear in mind. First, Goldman (1992: 44), whose book uses only perfume ads in order to make its arguments, points out that the 1970s was an era of 'celebrity ads', in which famous people were frequently used to promote products. In this sense, the Chanel and Babe ads are actually quite similar. So the criteria of 'similarity' and 'difference' in the relations between images may need to be carefully considered. Second, the self-referentiality of much contemporary advertising might mean that comparing adverts selling similar products may be too restrictive to pick up on an ad's resonances. Third, the meanings of adverts may also be established less in relation to other (dis)similar ads and more in relation to whatever other texts and images surround them in their place of display. This is a consideration ignored by all the semiologists of advertising whose work this chapter has so far cited. But Mieke Bal (1996: 117–28) offers an interesting interpretation of a visual image which argues that the context of its display is crucial to the meanings it accrues to its viewers (and more particularly to her as its viewer: an example of her reflexivity). Her example is a painting by Caravaggio hanging in the Berlin-Dahlem art gallery, and she suggests that both the surrounding paintings and the captions on the wall of the gallery, as well as the knowledge and feelings she brings to the painting, affect what it means to her.

If images gain meanings not only from their own signs then, but also from their relation with the signs of other images, it is necessary to consider what sort of relation to other images is most important for the images you are considering. Is it a relation based on 'content'? Or on a shared location of display? Or on explicit cross-referencing? Reaching this decision will help to clarify what other images you need to examine in relation to the ones of your case study. Even so, you will need to develop a broad knowledge of other images in order to be able to identify those which are in a relevant relation to the ones that constitute your case study.

3.4 signs and codes, referent systems and mythologies

Section 3.2 noted that certain sorts of signs – indexical, symbolic and connotive especially – refer to wider systems of meaning. These 'wider systems' can be characterized in a number of ways. They have been called 'codes' by Stuart Hall (1980), 'referent systems' by Williamson (1978) and 'mythologies' by Barthes (1973). Each of these terms means something rather different, and each has somewhat different methodological implications.

Code A **code** is a set of conventionalized ways of making meaning that are specific to particular groups of people. In the context of making television news programmes, for example, Stuart Hall (1980: 136) comments on what he calls the 'professional code' that is mobilized in the work of producers, editors, lighting and camera technicians, newscasters and so on. This professional code guides such things as 'the particular choice of presentational occasions and formats, the selection of personnel, the choice of images, the staging of debates'. It has a 'techno-practical nature' according to Hall because it operates with 'such apparently neutral-technical questions as visual quality, news and presentational values, televisual quality, professionalism and so on' (Hall, 1980: 136). The makers of adverts have their professional codes too, which result in the frequent occurrence visual structure described by Goldman (1992) as photographic image, text, mortise and graphics (see also Dyer, 1982: 135; Myers, 1983). Adverts depend on other sorts of codes too. Crucially, they depend on the codes held by the particular group of consumers to whom their makers want to sell the product (hence the use of focus groups by advertising agencies to find out what those codes are). Thus the Chanel ad analysed by Williamson (1978) depends for its effectiveness on its audience 'knowing' that Catherine **Encoded** Deneuve is beautiful, stylish and chic; she has to be already **encoded** as such for the advert to be able to transfer those signifiers from her to the perfume. An audience unfamiliar with Deneuve would not be able to make sense of this advert.

Codes can be researched in a number of ways. Goldman (1992), for example, seems to use a very informal (and implicit) kind of content analysis of the adverts to reach his fourfold characterization of advertising's visual code. Leiss, Kline and Jhally (1986), on the other hand, use content analysis explicitly to examine the visual structure of adverts. They also interview the producers of adverts to explore what codes they deploy in the production process. Similarly, Catherine Lutz and Jane Collins (1993), in their study of the photographs used in *National Geographic* which was examined in the previous chapter, supplemented their content analysis with interviews with the editors, writers and photographers at the magazine, in order to explore the codes they mobilized to make the publication look the way it does.

As Hall (1980) makes clear, codes allow the semiologist access to the wider ideologies at work in a society. 'At the connotive level, we must refer, *through* the codes, to the orders of social life, of economic and political power and of ideology', because codes 'contract relations for the sign with the wider universe of ideologies in a society' (Hall, 1980: 134). Thus Deneuve/Chanel are encoded as beautiful and glamorous, and that code is a particular expression of the ideology that all women should be beautiful and glamorous for men. Hall (1980) describes such ideologies as 'metacodes' or **'Dominant codes'** **'dominant codes'**. Williamson (1978), on the other hand, describes some- **Referent systems** thing similar as **referent systems**. Williamson (1978) says that there are three major referent systems on which the signs of adverts depend: Nature, Magic and Time. Referent systems, like dominant codes, are knowledges which pre-exist advertising and structure not only adverts but many other cultural and social forms. Thus of the referent system of Nature she says, 'Nature is the primary referent of a culture' (Williamson, 1978: 103). However, Williamson characterizes referent systems in a more rigid way than Hall does dominant codes. Following the work of the structuralist anthropologist Claude Lévi-Strauss, Williamson argues that referent systems are organized in binary terms. Hodge and Kress (1988: 30) refer to this structure as 'an abstract elemental binary principle, with infinite particular forms produced by this principle applied repeatedly to the material basis of the code'. Thus Nature, says Williamson (1978: 103–37) is in adverts represented in only two ways: it is either 'raw' or 'cooked' (that is, transformed by culture). Many adverts suggest that their products improve nature and picture this with images of 'cooked' nature. Many ads use images of 'science' to suggest that their products can order, investigate or overcome nature (again, in Williamson's terms cooking it). Many ads use images of 'raw' nature to confer apparently natural qualities on to their products, such as perfectibility, danger and obviousness. Thus Nature is for Williamson a referent system that underlies many of the particular signs and codes of adverts.

Using Willamson's notion of referent systems depends on a broader understanding of cultural more generally that is more likely to come from social theory than from empirical investigation. Indeed, Leiss, Kline and Jhally (1986: 165) find Williamson's referent systems just too huge to shed much light on adverts specifically. They imply that analyses of ads would be better based on some sort of 'middling level' structures of meaning, like 'fashion' or 'domesticity'. I suggest that this is what the notion of codes is useful for: referent systems can be accessed through codes, which themselves inform signs.

Mythology   Barthes's notion of **mythology** is different again. Barthes (1973: 117) says that 'myth is not defined by the object of its message, but by the way in which it utters this message: there are formal limits to myth, there are no 'substantial' ones'. That is, whereas Williamson's referent systems are substantive – her discussion of Nature, for example, is about how Nature is pictured in adverts – Barthes instead argues that mythology is defined by its form, not its content. Myth, he suggested, is a 'second-order semiological system' (1973: 123). By this he meant that myth builds upon denotive signs. Denotive signs consist of a signifier and a signified but they are fairly easy to understand, and Barthes suggests this is the first-order semiological system. The denotive sign, however, becomes a signifier at the second, or mythological, level of meaning. At this second level of meaning, this signifier is then accompanied by its own signified. These second-level signifieds and signifiers then form second-level signs. In order to avoid confusion, Barthes adopted a clear terminology for these different elements of signs. He called the sign at the first level, meaning; when it is referred to as the signifier of a mythical sign, he called it form. The signified is the concept. The second level of sign – at the level of myth – he called signification.

'In meaning', Barthes (1973: 127) writes, 'the meaning is already complete, it postulates a kind of knowledge, a past, a memory, a comparative order of facts, ideas, decisions.' Barthes elaborates what he means by this through an example. 'I am at the barber's, and a copy of *Paris-Match* is offered to me. On the cover, a young Negro in a French uniform is saluting, with his eyes uplifted, probably fixed on the fold of the tricolour' (Barthes, 1973: 125). This is the meaning of the image (at the denotive level). He suggests that the image contains a kind of richness at this level (remember Barthes's claim that the photograph carries its referent with it in ways that other forms of visual imagery do not); the black boy 'appears as a rich, fully experienced, spontaneous, *indisputable* image' (Barthes, 1973: 128). When this meaning becomes form, however, this richness is almost lost. 'When it becomes form, the meaning leaves contingency behind; it empties itself, it becomes impoverished, history evaporates' (Barthes, 1973: 127). The meaning is put at a distance, and what fills the gap is signification. In this case, signification produces the notion that

'France is a great Empire, that all her sons, without any colour discrimination, faithfully serve under her flag, and that there is no better answer to the detractors of an alleged colonialism than the zeal shown by this Negro in serving his so-called oppressors' (Barthes, 1973: 125). The contingency and the history of the meaning become remote, and instead a myth inserts itself as a non-historical truth. Myth makes us forget that things were and are made; instead, it naturalizes the way things are. Myth is thus a form of ideology. French imperialism is the drive behind this myth, says Barthes, and this image presents it as natural. But the myth is believable precisely because form does not entirely replace meaning. 'The meaning will be for the form like an instantaneous reserve of history, a tamed richness, which it is possible to call and dismiss in a sort of rapid alternation' (Barthes, 1973: 127); the meaning both hides and sustains the form.

As with dominant codes and referent systems, then, the interpretation of mythologies requires a broad understanding of a culture's dynamics.

3.5 slippery signs

This section has explored various ways of understanding how signs make what kinds of meanings. Not all these approaches are completely compatible with each other. However, they do share certain characteristics. Above all, they emphasize the relationality of signs: what one sign means depends on its relations with others. As Bal and Bryson (1991: 177) note, this makes the analysis of signs difficult because it is hard to know where to break into that relationality: 'Meaning [arises] exactly from the movement from one sign or signifier to the next, in a *perpetuum mobile* where there could be found neither a starting point for semiosis, nor a concluding moment in which semiosis terminated and the meaning of signs fully "arrived".' In semiology there is no stable point that can provide an entrance into the meaning-making process; all meanings are relational not only within the image but also in relation to other images and to broader dominant codes, referent systems and mythologies. Any point of entry will be artificial and arbitrary, then. But, providing this is borne in mind, this section has suggested a number of steps through which, faced with an image, a semiological analysis might be initiated. In summary, these are:

1 decide what the signs are.
2 decide what they signify 'in themselves'.
3 think about how they relate to other signs both within the image (here the vocabulary of section 3.2 is useful, and making a diagram of the movement of signifieds between the signifiers of an image may also help) and in other images.
4 then explore their connections (and the connections of the connections) to wider systems of meaning, from codes to dominant codes, referent systems or mythologies.

5 and then return to the signs via their codes to explore the precise articulation of ideology and mythology.

4 on audiences and interpretations

Polysemy

The meanings of signs are, therefore, extraordinarily complex. This complexity means that their meanings are multiple, and this multiplicity is referred to as **polysemy**. A sign is polysemic when it has more than one meaning. How is it then that Williamson (1978), for example, can speak of an advert as having a powerful meaning that positions its viewers in a specific imaginary social place? Is polysemy limited in some way? Williamson argues it is. This section explores how semiology argues that most images most of the time produce what Hall calls the **preferred meaning**.

Preferred meaning

> Any . . . sign is potentially transformable into more than one connotive configuration. Polysemy, however, must not be confused with pluralism . . . Any society/culture tends, with varying degrees of closure, to impose its classifications of the social and cultural and political world. These constitute a *dominant cultural order*, though it is neither univocal nor uncontested . . . The different areas of social life appeared to be mapped out into discursive domains, hierarchically organized into dominant or preferred meanings. (Hall, 1980: 134)

Preferred readings

These preferred meanings (or ideologies) become **preferred readings** when they are interpreted by audiences in ways that retain 'the institutional/ political/ideological order imprinted on them' (Hall, 1980: 134).

There are two ways in which semiologists explain the production of preferred readings. The first of these focuses on the visual and textual relation between an image and its viewer, and the second emphasizes the social modalities of the reception of an image.

4.1 the decoder of advertisements

In its discussion of advertising, this chapter has so far argued that the fundamental process through which adverts make meaning is by transferring signifieds between signs. But this elides a crucial part of Williamson's (1978) arguments. Adverts do not effect this transfer by themselves. The source of the movement of signifieds is not the ad itself, says Williamson, but the viewer of the ad. It is the viewer who makes sense of the advert, not the advert itself. Indeed, without a viewer to decode the advert, the ad would be, literally, meaningless. 'All signs depend for their signifying process on the existence of specific, concrete receivers, people *for* whom and in whose systems of belief, they have a meaning' (Williamson, 1978: 40). It is in this sense that Bal and Bryson argue that semiology is centrally concerned with the reception of images by audiences: 'semiotic analysis of visual art does not set out in the first place to produce interpretations of works of art, but rather to investigate how works of art are intelligible to those who view them, the processes by which viewers make sense of what they see' (Bal and Bryson, 1991: 184).

Williamson (1978) elaborates this argument in a way that has particular methodological implications. Unlike some other semiologists, she pays little attention to possible disjunctures between the systems of beliefs that viewers bring to adverts and what is encoded in the adverts. (Perhaps her estimation of the fundamental importance of referent systems to all forms of cultural expression is responsible for this uninterest in conflicts of meaning.) Instead, she develops an analysis of how adverts encourage their viewers to produce preferred readings. That is, *Decoding Advertisements* analyses the success of ideology. Williamson (1978) argues that ads invite their viewers to create meaning. But in that process of making meaning, the viewer is also made in specific, ideological ways.

> We [the advertiser viewer] must enter the space between the signifier and signified, between what means and what it means. This space is that of the individual as subject: he or she is not a simple receiver but a creator of meaning. But the receiver is only a creator of meaning because he/she *has been called upon to be so.* As an advertisement speaks to us, we simultaneously create that speech (it means to *us*), and are created by it *as its creators* (it assumes that it means to us). (Williamson, 1978: 41)

Thus, she continues, adverts 'invite us "freely" to create ourselves in accordance with the way in which they have already created us' (Williamson, 1978: 42). This sense of creative freedom is the most subtle form of adverts' ideology, says Williamson, because it deceives us into thinking that we can choose our social position through what we consume. That apparent choice is deceptive, says Williamson, not only because actual social position is determined by the class structure of capitalist societies and not by consumption, but also because adverts depend on codes and referent systems which precisely delimit our interpretive powers.

Williamson (1978) elaborates this argument by exploring the stages of a viewer's encounter with an ad. First, she says, the viewer creates the meaning of a product by making links between signs. Then, the viewer gives meaning to him or herself from the product; we believe we will become strong and dependable (though perhaps not irresistible – prams are not usually encoded as seduction devices) by buying a Silver Cross product. Third, we become created by the ad, in a process Williamson calls, after **Appellation**   Althusser, **appellation**. The advert hails us, 'hey you', often quite directly, and thus incorporates us into its signifying world:

> Every ad assumes a particular spectator; it projects out into the space in front of it an imaginary person composed in terms of the relationship

between the elements in the ad. You move into this space as you look at the ad, and in doing so 'become' the spectator, you feel that the 'hey you' *'really did'* apply to you in particular. (Williamson, 1978: 50–1)

Williamson suggests a number of ways in which adverts pull a spectator into their signifying effects:

1 the *spatial organization* of an image offers a particular position to its spectators. For example, Chapter 1 explored how a photograph by Robert Doisneau projects out into the space in front of it a spectator composed in terms of the relationship between the elements of the photograph.
2 ads contain or imply *visual absences* that the viewer is invited to fill. For example, the ad in Figure 4.3 doesn't show the products Silver Cross makes; it involves us by making us fill it in.
3 the *written text* draws us in.
4 many adverts rely on textual and visual *puns* or puzzles, that make us stop and look at them in order to work out 'what's going on'. Figure 4.2, for example, has a punning text. Ads can show incongruity, or use no words at all, again to attract our attention and involvement.
5 *calligraphy*. This is when the product is transformed into a word. The word then becomes a referent of a real object, the product.

Thus Williamson focuses on the compositional modality of the adverts themselves in her understanding of how they produce preferred meanings.

Finally, she suggests that we create ourselves in the advertisement itself. At this point in her argument she turns to certain ideas from psychoanalysis – including the imaginary – in order to explore the dynamics of precisely how we imagine adverts mirror our self. These arguments will be explored in the following chapter.

4.2 the social modality of making meaning

As the previous section noted, Judith Williamson (1978) explores the means by which adverts produce their viewers in particular ways. Even though she says it is the viewers doing the work, nonetheless her argument implies that adverts are themselves powerful in the sense that they produce certain kinds of ways of seeing through their visual and verbal organization and connotations. Other semiologists have paid more attention to other ways in which the polysemy of signs is limited, however. In particular, some prefer 'to interrogate which social and political pressures do check the actual dissemination' of meanings (Bal and Bryson, 1991: 193).

Perhaps the most sustained attempt to do this – or at least to assert its importance – is the book by Robert Hodge and Gunther Kress (1988) called *Social Semiotics*. They suggest that what they call 'mainstream semiotics' stresses 'system and product' (which is certainly true of Williamson's work, for example), whereas they prefer to emphasize 'speakers and writers or other participants in semiotic activity as connecting and inter*acting* in a variety of ways in concrete social contexts' (Hodge and Kress, 1988: 1). To do that, they refer to 'a second level of messages which regulates the functioning of ideological complexes' which **Logonomic system**   they term the **logonomic system** (Hodge and Kress, 1988: 4).

> A logonomic system is a set of rules prescribing the conditions for production and reception of meanings; which specify who can claim to initiate (produce, communicate) or know (receive, understand) meanings about what topics under what circumstances and with what modalities (how, when, why). Logonomic systems prescribe social semiotic behaviours at points of production and reception, so that we can distinguish **Production regimes**   between **production regimes** (rules constraining production) and **Reception regimes**   **reception regimes** (rules constraining reception). A logonomic system is itself a set of messages, part of an ideological complex but serving to make it unambiguous in practice . . . The logonomic rules are specifically taught and policed by concrete social agents (parents, teachers, employers) coercing concrete individuals in specific situations by processes which are in principle open to study and analysis . . . Logonomic systems cannot be invisible or obscure, or they would not work. (Hodge and Kress, 1988: 4)

This seems to me to be a crucial addition to the analytical lexicon of semiology, since, as Chapter 1 insisted, these sorts of social modalities are fundamental to the interpretation of visual images.

Let us briefly consider its implications for thinking about how adverts are interpreted (their reception regime; the discussion of professional codes in section 2.3 very briefly touched on their production regime). Perhaps one of the most important rules constraining the reception of adverts in their original places of display (that is, in magazines, on tv, in a cinema or on a billboard, for example, not in a gallery or in an academic text where different reception regimes apply; see Hodge and Kress, 1988: 68 for a useful discussion on the importance of the setting of a visual image to its interpretation) is that they are not to be taken too seriously. They are fun, entertainment, they're the gaps in the tv programme when you nip to the kitchen to make a drink. But they are not meant to deal with serious issues. Now of course semiologists would argue that adverts do indeed deal with serious issues: they engage with some of the most important issues, indeed, with questions of social difference and social hierarchy. But part of their power is precisely that they are not seen like that. Their reception regime suggests that they are pretty superficial things. This explains much of the controversy surrounding the advertising campaigns produced in the early 1990s by the clothing company Benetton (Back and Quaade, 1993; Ramamurthy, 1997: 188–96). Their ads showing a man dying from AIDS-related illness or of a bombed car in an Italian street caused outrage because these images challenged the reception regime of advertising. They were clearly asking their viewers to engage with 'big' issues – death, violence – and this violated the regime's rule that adverts do not do that. The ensuing efforts by other advertising agencies, by magazines and the rest of the media (that relies on advertising income) to re-establish the reception regime by branding these images immoral or obscene reasserted once more the apparent harmlessness of non-controversial advertising.

Metasigns   Hodge and Kress (1988) also explore the way signs are mobilized by social groups as markers of their difference from others; they call these metasigns. These are the kind of signs that the advertisers of products which are aimed at very specific audiences might try to encode into their adverts, with the aim of appellating that group through the advert and thus encouraging them to buy it.

Finally Hodge and Kress (1988) persistently make the point that all social identity is constructed through ideologies of social difference. Thus they insist that different social groups (however defined) encode the world in very different ways and may thus interpret visual images in very different ways. Their example is an advert for cigarettes that has been covered with grafitti by an anti-smoking organization. Bal and Bryson (1991) make the same point in their discussion of visual art. They suggest that there is probably always resistance to dominant scopic regimes, which might 'range from polite parody to outright defacement, from the clandestine inversion of existing rules of viewing to the invention of wholly new sets of rules, from subtle violations of propriety to blank refusal to play the game' – quite apart from the private languages of looking that are evoked, for example, by Barthes's notion of the *punctum* (Bal and Bryson, 1991: 187). However, there are very few semiological studies that pursue the diversity of interpretive practices, and the next section explores this and some other limitations of semiological approaches to visual images. Chapter 8 will return to the question of researching audiences' interpretations.

5 semiology: emphases and neglects

Despite the doubts voiced by some about the appropriateness of using semiology to interpret visual images, it seems that semiology can none-theless be a very productive way of thinking about visual meaning. Semiology demands detailed analysis of images, and its reliance on case studies and elaborate analytical terminology create careful and precise accounts of how the meanings of particular images are made. Moreover, semiology is centrally concerned with the construction of social difference through signs. Its focus on ideology, ideological complexes and dominant codes, and its recognition of resistance to those, means that it cannot avoid considering the social effects of meaning:

> Sign-events occur in specific circumstances and according to a finite number of culturally valid, conventional, yet not unalterable rules . . . The selection of those rules and their combination leads to specific interpretive behaviour. That behaviour is socially framed, and any semiotic view that is to be socially relevant will have to deal with this framing, precisely on the grounds of the fundamental polysemy of meaning and the subsequent possibility of dissemination. In the end, there is no way around considerations of power, inside and outside the academy. (Bal and Bryson, 1991: 208)

As Bal and Bryson's last sentence indicates, semiology can also imply the need for academic accounts of signs to reflect on their own meaning-making tactics. What kinds of truth does an interpretation of a visual image claim? Whose views are not being acknowledged in that interpretation? Is the process of double exposure admitted or denied?

Thus it would seem that semiology fulfils all the criteria for a critical visual methodology outlined in Chapter 1. It takes images seriously, providing a number of tools for understanding exactly how a particular image is structured. It considers the social conditions and effects of images, both in terms of how an image may have its own effects and how the logonomic system shapes its production and reception. And it is able to acknowledge that semiologists are themselves working with signs, codes and referent systems and are thus imbricated in nothing more, though certainly nothing less, than another series of transfers of meaning in which a particular image participates. This allows a certain reflexivity.

However, semiology also has some methodological drawbacks. First, its preference for detailed readings of individual images raises questions about the representativeness and replicability of its analyses. This is a doubt that Leiss, Kline and Jhally (1986: 165) have about Williamson's work. They are unclear about how or why Williamson chose the adverts she works with; are they representative of adverts in general? Would someone else using those same adverts have come to the same conclusions about them? Williamson would presumably respond that these questions are not important since she was using the ads to construct a general theory that could critique how adverts work; she was not trying to offer empirical generalizations about what they are. Certainly her book's illustrations are there to forward her argument about particular processes of meaning-making, not to exemplify particular types of adverts.

Another criticism often faced by semiology is its elaborate theoretical terminology. Ball and Smith (1992), Leiss, Kline and Jhally (1986: 165) and Wells (1992) all voice concern that semiology tends to invent new terminology for its own sake, and from my experience of writing this chapter I tend to agree. Often these terms are useful; they have particular meanings that are clearly defined, and refer to processes that are not easily described otherwise (this latter point is crucial). These sorts of neologisms are thus worth persevering with, no matter how clumsy their use might feel initially. However, sometimes new terms are confusing or unnecessary, and sometimes they are used to give a veneer of sophistication to something that is actually not particularly interesting. As Leiss, Kline and Jhally (1986: 165) remark, this can lead to an obscurantist text that does 'little more than state the obvious in a complex and often pretentious manner'. This sort of use of jargon should be avoided. If a simpler term will do, use the simpler term.

The use of a somewhat elaborate terminology leads to another issue that needs some thought when semiology is deployed as a method: reflexivity. I have commented, mostly in relation to the work of Mieke Bal, that semiology is capable of acknowledging its own interpretive practices. I would term such an acknowledgement reflexive. However, there is also a strong anti-reflexive strain in certain sorts of semiology, particularly those that claim to delve beneath surface appearances to reveal the true meaning of images. Thus Goldman (1992: 36), at the end of his first chapter which argues that adverts envehicle three key aspects of commodity form, says that 'the triumph of the commodity form is that we do not recognize its presence at all'. This statement immediately invites the question, 'who is this "we"?' It clearly excludes Goldman, since he has just spent 36 pages describing the commodity form in detail. So does 'we' refer to the rest of us poor dupes who don't know our Marx (and Goldman) well enough? What makes Goldman so insightful? How come he can see these ads differently to recognize their commodification of product and viewer? Goldman positions himself here as simply the one who sees and knows. He doesn't even clarify his methodology as a way of grounding his claims. This kind of non-reflexivity, I think, cannot be part of a critical visual methodology.

Finally, there is another omission in much semiological work, which is the empirical exploration of polysemy and logonomic systems. Semiology is very ready to admit to polysemy and to the contestation as well as the transfer and circulation of meaning in theory, but there are very few semiological studies that really get to grips with diverse ways of seeing. Don Slater (1983) has addressed this absence and suggests that it is not a coincidence: semiology is simply not concerned with the social practices, institutions and relations within which visual images are produced and interpreted. He blames this on the structuralist tradition within which much semiology was situated when he was writing, which, he says 'takes as assumed, as given, precisely what needs to be explained: the relations and practices within which discourses are formed and operated' (Slater, 1983: 258). This is certainly the case with Williamson's work. She does not explain how she decided that there were only three referent systems underpinning adverts, for example, nor how she decided that Nature, Magic and Time were the three. It seems that this was a theoretical decision that then informed her reading of the adverts. Neither does she pay any attention to the social institutions producing adverts, nor consider how different audiences might react to adverts differently or even simply not 'get' them (Myers, 1983; Wells, 1992). For the advert reproduced as

Figure 4.3 to work, for example, you need to know that Silver Cross is a company that makes prams and pushchairs. If you don't – and I imagine lots of readers of this book might not, although most readers of the magazine where it originally appeared probably would – the ad simply does not make its intended connections. Williamson (1978) does not talk about ads that fail like that; her focus on 'the image itself' produces what Slater (1983: 258) calls a 'radically internal analysis of signification' which cannot address these sorts of issues. This is perhaps the most telling criticism of semiology (and one that Bal and Bryson, 1991, for example, writing fifteen years after Williamson, are keen to dispel).

6 summary

- semiology depends on the distinction between the signifier and the signified of the sign. This distinction enables semiology to focus on the transfers of signifieds between signs.
- the transfer of signifieds is understood as structured through codes, and codes in turn give on to wider structures of meaning. These wider structures can be described as dominant codes, ideologies, mythologies or referent systems. These structures limit polysemy.
- signs, codes, dominant codes, ideologies, mythologies and referent systems can all be challenged by the diversity of ways of seeing.
- visual images have social conditions and social effects, which are articulated both through the image itself and through the social modality of the logonomic system.
- semiological studies focus on the image itself and there is thus little attention paid to audiencing and little concern for reflexivity.

further reading

Roland Barthes's *Mythologies* (1973) remains one of the best exemplifications of semiology; it consists mostly of short essays each looking at elements of post-war French culture, but the last section on 'Myth Today' is a more analytical account of his approach. Mieke Bal and Norman Bryson's essay in *Art Bulletin* (1991) is a good introduction to semiology's more recent themes.

5

psychoanalysis

visual culture, visual pleasure, visual disruption

1 a very brief introduction to psychoanalysis and visuality

Psychoanalysis consists of a range of theories that deal most centrally with human subjectivity, sexuality and the unconscious. Many of its key concepts were developed, and often then revised, by Sigmund Freud (1856–1939). Later writers have then taken his ideas and reworked them again, so psychoanalysis is now a very large and diverse body of work. This chapter cannot hope to cover all aspects of psychoanalysis; even more than other chapters in this book, this will be a very selective account. One element of its selectivity is that it will focus on those parts of psychoanalysis that address the visual. However, the visual is actually very important to **Scopophilia** psychoanalysis. Freud suggested that **scopophilia** – pleasure in looking – was one of the basic drives with which all (sighted) children are born, and the visual is especially important in the work of the psychoanalyst Jacques Lacan. Lacan, building on various claims of Freud, argues that certain moments of seeing, and particular visualities, are central to how subjectivities and sexualities are formed. For this reason, his work has become quite prominent in some approaches to visual culture.

Another aspect of this chapter's selective approach to psychoanalysis is its focus on a number of feminist authors who are using psychoanalysis, often in its Lacanian guise, to understand how the visual is imbricated in the production of sexual difference. These writers work with various kinds of psychoanalysis to produce readings of paintings and photographs, but most often of films. They pay close attention to these visual images and are centrally concerned with their social effects: the ways they produce particular spectating positions that are differentially sexualized and empowered. In this way their use of psychoanalysis conforms to the first two criteria for a critical visual methodology that the first chapter of this book outlined. As for the third criterion – reflexivity – the assumptions made by psychoanalysis about subjectivity raise some interesting questions in relation to reflexivity, and this chapter will explore these in section 8.

Psychoanalysis often takes the form of a therapeutic practice, with an individual talking to their analyst over a long period of time, hoping to find rest from some sort of psychic pain or blockage. However, the psychoanalytic skills brought to bear on the analysis of an individual are not those used in relation to visual culture. Psychoanalysis is not used to analyse the personality of the person producing a particular image, although this can be done; Freud himself wrote an essay on Leonardo da Vinci, for example. Those writers using psychoanalysis, like so many others currently addressing issues of visual culture, are not interested in the producer of images as an individual. Instead, psychoanalytic concepts are used to interpret aspects of visual images and in particular their effects on spectators. Psychoanalysis does not have a strict code of methodological conduct like content analysis, nor does it operate on a 'tool-box' model as the previous chapter suggested semiology does. Rather, psychoanalytic critics often work with just one or two psychoanalytic concepts, exploring their articulation – or rearticulation – through a particular image.

This close theoretical and empirical focus has consequences in relation to an important point raised in the introductory comments to this book and rather underplayed by the methods discussed in previous chapters: that there is no absolute right or wrong way to interpret a visual image. Different psychoanalytic concepts brought to bear on the same image can produce very different interpretations of that image. The case study discussed by this chapter makes the possibility of different interpretations of the same image clear: it is an examination of diverse feminist viewings of some of the films of Alfred Hitchcock. After beginning his film making in Britain, Hitchcock moved to Hollywood in the late 1930s and then directed many films which, as Tania Modleski (1988) observes, continue to fascinate their audiences – audiences which include feminist critics, some of whom have claimed the films for feminism while others have rejected them as irredeemably misogynist. Three films in particular have been the focus of feminist debate: *Rebecca* (1940), *Rear Window* (1954) and *Vertigo* (1958), and this chapter will focus on them too.

Film has proved particularly amenable to psychoanalytic interpretation, and from the mid-1970s through the 1980s the journal *Screen* carried many essays exploring particular films in relation to psychoanalytic ideas. Cinema is an especially powerful visual medium because a film can create a total world for its audience. Films manipulate the visual, the spatial and the temporal and, as Laura Mulvey (1989: 25) says, by 'playing on the tension between film as controlling the dimension of time (editing, narrative) and film as controlling the dimension of space (changes in distance, editing), cinematic codes create a gaze, a world and an object'. In particular, film is a powerful means of structuring looking, not only the looks between the film's protagonists but also the looks between its protagonists and its spectators. Since psychoanalysis in its Freudian and Lacanian forms argues that visuality is central to subjectivity, it follows that film can address our sense of self very powerfully – and that psychoanalysis can offer some powerful readings of films.

Feminist psychoanalytic film critics have of course been particularly concerned to see how films visualize masculinity and femininity in ways that disempower women, and how that visualization then positions the audience in gendered terms. However, for reasons the next section will explain, the relationship between feminism and psychoanalysis is an uneasy one. This has meant that psychoanalytic terms have not always been used by feminist film critics in strict accordance with their definitions by Freud or Lacan. Moreover, as Mieke Bal and Norman Bryson (1991: 210) suggest, if looked at attentively, images may well suggest modifications or resistances to some of the assumptions of psychoanalysis. They assume that 'the relationship between the [visual] work and psychoanalysis is an interaction . . . conducted among three subjects: the psychoanalytic theorist, the work, and the critic' (Bal and Bryson, 1991: 196). Thus feminist writers, among others, have also modified some psychoanalytic terms in order to see seeing differently. For there are issues that psychoanalysis is not concerned to address but that certain images may insist upon, and this chapter will conclude by exploring these absences in psychoanalytic theory. To expand on these comments, this chapter will:

- examine some of the founding assumptions of psychoanalysis's understanding of subjectivity, sexuality and the unconscious;
- focus on psychoanalytic arguments about how sexual difference is articulated visually;
- explore a number of different feminist psychoanalytic methods of interpreting visual representations of sexual difference;
- address the issues psychoanalysis raises for methodological reflexivity;
- assess the strengths and weaknesses of psychoanalytic approaches to visual images.

2   a longer introduction to psychoanalysis and visuality: subjectivity, sexuality and the unconscious

To say that psychoanalysis deals with subjectivity, sexuality and the unconscious provides a starting point for introducing the ways that psychoanalysis contributes to discussions about the visual. These three terms have implications for how psychoanalysis conceptualizes both the viewer of an image and the image itself, and these two sites – that of the *image itself* and its *audiencing* – are the two sites of meaning production that psychoanalysis examines. Discussion here will begin with their implications for understanding the audience of an image.

Subjectivity   To begin with, the use of the term **subjectivity** to refer to a viewer's characteristics – rather than, say, identity – has a number of consequences for psychoanalytic approaches. First, 'subjectivity' entails the acknowledgement that individuals are indeed *subjective*: that we make sense of our selves and our worlds through a whole range of complex and often non-rational ways of understanding. We feel, we dream, we fantasize, we take pleasure and are repulsed, we can be ambivalent and contradictory, panic-stricken and in love; and we can react to things in ways that feel beyond words. Psychoanalysis addresses these sorts of emotional states (and indeed would argue that rationality too is a kind of emotion often secretly dependent on these other non-rational states of mind). In relation to the visual, this means psychoanalysis often focuses on the emotional effects of visual images, on the way that the impact of an image may be 'immediate and powerful even when its precise meaning remains, as it were, vague, suspended – numinous' (Hall, 1999: 311).

But the notion of subjectivity in this context has further implications. In particular – and this is what distinguishes psychoanalytic approaches from others that engage with the emotional – psychoanalysis argues that understanding emotional reactions to, let's say, visual images requires the recognition that not all of those reactions are working at a wholly conscious level. **Unconscious**   Some reactions may be coming from the **unconscious**. Freud's elaboration of the unconscious is sometimes seen as the founding moment of psychoanalysis. Put simply, the unconscious is created when a very young child's drives and instincts start to be disciplined by cultural rules and values. The child is forced to repress the culturally forbidden aspects of those drives and instincts, and their repression produces the unconscious. The unconscious is thus a forbidden zone in two senses. It is forbidden because the conscious mind cannot access it. And it is forbidden because it is full of outlawed drives and energies and logics. But Freud insisted that it nevertheless has its effects on our conscious selves. Sometimes the boundary between the conscious and the unconscious leaks and the unconscious finds indirect expression in things like gestures, slips of the tongue (which the speaker does not notice), dreams, and so on. Thus because of the unconscious, subjectivity, in psychoanalytic terms, is never fully conscious, coherent or complete. We can never fully know ourselves, according to psychoanalysis, because the unconscious remains beyond self-consciousness; and our conscious selves are always likely to be infiltrated by excursions from the unconscious. As Jacqueline Rose (1986: 3) says: 'the unconscious is the only defence against a language frozen into pure, fixed or institutionalized meaning, and . . . in its capacity to unsettle the subject, is a break against the intolerable limits of common sense.' Psychoanalysis does not therefore concur with the modernist notion that to see is to know; indeed, Lacan (1977: 93) has commented that 'in this matter of the visible, everything is a trap'. Instead, the notion of the unconscious focuses attention on the uncertainties of subjectivity and on the uncertainties of seeing; psychoanalysis is especially interested in visual confusions, blindspots and mistakes.

There are two more implications of this particular understanding of subjectivity that need to be addressed before this chapter explores some of the more detailed methodological implications of psychoanalysis. As well as focusing on the subjective and the unconscious, psychoanalysis emphasizes that subjectivity is also always *subject* to certain disciplines. This should be clear from the previous discussion of the unconscious: the unconscious is formed by the disciplines of a culture, by its particular pattern of interdicts and permissions. Subjectivity is thus culturally as well as psychically constructed, and this process of subjection continues throughout our lives. We are made as subjects through disciplines, taboos and prohibitions. And in the sorts of psychoanalysis influenced by Lacan, visuality is one of those disciplines. We learn to see in particular ways, and this is a process that is reiterated every time we look. Thus visualities and visual images are given a kind of agency by psychoanalysis, because our immersion in a certain kind of visuality and our encounters with certain kinds of visual images tutor us into particular kinds of subjectivity. Thus psychoanalytic approaches, while centrally concerned with the psychic processes of subjectivity and visuality, can also address the *social modality* of these processes by considering their cultural constitution. (However, as section 8 of this chapter will explore, not all critics are happy with the way in which psychoanalysis deals with cultural processes.)

Psychoanalysis, then, has a dual emphasis: on the one hand, it examines the constant disciplining of subjectivity; on the other, it stresses the instabilities of the unconscious which always threaten those disciplines with disruption. Finally then, and concomitant with this, psychoanalytic approaches also emphasize that subjectivity is always *in process*. Never fully achieved, subjectivity must constantly be reiterated through its engagements with various structures of meaning, including visual images. As Griselda Pollock (1992: 10) says, 'visual representation is analysed . . . in terms of its continuing necessity as a site for the perpetual cultural process of shaping and working the subject, conceptualized as precarious and unfixed.'

As a consequence of this particular theorization of subjectivity, psychoanalysis understands the process of audiencing in a specific way. The viewer of an image is understood as bringing a certain subjectivity to bear on an image. But, as the previous two paragraphs have also been suggesting, that subjectivity is imbricated in the images it sees. It is formed through specific visualities, and these visualities are constructed through repeated encounters with images that invite specific ways of seeing. Psychoanalysis is therefore also concerned with the effects of visual images on spectators and pays careful attention to images themselves, especially their *compositional modality*. Stuart Hall summarizes this understanding of the relation between image and audience thus:

> The articulation between viewer and viewed is . . . conceptualized in this body of work . . . as an internal relation. Indeed, the two points in the

circuit of articulation privileged here – the viewer and viewed – are seen as mutually constitutive. The subject is, in part, formed subjectively through what and how it 'sees', how its 'field of vision' is constructed. In the same way, what is seen – the image and its meaning – is understood not as eternally fixed, but relative to and implicated in the positions and schemas of interpretation which are brought to bear upon it. Visual discourses already have possible positions of interpretation (from which they 'make sense') embedded in them, and the subjects bring their own subjective desires and capacities to the 'text' which enable them to take up positions of identification in relation to its meaning. (Hall, 1999: 310)

This understanding of the mutual constitution of visual images and spectators often encourages psychoanalytic accounts to take the form of case studies of particular visual images and the precise ways in which they subject the spectator. Even longer studies of a particular genre of films, for example, tend to depend on careful viewings of individual movies in order to develop an argument in relation to the genre as a whole.

In their emphasis on the image itself in its compositional modality as a site of meaning production, psychoanalytic approaches are similar to the previous three methods already discussed in this book. The differences between psychoanalysis, compositional interpretation and content analysis, however, should already be clear. Unlike compositional interpretation, psychoanalysis has an explicit interpretive framework. Content analysis, meanwhile, assumes the rational, scientific researcher who can be fully explicit about their methods; Lutz and Collins (1993: 89) in their study of *National Geographic* magazine, remember, advocated content analysis precisely as a means of 'protection against an unconscious search through the magazine for only those which confirm one's initial sense of what the photos say or do'. Psychoanalysis suggests that such a fully rational procedure (and researcher) is an impossible fantasy. Semiology, on the other hand, does have some connection to psychoanalysis. Indeed, Bal and Bryson (1991), in their discussion of semiology, suggest that psychoanalysis is simply a particular type of semiology. They suggest that psychoanalysis offers a way of interpreting the signs of an image in relation, not to particular referent systems, dominant codes or mythologies, but rather in relation to the unconscious and its dynamics. Judith Williamson (1978: 60–70) uses Lacan's notion of the imaginary to explain how she thinks adverts do produce preferred readings, and in particular how they offer us idealized images of ourselves (the imaginary will be discussed in section 3.2). One area where psychoanalysis and semiology do differ, though, is the specific things that a psychoanalytic approach picks out.

According to Bal and Bryson (1991: 197), psychoanalysis is 'a searchlight theory, allowing specific features [of an image] to be illuminated, sometimes explained but primarily read, by means of psychoanalytic concepts'. Again, the key concepts in psychoanalytic accounts of the

LRS: Somerset College

compositional modality of an image are concepts which offer particular understandings of subjectivity, sexuality and the unconscious. Images are interpreted in terms of their subjective effects; and one of the subjections that psychoanalysis has most to say about is that of **sexuality**. Psychoanalysis is centrally concerned with the process through which sexual difference is established and (often precariously) maintained. Freud elaborated what he termed the **castration complex** to explain the differentiation of babies into boys and girls. Freud assumes that all humans begin life in an undifferentiated relationship with their mother. He locates the break from the mother and the beginning of subjectivity with the intervention of the father. (Heterosexual) masculinity is constituted by the boy-child feeling threatened by the father with castration if he does not give up his closeness to the mother (a threat made effective by the sight of the mother's genitalia as apparently lacking); (heterosexual) femininity, in ways less convincingly theorized by Freud, is produced by girl-children seeing themselves as lacking – as already castrated – and transferring their attachment from the mother to the father. (More will be said about the castration complex in section 3.1.) It is this disciplining process, resolved by the Oedipus complex, that represses the child's profound drives and desires and thus produces the unconscious.

The psychoanalytic discussion of sexuality is extremely complicated and often hotly debated. Many feminists reject psychoanalysis outright because they see Freud's account as naturalizing the inferiority of girls or women by affirming them as lacking on biological grounds. Many gay and lesbian theorists reject psychoanalysis on the grounds that it assumes that heterosexuality established through the castration complex is the norm and that homosexuality is a deviation from it. Many black feminists reject psychoanalysis as a colonizing theory that simply erases race as an analytical and political category (see, for example, Iginla, 1992). However, many feminists and theorists of homosexualities and 'race' continue to struggle with psychoanalysis for all its difficulties because they see it as the only productive theory of sexuality that can speak of its complexity, its disciplines and its disruptions. In one of the first sustained explorations of the usefulness of Freudian psychoanalysis for feminism, Juliet Mitchell (1974: xv), for example, insisted that 'psychoanalysis is not a recommendation *for* a patriarchal society, but an analysis *of* one'. And that is the spirit in which the author discusses the approach to psychoanalysis here: as offering some helpful tools for analysing aspects of the intersection of subjectivity and visuality.

3 going to the movies with Laura Mulvey

One of the first – and still one of the most important – essays of psychoanalytic feminist film criticism is called 'Visual pleasure and narrative cinema', and was published by Laura Mulvey in *Screen* in 1975 (Mulvey,

1989: 14–26). By 'narrative cinema', Mulvey means mainstream Hollywood cinema. She cites a number of examples and pays some attention to two films directed by Alfred Hitchcock, *Vertigo* (1958) and *Rear Window* (1954).

The use of the term 'visual pleasure' in Mulvey's title immediately suggests that she is concerned with the subjective effect of narrative cinema. This is a subjectivity culturally constructed though: 'this paper intends to use psychoanalysis to discover where and how the fascination of film is reinforced by pre-existing patterns of fascination already at work within the individual subject and the social formations that have moulded him' (Mulvey, 1989: 14). Thus Mulvey is exploring the mutual constitution of the psychic and the social. As a feminist, though, Mulvey assumes that the most important of the social formations shaping the subject is patriarchy. She is thus concerned with the disciplining of subjectivity into a particular form of sexual difference. Mulvey is also exploring the mutual constitution of the movie and spectator. She does that by examining the visual, spatial and temporal construction of narrative cinema, and seeing how that effects both the representation of men and women in the movies and the gendering of the spectator. Thus Mulvey's essay addresses many of the key themes of feminist psychoanalytic film criticism. It does so by drawing on two psychoanalytic concepts – the castration complex and the mirror stage – in order to understand the visual articulation of subjectivity, sexual difference and the unconscious in particular ways.

3.1 the castration complex and visual pleasure

Mulvey's account depends on the notion of the castration complex, so, although section 2 briefly outlined Freud's discussion, it is pertinent to say a little more about that complex now. The previous section noted that Freud's account of the castration complex makes the assumption that all humans begin life in an undifferentiated relationship with their mother. However, this is only the first, and least problematic, of a number of assumptions in Freud's argument. Another, and much more problematic, is that all babies feel that to have a penis is normal. Thus when the father intervenes to break up the closeness of that primary relationship, the threat of castration feels real; the baby is threatened with the loss of something important. This notion that the penis is not simply a piece of anatomy but also something **Phallus** meaningful is emphasized by the concept of the **phallus**. Reference to the phallus rather than the penis is meant to indicate 'not that anatomical difference *is* sexual difference . . . but that anatomical difference comes to *figure* sexual difference, that is, it becomes the sole representative of what that difference is allowed to be' (Rose, 1986: 66). In the castration complex, the father asserts that the mother is 'his' and the threat that forces the boy to give up his closeness to his mother (in exchange for himself becoming a man and having 'his own' other woman in the future) is that he sees his mother as not having a penis. Here a third assumption in Freud's account comes into play: that when the boy sees his mother's genitalia, he sees them not simply as different from his, but as lacking. This assumption only works, however, if what Freud is talking about here is not simply vision, but visuality. The boy-child must already be seeing through a visuality that asserts that the masculine position is to look, the feminine is to be looked at, and that the feminine is to be seen as lacking.

Mulvey argues precisely that visuality is structured in this gendered way. She claims that 'in a world ordered by sexual imbalance, pleasure in looking has been split between active/male and passive/female. The determining male gaze projects its fantasy onto the female figure, which is styled accordingly' (Mulvey, 1989: 19). Thus sexual difference is understood relationally: visions of femininity depend on the vision of masculinity, and vice versa. As well as this active/male and passive/female distinction, Mulvey argues that the castration complex has implications for images of women in this patriarchal visuality. She says that 'the representation of the female form . . . in the last resort . . . speaks castration and nothing else' (Mulvey, 1989: 14). Thus Mulvey suggests that women cannot be represented in the movies on their own terms, but only in patriarchal terms, as castrated not-men. The analytical importance given to the (missing) phallus in this sort of account

Phallocentrism often leads to the use of the term **phallocentrism** rather than patriarchy to describe the way cultural meaning is structured around masculine terms. Thus Mulvey's use of Freud's formulation of the castration complex mobilizes not only a set of ideas about sexual difference in relation to subjectivity, but also in relation to visuality.

---

focus

The art historian Linda Nochlin (1989: 138, 142) offers an example of this gendered visuality, reproduced here as Figure 5.1.

[Above] is a late nineteenth-century soft porn postcard showing a woman offering some fruit to the spectator; she is clearly offering herself for 'picking' too. [Below], Nochlin has constructed an apparently equivalent image with a man offering fruit/himself. Nochlin's point, though, is that of course these are not equivalent images because the visuality that constructs women as objects to be seen does not allow the spectator to make sense of a man being shown in the same terms; the photo of the man is therefore a joke, laughable. Hence we can see that the dominant form of visuality tutors us into finding only women suitable objects for sexual display.

To what extent might this claim be challenged by more recent ways of visualizing masculinity? Nochlin wrote her essay in 1972. Since then, it has become much more common to use men in advertising apparently as 'sex objects'. Look at the adverts in some recent glossy magazines and consider the ways you, as the reader, are invited to look at the male and female bodies used there. Are both sexualized? How? Are they sexualized in the same way?

Figure 5.1

*(a) Nineteenth-
century soft porn
postcard
(b) Nochlin's
construction of
equivalent male
image* (Nochlin,
1989: 138, 142)

(a)

(b)

Now, it would seem that the sight of women as castrated not-men in the movies would not be very appealing to the movie-goer, and Mulvey has already asserted the pleasurability of the cinema. She resolves this paradox by arguing that cinematic visual pleasure stems precisely from its assuaging of the fear of castration – for men (the role of the female spectator is somewhat problematic in her account, a point to which I will return). 'In the highly developed Hollywood cinema . . . the alienated subject, torn in his imaginary memory by a sense of loss, by the terror of potential lack in fantasy, came near to finding a glimpse of satisfaction: through its formal beauty and its play on his own formative obsessions' (Mulvey, 1989: 16). She argues that this is achieved in narrative cinema in two ways (Mulvey, 1989: 21–2). Both these ways involve structuring how the spectator sees images of women in narrative cinema.

Voyeurism　　The first way she describes as **voyeurism**. Voyeurism is a way of seeing that is active; it distances and objectifies what is looked at. It is controlling and even sadistic, says Mulvey. It is a look that is only given to men by films (whether as characters in the film or as the film's audience). It deals with castration anxiety by investigating the woman and then punishing or saving her. Mulvey notes this is typical of how the women in the film noir genre are represented: as threatening but ultimately guilty and weak. The particular ways in which voyeurism is produced by the spatial and visual organization of a film are various, and some of the tools of compositional interpretation are useful here to describe them (see Chapter 2). What Mulvey looks for is how that relationality between masculinity and femininity is constructed. Particular filmic techniques can include:

1　*putting distance between the male and female protagonists of a movie.*
In Hitchcock's film *Vertigo*, for example, the retired policeman Scottie becomes obsessed with the beautiful woman he has been asked to follow, and the first part of the film shows him trailing her, always keeping his distance to remain hidden from her. In *Rear Window*, photo-journalist Jeffries is immobilized with a broken leg and becomes fascinated with what he sees going on in the apartment opposite his; Mulvey says that his erotic interest in his girlfriend is rekindled only when she enters that other apartment and Jeffries sees her over there, away from him (Figure 5.2).
2　*putting distance between the female protagonist of a movie and the movie audience.* In both *Vertigo* and *Rear Window*, the camera often occupies the position of the hero. Thus the audience sees what he sees, and the women in the film (Madeleine/Judy in *Vertigo* and Lisa in *Rear Window*) are distanced from the audience just as they are distanced from him.

The second way that the image of the castrated woman is disavowed **Fetishistic** by narrative cinema, according to Mulvey, is **fetishistic scopophilia**. This is **scopophilia** when the female figure is represented simply as a beautiful object of display

Figure 5.2 *Still from Hitchcock's* Rear Window

(her objectification shows how voyeurism and this kind of fetishism can overlap). Again, this is a mode of representation directed both at the hero of the film and at the male spectator: she is on display for both of them. Her beauty is so overwhelming, often pictured in huge close-ups, so perfect that the threat of castration is assuaged as she is turned into a reassuring object in an intimate relation to the spectator. Drawing on Mulvey's work, Mary Ann Doane (1982: 76) says that 'the woman's beauty, her very desirability, becomes a function of certain practices of imaging – framing, lighting, camera movement, angle. She is thus . . . more closely associated with the surface of the image than its illusory depths'. Again, the particular ways in which fetishism is produced by the spatial and visual organization of a film are various. They can include:

1 *framing*. The obvious framing device is the use of close-up shots, that exclude everything from the viewer's gaze except the body, or parts of the body (often the face) of the female star.
2 *lighting*. Doane (1991) describes the way lighting was used in many of Greta Garbo's films to make her face luminous, and so to convey a sense of her almost ethereal, fascinating beauty.
3 *camera movement*. Modleski traces the various ways in which the camera shows Madeleine/Judy for the first time in *Rear Window*:

> The camera itself takes over the enunciation . . . it first shows Scottie sitting at a bar and then detaches itself from his searching gaze to conduct its own search for the woman through the restaurant. Finally it comes to rest in a long shot of a woman seated . . . at a table, with her back to the camera. Romantic music emerges slowly on the soundtrack, and the camera moves slightly forward. It cuts back to Scottie looking and to a point of view shot of Madeleine, who gets up from her chair and walks into a closeup shot of her profile. Only much later will we be able to see her entire face and only at that time will we get to hear her speak. (Modleski, 1988: 91)

This camera movement establishes Madeleine, says Modleski (1988: 92) as the 'mute, only half-seen object of man's romantic quest'.

Mulvey also notes that the fetishism and voyeurism through which women are represented in narrative cinema often works to halt the narrative flow of the film; women are represented as passive spectacle.

focus

If you can, watch the opening half an hour of *Vertigo*. How does it invite voyeuristic and fetishistic ways of seeing? If you can't get to see that film in a cinema or on video, then think about the same question the next time you watch a mainstream Hollywood film. If you're not watching it in a cinema, think about whether the seductive power of film is reduced when it's being shown on a tv screen.

3.2 the mirror stage and visual pleasure

The other major psychoanalytic concept used by Mulvey in 'Visual pleasure and narrative cinema' is the mirror stage. The idea of the mirror stage was developed by Lacan and it is one of the ways in which his work has impacted on some accounts of visual culture.

Mirror stage

According to Lacan, babies go through the **mirror stage** when they recognize an image in a mirror as their self. However, as with the baby's 'recognition' of their mother's castration, this other recognition happens through a particular visuality, and also through a particular construction of spatiality. On the one hand, the mirror image and the body it apparently simply reflects are seen by the baby as complete and whole. This is fascinating and seductive, for the baby's own bodily co-ordination is still incomplete. As Malcolm Bowie (1991: 23) says, 'the child's attention is seized . . . by the firm spatial relationships between its real body and its specular body and between body and setting in the specular image'. Thus the child sees a coherent body in a coherent, three-dimensional space. As well as giving the baby a certain pleasing sense of his or her own bodily image and space, this vision also allows the identification of other objects in that space. This is the founding moment therefore of the **Imaginary**, which is

Imaginary

the field of interrelations between subject and other people or objects. On the other hand, the mirror image also involves a misrecognition, since the baby knows that the image is not actually itself. The mirror image involves a certain alienation from what is seen: 'identification of an object world is . . . grounded in the moment when the child's image was alienated from itself as an imaginary object and sent back to it the message of its own subjecthood' (Rose, 1986: 173). Thus the mirror stage involves both identification with an image, and alienation from it: both recognition and misrecognition.

Lacan suggests that the dynamics of the mirror stage continue to structure subjectivity, and that they explain the importance of the visual to our sense of self. (Hence Judith Williamson's 1978 use of the Imaginary in her account of the power of advertisements to produce a sense of their spectator's self.) But clearly these dynamics are complex, and the contradiction between identifying with the mirror image and being alienated from it is one of those moments of visual uncertainty that psychoanalytic accounts tend to emphasize.

Mulvey uses the mirror stage to explore the representation of male figures in narrative cinema, and the ways in which the audience is positioned by that representation. The male movie star, the hero of the film's narrative, occupies that coherent space seen during the mirror stage. 'The active male figure . . . demands a three-dimensional space corresponding to that of the mirror recognition, in which the alienated subject internalized his own representation of his imaginary existence'; he is 'free to command the stage, a stage of spatial illusion in which he articulates the look and creates the action' (Mulvey, 1989: 20). Thus the male hero of the movie occupies a space of depth (compared to the surficiality of representations of women), in which he actively looks. The masculine figure is not therefore himself subject to looking, according to Mulvey. He also propels the narrative; he is active, unlike the passive figure of woman. Ways in which a film's space and gazes produce this effect include:

1 *deep focus*. A deep focus emphasizes the apparent depth of the scene being shown by the film, and allows the hero to move through a space that is extensive. Even in *Rear Window*, a film in which the hero is immobilized by a broken leg, Modleski (1988: 79) suggests that the deep focus given to his view from his apartment window constructs that view as 'an image of wholeness and plenitude' over which his gaze can roam freely.

2 *camera movements determined by male hero*.

Mulvey argues that the spectator identifies with the movie hero because he embodies the spectator/subject's mirror stage self-image:

> A male movie star's glamorous characteristics are . . . those of the more perfect, more complete, more powerful ideal ego conceived in the original moment of recognition in front of the mirror. The character in the story can make things happen and control events better than the subject/spectator, just as the image in the mirror was more in control of motor co-ordination. (Mulvey, 1989: 20)

This identification is encouraged by the way the cameras assume the male protagonist's position when picturing the film's narrative. This can involve:

1 *camera position*. The camera literally is in the same position as the male protagonist is shown to be, so the audience sees (apparently) exactly what he sees. For example, in the first scene of *Vertigo*, Scottie is trying to overcome his vertigo by slowly climbing up a small stepladder next to a window; we see him look out and down from the window and the next shot is of the view downwards, which rapidly zooms forward/down and then back again to show what Scottie's vertigo looks like to him.

2 *points of view*. Reverse shots often establish which character's view the camera is showing. In *Vertigo*, the camera persistently shows the spectator what Scottie sees during his surveillance of the mysterious woman he is following. Moreover, the audience never sees what she sees as she sees it: we are given a good look only when Scottie goes to look at it too.

Mulvey thus uses two central psychoanalytic concepts – the castration complex and the mirror stage – to explore the way in which narrative cinema produces 'woman as image, man as bearer of the look' (Mulvey, 1989: 19). Her use of both these concepts assumes a phallocentric scopic regime in which woman can only figure passively as a castrated man, and men appear as active and powerful, controlling the visual, the spatial and the temporal. This, she says, is 'the way the unconscious of patriarchal society has structured film form' (Mulvey, 1989: 14). Mulvey suggests that Hitchcock's movies explore this unconscious. In her brief discussion of *Vertigo* and *Rear Window*, she notes that their heroes are voyeurs of one kind or another:

The power to subject another person to the will sadistically or to voyeuristically is turned onto the woman as the object of both. I backed by a certainty of legal right and the established guilt of the woman (evoking castration, psychoanalytically speaking). True perversion is barely concealed under a shallow mask of ideological correctness – the man is on the right side of the law, the woman on the wrong. Hitchcock's skilful use of identification processes and liberal use of subjective camera from the point of view of the male protagonist draw the spectators deeply into his position, making them share his uneasy gaze. The spectator is absorbed into a voyeuristic situation within the screen scene and diegesis, which parodies his own in the cinema. (Mulvey, 1989: 23)

3.3 Mulvey's searchlight

Mulvey focuses on certain aspects of the cinematic image – its spatial organization, the scale of what it shows, its orchestration of looks both between the actors on the screen and between the audience and the screen, and in particular the gendering of who sees and who is seen in certain ways – in order to characterize a way of cinematic seeing that is both gendered and gendering. The pleasure of these ways of seeing for the audience is then also understood in a particular way, as a denial of the threat of castration.

Male gaze   Mulvey's essay has been enormously influential on feminist film theory and feminist theory more widely. Indeed, notions of a voyeuristic **male gaze** remain extensive in feminist work, and are often used without reference to the specifically psychoanalytic ideas through which Mulvey formulated her arguments. But Mulvey's arguments, though polemical, are nuanced. She suggests that voyeurism and fetishism have quite particular visual, temporal and spatial articulations. These conceptual details are important to remember when utilizing psychoanalytic arguments. Psychoanalysis in many ways depends on the details of an image for its interpretive insight; and it is necessary to be similarly attentive to the detail of psychoanalytic concepts.

Mulvey's arguments are not without their problems, however. She seems to assume that not only can women be seen only as castrated, women can see themselves only like that too. This is because she assumes that all the members of a cinema audience, whether male or female, are positioned in the same way in relation to the figures on the screen and that all see them in the same way; the implication is that all of a film's spectators are made to be fetishistic and voyeuristic by the visual and spatial structure of the film. In that sense, Mulvey's argument positions all cinema spectators as male. But is she too quick to suggest that women represent castration and nothing else? Or can women be represented differently? Can women also see actively? Moreover, are all men only voyeurs and fetishists when they look at women? Are other ways of seeing possible, less powerful, less pleasurable too perhaps? And what about men who want to look at men, and women who want to look at women, pleasurably?

None of these questions can be addressed in Mulvey's framework. She assumes a powerful, patriarchal and heterosexual narrative cinema, and places her faith for critique and change in avant-garde cinematic practices that refuse the visual and spatial organization of Hollywood's narrative cinema. However, other feminist critics have been less willing to give up on what are, after all, hugely popular cultural practices like mainstream Hollywood film. They have looked for other psychoanalytic ways of seeing films, and have brought other theoretical terms to bear on them.

4   from the fetish to the masquerade: other representations of femininity

There are many ways in which psychoanalysis can be used to explore ways of seeing. Many feminists, not surprisingly, have been particularly concerned to see images of femininity that do not 'speak castration and nothing else', for example. Indeed, the notion that femininity can be represented only as lacking – as castrated – has been contested by many feminists, who have turned to other psychoanalytic notions to see femininity in other ways.

Elisabeth Bronfen (1992: 43), for example, has noted that 'one of the theoretical problems inherent in Freud's definition is how the castration complex can be applied to both sexes when for the girl there appears to be no threat in losing something she never possessed'. This does not appear to be a problem for Mulvey, for example, but other feminists have tried to rework the castration complex in order to displace its implication that women can be represented only as castrated. Bronfen (1992), for example, suggests that what Freud explored through the castration complex was the universal process of leaving the primary carer, and anatomical parts other than the penis/phallus might symbolize that process: the navel, for example. Through such strategies, images of women may not necessarily represent 'castration and nothing else'.

One possibility that has been pursued in relation to visual images is to suggest that if women are indeed often represented as smooth surfaces on display for a male gaze, fetishization might not be the only way to interpret that representation. Perhaps that smooth surface does not hide something horrible, does not conceal a castrated body. Perhaps it hides something else. Or perhaps it is simply that, a surface, that hides nothing: a **Masquerade** masquerade. This latter possibility was most famously proposed by the psychoanalyst Joan Riviere in an essay first published in 1929 (Riviere, 1986). Riviere's essay took off from her analysis of an academic woman who, after her articulate and professional presentations of her work to her peers, would feel compelled to flirt with the men in her audience. Riviere suggested that this woman saw her success in terms of being successful in a man's world and therefore in a sense, for the duration of her performances, becoming a man. This, though, she knew her mostly male audiences would find very threatening (the only thing more threatening than a castrated woman being a non-castrated one), so after her lectures she would conform to their expectations of female behaviour, and flirt and be charming and non-confrontational. From this Riviere concluded:

> Womanliness could therefore be assumed and worn as a mask, both to hide the possession of masculinity and to avert the reprisals expected if she was found to possess it – much as a thief will turn out his pockets and ask to be searched to prove that he has not stolen the goods. The reader may now ask how I define womanliness or where I draw the line between genuine womanliness and the 'masquerade'. My suggestion is not, however, that there is any such difference; whether radical or superficial, they are the same thing. (Riviere, 1986: 38)

Riviere is suggesting that since femininity is not natural but constructed – through processes such as the castration complex but also, we might add, through things like watching movies – there are ways of thinking about femininity as just that, a construction. Femininity can be seen as a mask, a masquerade, performed by mimicking what being a woman is meant to be about. Femininity might be thought of as 'a decorative layer which conceals a non-identity' (Doane, 1982: 81). Luce Irigaray has taken this argument even further to suggest that masquerade – or what she calls mimesis – might even be an evasion, in part at least, of those disciplines of femininity. She suggests that 'if women are such good mimics, it is because they are not simply resorbed in this function. *They also remain elsewhere*' (Irigaray, 1985: 76).

What are the methodological implications of these arguments about masquerade? Doane (1982) raises the possibility (although she is not herself persuaded by it) that masquerade might provide a way of thinking about how women see themselves and each other which does not depend on the way of seeing outlined by Mulvey. Other critics are more confident that here may be traces of a manipulation of the position of femininity, or its parody, in visual images like films, marked by strategies such as:

1 *excess*. The film performances of Marlene Dietrich have been characterized as so excessively feminine that the audience is 'watching a woman demonstrate the representation of a woman's body' (Bovenschen, cited in Doane, 1982: 82).

2 *construction*. A film may show moments when the female body is quite literally donning the mask of femininity: make-up, hairstyle, dress, comportment. An example from a Hitchcock film could be a scene in his 1940 movie *Rebecca*. The heroine of this film (who is never named) is shown at first as a gauche and nervous young woman whose qualities are characterized only by what she cannot do. Thinking that she has lost

the love of her husband Maxim (whose first, dead wife was called Rebecca), she attempts to win it back by dressing for a fancy dress ball in the costume of one of his ancestors whose painting hangs in their grand house, and she is thus shown as constructing herself as glamorous.

3 *repetition*. In film, repetition may take narrative or visual form. The heroine of *Rebecca* is shown using visual repetition as a means of becoming glamorously attractive too, since her masquerade is a copy of an already existing image of glamour.

Or there may be traces of the 'elsewhere' mentioned by Irigaray: hints at spaces other than those constructed through objectifying distance or fetishizing intimacy.

1 *distorted spaces*.
2 *points of view impossible in coherent space*.
3 *(in)visible absences*. Modleski (1988) persuasively argues that in *Rebecca*, although the character Rebecca is dead, her presence continues to haunt the film in ways that refuse the usual representations of femininity. In particular, her disruptive sexuality is marked by traces of her own masquerades: her clothing, her unfaithfulness to her husband while appearing to be the perfect wife, the way the housekeeper evokes Rebecca's thoughts and actions in the film. Finally, in what Modleski (1988: 53) calls 'one of the film's most extraordinary moments the camera pointedly dynamizes Rebecca's absence. When Maxim tells the heroine about what happened on the night of Rebecca's death ("She got up, came towards me", etc.), the camera follows Rebecca's movements in a lengthy tracking shot'. This is a flaunting of lack, not its hiding, and it suggests that the representation of femininity need not represent absence in the phallocentric way that Mulvey suggests.

focus

Some feminists have criticized the notion of masquerade, suggesting that it is naïve to think that constructions of femininity can escape the disciplines of cultural representation. Judith Butler (1990), for example, has chastised Irigaray in these terms, and even Modleski (1988: 53) in her discussion of *Rebecca* has to admit that 'in the film's narrative, Rebecca is subjected to a brutal devaluation and punishment'.

Watch *Vertigo* if you can. The central female figure – Madeleine/Judy – might be seen as exemplifying femininity as masquerade since Madeleine is apparently copying a dead ancestor, 'Madeleine' is being impersonated by Judy, and Scottie forces 'Judy' to dress up as Madeleine again. The movie thus has a narrative and scenes that show the construction of femininity. But does the movie suggest that in being able to make these transformations Madeleine/Judy is occupying an 'elsewhere' beyond phallocentric visions of femininity? Are there other visual or spatial suggestions in the film that this is the case? Or are those transformation scenes embedded in a filmic organization of the visual and spatial that captures Madeleine/Judy in Scottie's terms?

Mary Ann Doane's (1987) discussion of *Rebecca* raises a similar question in relation to the liberating possibilities of disorientating spaces. She describes the incoherent domestic spaces of a cycle of post-war Hollywood movies not as elements of subversive masquerades of femininity, but as representing a paranoia deeply threatening to the film's female protagonists. Thus in *Rebecca*, the bedroom of Rebecca has been kept as it was before her death by the housekeeper, and when the heroine finally gathers the courage to enter it, it is a strange and disorienting space. Everything is slightly too large for the heroine (implying she is childlike), curtains blow oddly, the housekeeper appears from nowhere and forces the heroine to touch Rebecca's clothes, to sit at her dressing table, to let the housekeeper brush her hair as she brushed Rebecca's (Figure 5.3).

The room disorientates the heroine, and what goes on there threatens to replace her own subjectivity with that of Rebecca. Thus, as Doane (1987) notes, this particular distorted space is hardly a subversive space for articulating the heroine's subjectivity. However, Modleski (1988) prefers to emphasize that it is a space in which Rebecca remains powerful, even if the heroine does not. Section 7 returns to the different ways they interpret *Rebecca*.

Clearly the interpretation of masquerade and incoherent spaces needs to take many other aspects of a film into account before an account of their effects can be persuasive.

Notions of masquerade have been employed to disrupt the apparent hegemony of the male gaze as characterized by Mulvey, then. However, they disrupt by offering a supplement to that gaze. That is, they do not fundamentally challenge Mulvey's characterization of that gaze; they simply suggest that this might not be the full story.

5 from the voyeuristic gaze to the Lacanian Gaze: other ways of seeing

The 'male gaze', then, has become a staple of certain feminist critiques of patriarchal visuality; even those feminist strategies that are more critical of Mulvey's reliance on Freud's theorization of the castration complex have tended to take that gaze for granted, even as they search for other ways of seeing. But did Mulvey's polemic exaggerate the power of that gaze? There are hints, even in her original essay, that the voyeuristic and fetishistic gaze produced its own difficulties. After all, the 'hero' of *Vertigo* goes nearly mad in his obsession with the woman he follows. Did Mulvey underestimate the inherent difficulties of masculine looking, then? Other feminists have chosen psychoanalytic materials other than castration, voyeurism and fetishism to work with, precisely in order to theorize a visuality that, while dominant, is not all-powerful. If women are not necessarily castrated not-men, then neither are all men necessarily voyeuristic fetishists (Figure 5.4).

Gaze

The psychoanalytic term used to develop this possibility is Lacan's version of the **Gaze**. As Joan Copjec (1989) insists, the Lacanian Gaze is not the same as the 'male gaze' initially theorized by Mulvey and then popularized in many feminist discussions. The most important difference is that the Gaze is striated by inherent failure. Lacan elaborated his notion of the Gaze some time after his exploration of the mirror stage (for a detailed exegesis, see Silverman, 1992: 145–53). In this later work, he is less interested in how the subject sees and more interested in how the subject is seen. The Gaze thus supplements his earlier account of the mirror stage. The Gaze is a form of visuality that pre-exists the individual subject; it is a visuality into which subjects are born. Like the visuality that subjects adopt as their own, though, the Gaze is culturally constituted:

> Between the subject and the world is inserted the entire sum of discourses that make up visuality, that cultural construct, and make visuality different from vision, the notion of unmediated visual experience. Between the retina and the world is inserted a *screen* of signs, consisting of all the multiple discourses of vision built into the social arena . . . when I learn to see socially, that is, when I begin to articulate my retinal experience with the codes of recognition that come to me from my social milieu(s), I am inserted into systems of visual discourse that saw the world before I did, and will go on seeing after I see no longer. (Bryson, 1988: 91–2)

Following this assertion, there are three ways in which this Gaze fails to offer visual mastery. The first is suggested by Bryson. Since the Gaze 'will go on seeing after I see no longer', Bryson says that it 'casts a shadow of *death*' (Bryson, 1988: 92). It reminds us of our own mortality. Second, the Gaze cannot offer visual mastery because it is diffuse, evanescent and irridescent, says Lacan. Indeed, given the way it predates and will outlast the subject, in a sense it looks at the subject rather than the subject looking at or through it. 'In the scopic field, the gaze is outside, I am looked at, that is to say, I am a picture . . . What determines me, at the most profound level, in the visible, is the gaze that is outside' (Lacan, 1977: 106). The consequence of the externality of the Gaze is that when 'I solicit a look, what is profoundly unsatisfying and always missing is that – *You never look at me from the place which I see you*' (Lacan, 1977: 103). Finally, the Gaze fails precisely because it is structured through a screen of signs. Signs, as semiology notes, are substitutes for their referents. As representations, they are different from that to which they refer. For Lacan, the child's entry into culture – into the signs that constitute language, visuality and **Symbolic** what he called the **Symbolic** – is a traumatic separation from intimacy with referents. (Lacan's term for a world of referents before the Symbolic was the Real.) Indeed, Lacan reworked Freud's account of the castration

Figure 5.3 *Still from Hitchcock's* Rebecca

complex to suggest that what that complex deals with is not perceptions of anatomical difference but rather the entry into the Symbolic and the substitution of signs for referents which all babies, boys and girls, go through. Hence the Gaze, as part of the Symbolic, is also marked by the lack inherent in that substitution.

Lacan uses a painting to emphasize the lack that haunts the Gaze: *The Ambassadors*, painted at the court of Henry VIII in London in 1533 by Hans Holbein (Figure 5.5).

The painting shows two men in luxurious dress, surrounded by the instruments of scientific knowledge and artistic expression: they are shown

Figure 5.4 *Still from Hitchcock's* Vertigo

as powerful, socially, artistically and scientifically. But in front of them, at their feet, is a strange oval shape, incomprehensible in terms of the coherent, perspectively represented space of the rest of the painting. This oval only makes visual sense if the spectator stands to one side of the painting, when it then appears as a skull. It is a reminder of death, a popular device in seventeenth-century paintings that otherwise celebrated the richness of life. However, its disruption of the coherent space of the ambassadors and the spectator is a reminder for Lacan (1977: 88) of 'the subject as annihilated', not only by death, but by the lack that structures the (visual) Symbolic.

This definition of the Gaze has some profound implications for Mulvey's argument about sexual difference in the field of vision. As Kaja Silverman (1992: 151) for one notes, 'since the gaze always emerges for us within the field of vision, and since we ourselves are always being photographed by it even as we look, all binarizations of spectator and spectacle mystify the scopic relations in which we are held'. Hence, since the Gaze looks at everyone, men as well as women are turned into spectacles through it; and since its status as a screen of signs means it is never a complete vision, neither women nor men can attain visual mastery through it.

For feminists like Silverman, this is a much more satisfactory formulation of the dominant scopic regime than Mulvey's analysis of the male gaze. It breaks down the binary distinction between 'woman as image, man as bearer of the look' to suggest that man may be image too, and that both men and women may look, but neither and never all-powerfully. For Silverman (1996: 2), this opens the door to what she calls 'an ethics of the field of vision' that might 'make it possible for us to idealize, and, so, to identify with bodies we would otherwise repudiate'. In other words, the Gaze allows a greater range of ways of seeing to become possible, some of which may work against the cultural construction of some visualized identities as inferior.

Some of the methodological implications of working with the Gaze also become evident in Silverman's work, especially her 1992 book *Male Subjectivity at the Margins*. Here, she explores what she calls 'deviant masculinities' – those which do not conform to the dominant fiction of phallic masculinity – 'some of which do indeed say "no" to power' (Silverman, 1992: 2). For Silverman, these are masculinities which embrace those qualities that the dominant fiction ascribes to femininity. She thus provides some methodological pointers. She is interested in representations of masculinity that:

1 *acknowledge and embrace castration*. Silverman's (1992: 52–121) own example of a film which explores 'the castrations through which the male subject is constituted' (Silverman 1992: 52) is a 1946 film directed by William Wyler called *The Best Years of Our Lives*. It traces the return home of three soldiers at the end of World War II and, according to Silverman (1992: 67), 'male lack is so fully displayed in that film that even four decades after its original release it remains profoundly disturbing, and at times almost unwatchable'. As just one instance, she notes the way in which the aircraftman who has lost both hands eventually shows his amputated arms to his girlfriend, unable to look at her as he does so. His bodily loss is paralleled by his loss of vision, and it is the female subject who can see this. Modleski (1988) argues strongly that Hitchcock's heroes are also much less secure in their masculinity than Mulvey's argument allows. She points to a number of ways in which the films assert the fragility of masculine subjectivity: in

Figure 5.5 *Hans Holbein,* The Ambassadors, *1533* (National Gallery, London)

Jeffries's broken leg, in his passivity as opposed to his girlfriend's increasing activity in *Rear Window*, in Scottie's vertigo, in Scottie's obsession with Madeleine which comes close to driving him mad, in his inability to see properly after he thinks he has witnessed her death.

2 *are specular.* Silverman (1992) offers another example from *The Best Years of Our Lives.* Another of the soldiers returning home in uniform and medals is greeted by his wife '*as spectacle* – as a glamorous and heroic image . . . However, the first time she sees him in civilian clothes she visibly recoils, appalled by his shabby and unfashionable suit' (Silverman, 1992: 77; for more general discussions of spectacularized masculinities in film, see Cohan and Hark, 1993; R. Dyer 1982; Neale 1983).

Mobilizing Lacan's notion of the Gaze, then, permits a more complex visuality to be seen than that proposed by Mulvey (1989).

6 from the disciplines of subjection to the possibilities of fantasy

Another tactic adopted by some feminist film theorists to explore a wider range of ways of seeing than that allowed by Mulvey's account is to draw on the psychoanalytic understanding of fantasy. In psychoanalytic work, fantasy is not used in the popular sense of something that is quite distinct from 'reality'. Instead, fantasy is seen as something that partly structures a subject's reality.

Fantasy   **Fantasy** is located between the conscious and the unconscious; it is where the transactions between these two zones occur (Burgin, 1992). In fantasy – daydreams, for example – the unconscious is given some sort of temporal, spatial and symbolic form by the conscious. Certain lost objects are dreamt about, given a particular spatial arrangement and placed in a particular narrative. Thus fantasy is often described as a kind of staging. This sense of a fantasy being staged is also appropriate because the subject often feels, in part, that they are looking on at the fantasy: they are its audience. A parallel with cinema is immediately obvious, since cinema too stages objects, times and spaces through particular codes of representation for an audience in ways that depend, according to feminist psychoanalytic critics, on fantasies about sexual difference in particular. Elizabeth Cowie (1990: 150) notes, however, that Mulvey, for example, only allows for one fantasy in cinema: that concerning the masculine fear of castration.

There is another connection too between cinema and fantasy: visual pleasure. Freud suggested that fantasy begins when the infant dreams of lost pleasurable objects, their mother's milk or breast, for example. The

Desire   pleasure gained from fantasizing about lost objects is called **desire**. Cowie (1990: 149) describes fantasy as 'the mise-en-scène of desire, the putting into a scene, a staging, of desire'. These emphases on the spectator's visual pleasure suggest why fantasy has tended to be used to address questions of spectatorship in cinema. Mary Ann Doane's (1987) book about the so-called 'women's films' made by Hollywood in the 1930s and 1940s is called *The Desire to Desire*. Like Mulvey though, Doane does not see narrative cinema allowing women to see films, or be seen in them, in terms other than those set by phallocentric visuality. Thus, in relation to these movies, women can only desire desire.

Cowie sees the reliance of Mulvey and Doane on the implications of the castration complex as too restrictive in the way it fixes the spectator into a particular, masculinized viewing position. Cowie (1990) instead turns to the notion of fantasy because she thinks it provides a way of loosening that fixity. In that sense, her aims are the same as those feminists who have deployed the masquerade or the Gaze. All want to suggest that even within a phallocentric cultural form like mainstream Hollywood cinema, there are traces of non-dominant ways of seeing, in both the film and in its audience.

Cowie's (1990) key point about fantasy is that the subject need not only be the audience of a fantasy. The subject may also imagine that they participate in the fantasy as well, and in perhaps more than one role. All fantasies, she says, 'present a varying of subject positions so that the subject takes up more than one position and thus is not fixed' (Cowie, 1990: 160). This is because the fantasy consists, not of objects per se, but of their interrelations, their staging. Thus 'the subject is present or presented through the very form of organization, composition, of the scene' (Cowie, 1990: 160); the subject is positioned through the scenic organization of the fantasy and is therefore part of each object in it. The implications for cinema spectatorship are that audiences may refuse to be positioned in the ways that Mulvey suggested they would be, as men. Instead, men and women in the audience may be positioned while watching a film in ways that correspond to the dynamics of their own fantasies.

Cowie's (1990) essay contains an extended discussion of one of the 'women's films' of the 1940s, *Now Voyager*, directed by Irving Rapper and starring Bette Davis. She begins by noting what sort of fantasies the film addresses, and she detects these fantasies by looking at three aspects of the film:

1 *narrative.* Cowie notes how the story of the film contains a number of wishes for rather conventional kinds of success: erotic success and social success in particular. But the film also presents some more prohibited fantasies. Cowie (1990) argue that fantasies very often do just this, because of their borderline location between the conscious and the repressions of the unconscious. The prohibited desires often centre on the relations between parents and children. Thus in *Now Voyager* the Bette Davis character rejects her own domineering mother as head of the household, and mothers in her turn without a male partner.

2 *equivalences between characters.* In a discussion of another film, Cowie (1990) suggests another way in which a film may allow multiple entry points for fantasied identifications with several characters. She notes that both narratively (in terms of what they do, especially in relation to other characters) and visually (in terms of how they are seen), a film may suggest that certain characters are equivalent: two characters may be shown as 'fathers' in relation to a family, for example, even though only one 'really' is. Thus spectators may respond to both characters as 'fathers'.

3 *visual substitutions.* If fantasies often articulate repressed desires, they must do so seductively in ways that do not invite rejection, says Cowie. Hollywood movies can achieve this by making visual substitutions: visual moments that repeat themselves but with a difference. Cowie (1990: 178–9) explains this with an example from *Now Voyager*. Bette Davis's transformation from dowdy daughter to glamorous independent woman (an articulation of both her erotic and social success) is marked by a tilt shot that starts at her legs and ends at her head. The first time, it shows flat shoes, thick stockings, glasses: the second time, beautiful shoes, silk tights, a stunning hat and no glasses. Such visual puns entice the audience into accepting the film's terms, says Cowie.

Cowie's last example is, as she notes, also an example of the masquerade of femininity. But she argues that the subversiveness of the masquerade can be understood only if the fantasies in which it is embedded are also made clear. (Modleski, 1986: 129 also notes that the 'elsewhere' central to Irigaray's account of masquerade needs to be specified if its potential for critique is to be fulfilled.) In particular, Cowie (1990: 180) argues that the narrative resolution of *Now Voyager* – in which Bette Davis agrees to mother the daughter of the married man she spent one night with – is a woman's fantasy of having a child without accepting the (rule of) the father. It thus sidesteps the position offered to women in Freud's account of the castration complex.

Cowie's discussion of fantasy clearly remains within psychoanalysis. Fantasy, it is argued, still deals with subjectivity, sexuality and the unconscious, with the dynamics of the child's relation to its early carers and of sexual difference. Teresa de Lauretis (1995: 75) insists on this, and warns against 'the optimistically silly notion of an unbounded mobility of identities for the spectator-subject . . . the film's spectator [cannot] pick and choose any or all of the subject-positions inscribed in the film regardless of gender or sexual difference, to say nothing of other kinds of difference'. However, in its engagement with the repressions of the unconscious, fantasy also allows a greater range of interpretive possibilities in relation to films and their audiences.

focus

Watch *Rebecca* if you can.

What are the fantasies of success (and failure) that structure the film?

How are characters made equivalent? For example, in an early scene the heroine describes to Maxim her close relation to her father, and is shown as childlike as she does so: clumsy, gauche, eating runny eggs. Does Maxim become equated with her father? And if that is the case, is the heroine's struggle to become a 'proper' wife also a struggle to overcome Rebecca as some sort of powerful mother? Modleski (1988) suggests this is the case.

Are there visual substitutions? What are the implications of both Rebecca and the heroine dressing up in the same costume in terms of fantasy, and for whom?

7 queer looks

Much psychoanalytic feminist film theory (and certainly that of Mulvey) assumes that the structure of gendered differences in visuality and representation is heterosexual: that is, that the important structure is that articulated between masculine and feminine, or male and female. This assumption clearly produces a number of omissions in Mulvey's account, and these have been criticized by gay and lesbian critics. Writers adopting

Mulvey's analysis are unlikely to pay much attention to how gay and lesbian characters might be represented in a film, and nor are they likely to consider the possible ways that lesbian and gay moviegoers might see certain scenarios or narratives in particular ways.

Psychoanalysis does have something to say about homosexuality, but this is often to position lesbian and gay sexuality as in some way perverse or deviant. This means that the psychoanalytic concepts that might be useful in focusing on the possibility of gay and lesbian desires in the cinema usually need to be heavily reworked. As Patricia White (1995: 87) says of psychoanalysis, 'lesbianism can not be fully "explained" in its terms'. However, some of that reworking has been done, and one starting point has been the difficult position of little girls in relation to the castration complex (a point already made by Bronfen in section 4 of this chapter).

> Unlike the little boy, who must simply displace his love for the mother to other women and thereby consolidate his identification with the father and all that he represents, the little girl is asked to change her object from mother to father, her disposition from active to passive, and her sexual zone from clitoris to vagina, in order to become woman, post-Oedipal and heterosexual. (White, 1995: 86)

Given the elaborateness of this change, it is not surprising that the little girl might not manage all of it successfully, and might retain her desire for her mother. Freud certainly thought this could and did occur, although he tended to see it as a problem in the path towards 'normal' heterosexual womanhood. Silverman (1988) has picked up on this however and, far from seeing it as a 'problem', has suggested that elaborating this desire between mother and daughter could provide a way of inserting desire between women into psychoanalytic accounts of sexuality.

This is a controversial suggestion. Teresa de Lauretis (1994) in particular has criticized it for evoking a general feminine subjectivity and thus erasing the specificity of lesbian desire. For her own part, de Lauretis suggests that what defines lesbian desire is a desire for a lost female body which is actually the subject's own lost body image (de Lauretis, 1994: 231). Sue Thornham (1997: 128) responds in turn that de Lauretis's concern with the particularity of lesbian desire ends up reasserting a fixed boundary between lesbian and heterosexual women which denies the mobility of desire and fantasy.

These debates are theoretically complex, and this is not the place to attempt their resolution. Their insistence that filmic structures of sexuality, difference and desire are not always heterosexual does, however, offer some further methodological pointers for thinking about visual culture, visual pleasure and visual disruption (and there are parallel debates made by theorists of gay movies and spectators; see, for example, Dyer, 1990). They suggest the need to be alert for narratives, scenes, looks and spaces that do not articulate heterosexual visualities or spatialities.

Modleski (1988) offers an example of this need in her discussion of *Rebecca*. She suggests that there is a strong suggestion in the film that the housekeeper – Mrs Danvers – was sexually attracted to Rebecca. She points to the scene in which Mrs Danvers shows the heroine of *Rebecca* her predecessor's wardrobe and all its beautiful clothes, which Mrs Danvers caresses and strokes. Modleski suggests that this is disruptive of Mulvey's analysis of narrative cinema, not only because it is another evocation of the absent Rebecca's powerful and sexual presence, but also because that sexuality is shown to be attractive to women as well as to men.

focus

Read Modleski's (1988: 43–56) account of *Rebecca*, then Mary Anne Doane's (1987: 123–75) and her later response to Modleski (Doane, 1991: 33–43). Both Doane and Modleski have watched the film carefully and both ground their interpretations in psychoanalytic theory. Modleski argues that Hitchcock's films are ambivalent in their representation of femininity. It is because they show femininity as threatening that they punish their female characters, she says; feminist interpretations, she argues, should therefore focus on that threat. Doane argues that this is an overly optimistic viewing of Hitchcock's oeuvre. She sees the films as fundamentally phallocentric, and insists that, no matter how popular they are, that should not be an excuse for feminists to argue for meanings in them that the films themselves cannot sustain.

Clearly this debate is about more than methodology: it is also about more than abstract theory. It is about the critical effects of different sorts of theory. Modleski demands a kind of viewing of Hitchcock's films that can recover some feminine power for both their characters and their female audiences; Doane argues that these films deny such power and that feminist efforts should be directed at finding new forms of visuality that do give feminine subjectivities power. These are in effect different politics of critique.

8 reflexivity

This chapter has structured its discussion around certain developments in psychoanalytic feminist film criticism since Laura Mulvey's key essay. In many ways, Mulvey's essay has been a point of departure for subsequent critics; they have accepted some of her premises but have sought a less restrictive interpretation of both film and spectatorship. However, there is one thing that later writers share with Mulvey, and that is a certain sort of reflexivity.

In the social sciences, reflexivity is claimed to be unnecessary for work that defines itself as scientific. Thus the practitioners of content analysis and semiology – discussed in Chapters 3 and 4 here – do not engage in reflexivity, since both, for different reasons, claim their work is scientific. However, reflexivity is a crucial aspect of work that participates in the so-called cultural turn. There, reflexivity is an attempt to resist the universalizing claims of academic knowledge and to insist that academic knowledge, like all other knowledges, is situated and partial. Reflexivity is thus about the position of the critic, about the effects that position has on the knowledge that the critic produces, about the relation between the critic and the people or materials they deal with, and about the social effects of the critic's work. Frequently now, it is assumed that before the results of a piece of research can be presented, the author must explain how their social position has affected what they found; a kind of auto-biography often precedes the research results.

There are a number of ways in which psychoanalytic approaches are incompatible with this autobiographical reflexivity (for a fuller discussion, see Rose, 1997). To begin with, autobiographical reflexivity implies a full understanding of the researcher's self. It implies that self-knowledge is possible (even if the researcher chooses not to reveal all that knowledge in their reflexive moment). But of course psychoanalysis claims that this is an impossible a goal. Full self-knowledge is impossible because a central part of our subjectivity – the unconscious – is not accessible to consciousness. Second, psychoanalysis's emphasis on the relationality of subjectivity – the relations between carers and babies, between masculinity and femininity, between movies and their audiences, for example – means that to split an account of 'who I am' from 'what I studied' is also impossible. Who you are depends, in part, on what you study, what you watch, who you talk to. This split is also impossible to sustain because of the psychoanalytic emphasis on the subject in process. Again, who you are depends on what you relate to. It's a process of mutual constitution, not one of a pre-existing person impacting on other people or images. Moreover, the psychoanalytic account of visual culture also recognizes that audiences bring their own ways of knowing to the images they encounter, and the same is true of the audiences for academic work. Thus autobiographical reflexivity may over-emphasize the writer at the expense of the critical agency of their audiences.

So none of the critics whose work I have cited offer any sort of autobiographical account before their interpretation of a movie (although Doane, 1991: 1–14 offers an interesting discussion of some of the theoretical and institutional relations within which her work is embedded). None start by saying 'this is who (I think) I am, and this is how that's shaped me as a spectator of this film'. They are however theoretically explicit and, while none offer methodological tool-kits, it is usually possible to trace quite clearly the methodological implications of their conceptual tools in their work. Their theoretical starting points make clear the particular way of seeing this work invites. The reader can trace the interpretive implications of the theoretical position adopted. This theoretical explicitness has the effect of positioning their work in some way. The frequent use of case studies also often enhances this sense of the particularity of each psychoanalytic study.

However, the positionality of these critics is more strongly marked in another way. Almost all of them say quite clearly that they are writing with political – that is, feminist – aims in mind. Mulvey (1989: 14), for example, begins by saying that in her essay, 'psychoanalytic theory is . . . appropriated here as a political weapon, demonstrating the way in which the unconscious of patriarchal society has structured film form'. Modleski (1988: 121) says her readings are without doubt partial, because she wants to place the evidence in Hitchcock's films of men's guilt in women's hands. And there is Kaja Silverman's (1996) project for an ethics of the field of vision. The reflexivity of this work, then, rests in part on its theoretical explicitness and its reliance on detailed case studies, but mostly on the articulation of its critical aims. It uses its awareness of its status as a particular kind of politics of critique to position itself (as the previous section's discussion of the disagreement between Modleski (1988) and Doane (1987, 1991) implied).

9 what the psychoanalytic searchlight doesn't see

The three criteria for a critical visual methodology outlined in Chapter 1 of this book would seem to be fulfilled by the psychoanalytic work discussed in this chapter. That work pays detailed attention to the images with which it is concerned, often in the form of case studies. It allows visual images to have their own effects, and these effects are seen as both psychic and social. Discussions of sexual difference, for example, work at both the latter levels; they engage with questions of fantasy but also the cultural coding of masculinity and femininity. The effect of visual images on spectators is a central concern of psychoanalytic approaches too. And there is a certain reflexive effect in their work, even if the explicitly reflexive moments are limited to claims of allegiance to feminist goals. However, all of these criteria are dealt with by psychoanalytic writers in quite specific ways, which do have some omissions for which psychoanalysis has been criticized. And there are some issues about which psychoanalytic methods have almost nothing to say.

Psychoanalytic approaches to the way visual images produce social difference through their picturing of subjectivity are very much dominated by studies of sexuality. This is hardly surprising, since sexuality was the main concern of both Freud and Lacan. However, sexuality is not the only axis through which social difference and social power relations are articulated: far from it. Hence psychoanalytic film theory has been criticized for neglecting issues of class and race. As Jane Gaines (1988) points out, at a certain historical period in the USA, men were lynched for looking at women – black men were hung for looking at white women. Indeed, Gaines (1988) argues that racialized aspects of subjectivity are not just neglected by psychoanalysis, but actively erased from consideration, particularly in generalizing accounts of the so-called 'male gaze'. Gaines suggests that the erasure of 'race' from psychoanalytic film theory is produced by the white middle-class norms of family relations that psychoanalysis implicitly assumes; and in her discussion of the film *Mahogany* starring Diana Ross, she shows that the only men whose gaze at Ross is sanctioned by the film are white. 'Race', she insists, must therefore intersect with sexual difference in accounts of spectatorship, but Gaines (1988) sees psychoanalyisis as actively unhelpful in this regard. Lola Young (1996), among others, has nevertheless explored the possibility that psychoanalytic ideas may address issues of racialization as well as sexuality. She draws on the work of Frantz Fanon (1986) to make this claim. Doane justifies addressing issues of racialization through psychoanalytic concepts thus:

> For Fanon, a psychoanalytic understanding of racism hinges on a close analysis of the realm of sexuality. This is particularly true of black–white relations since blacks are persistently attributed with a hypersexuality. Why is it sexuality forms a major arena for the articulation of racism? From a psychoanalytic point of view, sexuality is the realm where fear and desire find their most intimate connection, where notions of other-ness and the exotic/erotic are often conflated. (Doane, 1991: 217)

Clearly this remains a contested claim, and theorizing 'race' through psychoanalytic terms is likely to remain as controversial as theorizing gender and sexuality. As for class, there is nothing that I know of in psychoanalytic feminist film criticism that addresses the possible class specificity of certain ways of seeing (but see Pollock, 1994 for a psycho-analytic discussion of this in relation to other visual media). These absences clearly weaken the critical potential of psychoanalytic theory.

Moreover, there are some worries that, although psychoanalysis asserts the intersection of the cultural with the psychic, in practice its emphasis is very much on the latter. Evidence of the neglect of the social and cultural in psychoanalytic film theory can be found in two places. The first of these is, paradoxically, in its treatment of the audience. While psychoanalytic film theory argues that the audience is central to its accounts of the effects of films, there has been very little work that tries to explore empirically the workings of specific fantasies, say, for certain spectators constituted by particular mediations of both cultural and psychic dynamics. De Lauretis, for example, is very unusual in her insistence that not all of a fantasy's spectators will get pleasure from it:

> A particular fantasy scenario, regardless of its artistic, formal, or aesthetic, excellence as film representation, is not automatically accessible to every spectator; a film may work as fantasy for some spectators, but not for others . . . the spectator's own sociopolitical location and psycho-sexual configuration have much to do with whether or not a film can work for her as a scenario of desire, and as what Freud would call a 'visualization' of the

subject herself as subject of the fantasy: that is to say, whether the film can engage her spectatorial desire or, literally, whether she can see herself in it. (de Lauretis, 1995: 64)

Because this possibility is rarely acknowledged, let alone investigated, the psychoanalytic claim that the film and its audience are mutually constitutive remains one that is asserted rather than demonstrated. Since it is the film that is paid most attention in psychoanalytic accounts, the effect is to suggest that the film positions the audience.

Second, the focus in psychoanalytic film theory on the film itself produces a further absence, which is any consideration of the social institutions which produce films and the social contexts in which movies – or any other visual image – are shown. As the first chapter here suggested, the spaces in which visual images are displayed usually entail quite specific visual practices. How might the social practices of cinema-going intersect with these arguments about cinematic visualities? How might the effects of a film change between its screening in a cinema and its showing as a video on a home tv screen? I'm thinking here not just of things like the size of the screen and so on – which Mulvey for one does mention as part of the visual pleasure of narrative cinema – but of the ways that people watch differently in different places, and how these social practices are disciplined. Psychoanalysis, like the other methods discussed so far in this book, has nothing to say about these questions either. Thus it is not surprising to find that some psychoanalytic accounts of film spectatorship are turning to other theorists – most notably perhaps to Foucault – to ground their accounts of visuality in social practices and institutions (Mayne, 1993 discusses this shift). The next two chapters will turn to Foucault's work for the same end.

10 summary

- the key concerns of psychoanalytic film criticism are subjectivity, sexuality and the unconscious.
- sexual difference is a key substantive focus; other kinds of difference are neglected. Sexual difference is understood as relational, and structured between both the male and female characters in a movie, and the members of the film's audience.
- these relationalities are articulated by different kinds of looks, temporalities and spaces. The methodological pointers offered by psychoanalytic accounts of film consist of interpreting the structures of these looks, temporalities and spaces.
- initial formulations of the male gaze as voyeuristic and fetishistic, and of images of women as representing only the disavowal of castration, have been supplemented by concepts such as masquerade, fantasy and the Gaze.

- psychoanalysis has a detailed vocabulary for exploring the possible subjective effects of images on their audiences, but there is little work exploring these empirically.
- psychoanalysis cannot address the social practices of the display and audiencing of visual images.

further reading

Sue Thornham's (1997) *Passionate Detachments: An Introduction to Feminist Film Theory* provides some very useful surveys of the debates within psychoanalytic feminist film criticism.

discourse analysis I

text, intertextuality and context

1 discourse and visual culture: an introduction

The previous chapter examined certain psychoanalytic approaches to visual images, and ended with the concerns expressed by some writers that psychoanalysis does not pay enough attention to the social construction of difference. This claim is made on two grounds: first, that psychoanalysis has very little to say about some forms of social difference, such as 'race' and class; second, that it concentrates on the psychic and visual construction of difference at the expense of considering the social construction and consequences of difference. Very little attention is paid either to the ways of seeing brought to particular images by specific audiences, or to the social institutions and practices through which images are made and displayed.

One writer whose work is often turned to in order to address these absences in psychoanalytic theory is Michel Foucault. For various reasons, Foucault was quite hostile to psychoanalysis, but Foucault's approach does have some compatibilities with that of Freud. Most importantly, perhaps, Foucault's understanding of the subject is in some ways similar to that of psychoanalysis. Like psychoanalytic approaches to the subject, Foucault too considered that human subjects are produced and not simply born. Human subjectivity is constructed through particular processes, he argued, and much of his work consists of detailed historical studies of some of those processes at particular periods in Western history (actually, mostly French history). He wrote books on the emergence of the human sciences in modern Europe, on the development of modern clinical and psychiatric medicine, on the birth of the prison, and on attitudes towards sexuality. In all of these he paid close attention to the ways in which various practices and institutions defined what it was to be human (and therefore also what it was to be sub-human, abnormal or deviant) in very particular ways.

Thus his work has appealed to those writers cited in the previous chapter who are concerned that psychoanalysis, for all its other analytical insights, does not pay enough attention to the social processes through which a range of subjectivities are constituted. Stuart Hall (1996: 7), for example, argues that 'if ideology is effective, it is because it works at *both* the 'the rudimentary levels of psychic identity and the drives' *and* at the level of the discursive formation and practices which constitute the social field'. Teresa de Lauretis (1994), too, concludes her Freudian account of 'perverse desire' by emphasizing the need to connect Foucault and Freud; Freud, she says, provides an account of how the social processes described by Foucault are subjectively articulated. Kaja Silverman (1992), in the opening pages of her study of *Male Subjectivity at the Margins*, also argues that the work of Foucault and Freud needs to be brought together, although she suggests a rather more complicated relation between the psychic and the social than does de Lauretis.

Discourse Although many of Foucault's ideas are now broadly disseminated, it is still useful to begin a discussion of the methodological implications of his work by examining some of his theoretical terms. The notion of **discourse** is central to both Foucault's theoretical arguments and to his methodology. Discourse has a quite specific meaning. It refers to groups of statements which structure the way a thing is thought, and the way we act on the basis of that thinking. In other words, discourse is a particular knowledge about the world which shapes how the world is understood and how things are done in it. Lynda Nead (1988: 4) defines discourse as 'a particular form of language with its own rules and conventions and the institutions within which the discourse is produced and circulated', and she gives medical discourse as an example: 'in this way, it is possible to speak of a medical discourse . . . which refers to the special language of medicine, the form of knowledge it produces and the professional institutions and social spaces which it occupies'. Discourse also produces subjects: hence medical discourse produces, among other subject positions, doctors, nurses and patients. Nead suggests that 'art' can also be understood as a discourse, as a specialized form of knowledge. She says that 'the discourse of art in the nineteenth century [consisted of] the concatenation of visual images, the language and structures of criticism, cultural institutions, publics for art and the values and knowledges made possible within and through high culture' (Nead, 1988: 4). On this understanding, 'art' becomes not certain kinds of visual images but the knowledges, institutions, subjects and practices which work to define certain images as art and others as not art. Discourses are articulated through all sorts visual and verbal images and texts, specialized or not, and also through the practices that those languages permit. The diversity of forms through which a discourse can be

Intertextuality articulated means that **intertextuality** is important to understanding discourse. Intertextuality refers to the way that the meanings of any one discursive image or text depend not only on that one text or image, but also on the meanings carried by other images and texts.

It is possible to think of visuality as a sort of discourse too. A specific visuality will make certain things visible in particular ways, and other things unseeable, for example, and subjects will be produced and act within that field of vision. Some of the arguments made by psychoanalytic feminist film critics and discussed in the previous chapter can be recast in these Foucauldian terms. Thus the visuality that, according to Laura Mulvey (1989: 19) makes 'woman as image, man the bearer of the look', could be described as a visual discourse that has effects on the making of masculinity and femininity, men and women. John Berger (1972: 46) points out some of the implications for everyday practice of that discourse: 'a woman must continually watch herself. She is almost continually accompanied by her own image of herself'. This example is also relevant to another Foucauldian term, that of discursive formation. A **discursive formation** is the way meanings are connected together in a particular discourse. Foucault (1972: 37) describes discursive formations as 'systems of dispersion', in that they consist of the relations between parts of a discourse. 'Whenever,' he says, 'one can define a regularity (an order, correlations, positions and functionings, transformations), we will say, for the sake of convenience, that we are dealing with a *discursive formation*' (Foucault, 1972: 38). Thus, to continue for a moment to translate psycho-analytic work into Foucauldian terms, Mulvey argues that phallocentric visuality has a structure in which images of women depend on particular forms of masculine seeing. This is a relational argument in that masculinity and femininity depend on each other for their characteristics: woman always signifying castration, and man always enacting voyeuristic and fetishistic ways of seeing. That relation – that correlation and those positions – could be described as a discursive formation.

Discursive formation (margin note)

Foucault was quite clear that discourse was a form of discipline, and this leads us to his concern with **power**. Discourse, he says, is powerful, but it is powerful in a particular way. It is powerful, says Foucault, because it is productive. Discourse disciplines subjects into certain ways of thinking and acting, but this is not simply repressive; it does not impose rules for thought and behaviour on a pre-existing human agent. Instead, human subjects are produced through discourses. Our sense of our self is made through the operation of discourse. So too are objects, relations, places, scenes: discourse produces the world as it understands it. Thus, to translate once more some of the arguments of the previous chapter, it might be said that certain kinds of masculinity are produced through a discursive visuality that is voyeuristic and fetishistic.

Power (margin note)

An important implication of Foucault's account of power is that power is not something imposed from the top of society down on to its oppressed bottom layers. Power is everywhere, since discourse too is everywhere. And there are many discourses, some of which clearly contest the terms of others. Foucault (1979: 95) claimed that 'where there is power, there is resistance . . . a multiplicity of points of resistance', and by this he meant that there are many discourses which jostle and compete in their effects. We might define the efforts of feminist film critics like Silverman and de Lauretis, for example, as efforts to develop visual discourses that do not discipline looking in a phallocentric manner, but that produce other (ways of visualizing) masculinities and femininities. But certain discourses are nonetheless dominant, and Foucault was particularly concerned in his own work with the emergence of institutions and technologies that were structured through specific, even if complex and contested, discourses. He suggested that the dominance of certain discourses occurred not only because they were located in socially powerful institutions – those given coercive powers by the state, for example, such as the police, prisons and workhouses – but also because their discourses claimed absolute truth. The construction of claims to truth lies at the heart

Power/knowledge   of the intersection of **power/knowledge**:

> We should admit . . . that power produces knowledge (and not simply by encouraging it because it serves power or by applying it because it is useful); that power and knowledge directly imply one another; that there is no power relation without the correlative constitution of a field of knowledge, nor any knowledge that does not presuppose and constitute at the same time power relations. (Foucault, 1977: 27)

Foucault insisted that knowledge and power are imbricated one in the other, not only because all knowledge is discursive and all discourse is saturated with power, but because the most powerful discourses, in terms of the productiveness of their social effects, depend on assumptions and claims that their knowledge is true. The particular grounds on which truth is claimed – and these shift historically – constitute what Foucault called a

Regime of truth   **regime of truth.** Some historians of photography have argued, for example, that the 'realism' of the photographic image was produced, not by new photographic technology, but by the use of photographs in a specific regime of truth, so that photographs were seen as evidence of 'what was really there'. This argument will be examined a little more fully in the next chapter.

Foucault's work is radical in many ways. It has been adopted with enthusiasm by many working in the social sciences and humanities, but has also been greeted with hostility and even derision by others. His controversial status is in small part explained by his methodological programme (which is perhaps spelled out most clearly in *The Archeology of Knowledge* (1972); see also Kendall and Wickham, 1999). Foucault refused the premise which forms the basis of all the analytical methods that this book has examined so far. Content analysis, semiology and psychoanalysis all assume that analysis needs somehow to delve behind the surface appearance of things in order to discover their real meaning. Content analysis seeks out latent meanings that it claims become evident only from systematic quantitative study; semiology searches for the dominant codes or myths or referent systems that underlie the surface appearance of signs;

and psychoanalysis looks for signs of the unconscious as they disrupt the conscious making of meaning. This approach to the interpretation of meaning is widespread in the humanities and social sciences, and subtends many other methods apart from these three. Foucault rejected such 'penetrative' models of interpretation at the level of method, but also at the level of explanation, since he also wanted to avoid explanatory accounts of why power works in the way it does. He explicitly rejected the Marxist claim that meaning was determined by the system of production, for example; he was always vague about how discourses connected to other, non-discursive processes such as economic change; and while he acknowledged that power has aims and effects, he never explained these by turning to notions of human or institutional agency. Michele Barrett (1991: 131) says that his notion of causality and dependency was 'polymorphous'. Both methodologically and theoretically, then, Foucault rejected approaches that look behind or underneath things and practices for other processes that would explain them. Instead, as Barrett (1991) makes clear in her account of his work, he focused on the question of how power worked. How does it do what it does, how did it do what it did? Certainly his most satisfying works, to me, are his empirical accounts of particular texts and institutions, often focusing on their details, their casual assumptions, their everyday mundane routines, their taken-for-granted architecture, their banalities. It is these detailed descriptions that produce his most startling accounts of how subjects and objects were and are discursively produced.

Elaborating Foucault's method is not easy however. As Barrett (1991: 127) notes, his methodological statements are rather vague. Nor are more recent discourse analysts much more forthcoming about their methods. Jonathan Potter (1996: 140), for example, describes discourse analysis as a 'craft skill' and suggests that the only way to learn it is to get on and do it (although elsewhere he does offer some guidelines; see Potter and Wetherell, 1987: 158–76). This vagueness, combined with the huge amount of Foucault's work now available – which includes many interviews and pieces of journalism quite apart from his books and papers – and the fact that, not surprisingly, his ideas changed as his projects shifted, means that his methodological legacy has been complex and diffuse. This chapter and the next will focus on two methodologies, both of which owe allegiance to Foucauldian arguments – especially to his notion of discourse – but which have rather different results when used. I will call these discourse analysis I and discourse analysis II.

2   discourse analyis I and discourse analysis II

I have suggested that Foucault's work has produced two somewhat different methodological emphases, which I am calling discourse analysis I and discourse analysis II. I distinguish between them thus:

- *discourse analysis I*. This form of discourse analysis tends to pay rather more attention to the notion of discourse as articulated through various kinds of visual images and verbal texts than it does to the practices entailed by specific discourses. As Rosalind Gill (1996: 141) says, it uses 'discourse' to 'refer to all forms of talk and texts'. It is most concerned with discourse, discursive formations and their productivity.
- *discourse analysis II*. This form of discourse analysis tends to pay more attention to the practices of institutions than it does to the visual images and verbal texts. Its methodology is usually left implicit. It tends to be more explicitly concerned with issues of power, regimes of truth, institutions and technologies.

This distinction is not clear-cut. It is not difficult to find work that examines visual images, verbal texts, institutions and social practices together (see Green, 1990 for example). However, in terms of current discussions of methodologies in the social sciences, it does seem to me that there is a case to be made for discussing these two methodological emphases separately, since they do produce rather different kinds of research work. Thus this chapter will examine the first type of discourse analysis, and the next chapter will examine the second. For convenience, whenever this chapter mentions discourse analysis, it is referring to what has just been characterized as discourse analysis I, unless the text specifies otherwise.

This first type of discourse analysis is centrally concerned with language. But, as Fran Tonkiss emphasizes:

> Language is viewed as the topic of research . . . Rather than gathering accounts or texts so as to gain access to people's views and attitudes, or to find out what happened at a particular event, the discourse analyst is interested in how people use language to construct their accounts of the social world. (Tonkiss, 1998: 247–8)

Discourse analysis can also be used to explore how images construct specific views of the social world, in which case, to paraphrase Tonkiss, visuality is viewed as the topic of research, and the discourse analyst is interested in how images construct accounts of the social world. This type of discourse analysis therefore pays careful attention to an *image itself* (as well as other sorts of evidence). Since discourses are seen as socially produced rather than created by individuals, this type of discourse analysis is especially concerned with the *social modality* of the image site. In particular, discourse analysis explores how those specific views or accounts are constructed as real or truthful or natural through particular regimes of truth. As Gill (1996: 143) says, 'all discourse is organized to make itself persuasive', and discourse analysis focuses on those strategies of persuasion. It also pays attention to the more socially constituted forms of discursive power, looking at the social construction of difference and authority, for example. Discourse analysis is thus concerned too with the social production and effects of discourses.

This chapter will explore the usefulness of these methodological foci through a case study of the work of several historians who have examined the discursive construction of the East End of London in the 1880s. These historians work with a variety of images and texts in order to examine the way bourgeois commentators produced an apparently truthful account of this working-class area, and to explore the effects that had on its residents in terms of the various institutional interventions legitimated by that 'truth'. Gareth Stedman Jones (1976: 10–11) points out that in the 1870s and 1880s, most British social thinkers assumed that economic progress would eliminate poverty. The fact that it did not – most blatantly in London's East End, an area with a seasonal and casual labour market and high levels of poverty – was blamed on what were seen as 'the still unregenerate poor: those who had turned their back on progress, or been rejected by it'. Jones continues:

> This group was variously referred to as 'the dangerous class', the casual poor or, most characteristically, 'the residuum' . . . In the explanation of the existence of the residuum the subjective psychological defects of individuals bulked even larger than before . . . The problem was not structural but moral. The evil to be combated was not poverty but pauperism; pauperism with its attendant vices, drunkenness, improvidence, mendicancy, bad language, filthy habits, gambling, low amusements and ignorance. (Jones, 1976: 11)

This particular definition of the problem led to specific strategies to combat it: strategies which aimed to alter the morality of the poor rather than their standard of living.

Discourse analysis thus addresses questions of power/knowledge. Because of this, it also fulfils two of the three criteria for a critical visual methodology that were outlined in the first chapter. As a method, discourse analysis pays careful attention to images, and to their social production and effect. However, discourse analytic methods are not much concerned with questions of reflexivity. Certainly in his early work, Foucault seemed to separate his own practices as an academic from those of the thinkers he was discussing and, in another parallel with psychoanalytic approaches, in the introduction to *The Archeology of Knowledge* he derided autobiographical efforts at reflexivity: 'do not ask me who I am and do not ask me to remain the same: leave it to our bureaucrats and our police to see that our papers are in order' (Foucault, 1972: 17). In the section on reflexivity in their book on Foucault, Gavin Kendall and Gary Wickham (1999: 101–9) echo this refusal and say very little about reflexivity as it is currently debated in the social sciences.

In order to discuss more fully what this type of discourse analysis entails, and to assess it critically, this chapter will:

- explore more fully the notion of discourse and discursive formation and its implications for finding sources for discourse analysis;
- examine how discourse analysis addresses the discursive construction of truth claims, through both the structure of discourse and its institutional location;
- examine why discourse analysis refuses to be reflexive.

3 finding your sources

Doing a discourse analysis assumes that you are concerned with the discursive production of some kind of authoritative account – and perhaps too about how that account was or is contested – and with the social practices both in which that production is embedded and which it itself produces. Discourses are articulated through a huge range of images, texts and practices, however, and any and all of these are legitimate sources for a discourse analysis. When beginning a piece of discourse analysis, then, it is necessary to think carefully about what sorts of sources you need.

3.1 finding your sources: in general

For most sorts of research questions, some key sources will be immediately obvious, either from your own knowledge or from the work of other researchers. In the work of historians looking at the discursive construction of the East End of London in the 1880s, for example, a number of sources recur (Cowling, 1989; Fishman, 1988; Jones, 1976, 1989; Keating, 1976; Nead, 1988; Walkowitz, 1992). These are: contemporary newspapers, often London ones rather than national ones; contemporary accounts of visits to the East End by journalists, clerics, philanthropists and others, which often take the form of travel diaries and could be published in pamphlet or book form as well as in newspapers; novels and, less often, poems; documents produced by various branches of government such as the census, reports by local medical officers of health, and other sorts of government reports. Many of these written sources are illustrated with figurative images – often engravings – or with maps, cartoons or other visual images. Almost all of these historians also use photographs of the area, some taken by philanthropic institutions and some by journalists, but the provenance of many of these is now hard to trace. It is important to note the seeming eclecticism of these sources. They are not constrained by notions of genre, for example, or technology. Even a study concerned to examine just one sort of visual construction relevant to the production of the East End, such as Nead's (1988) study of 'art', uses a wide range of sources, including paintings, engravings and drawings, but also journalism, parliamentary reports and fictional and non-fictional writing. This eclecticism is demanded by the intertextuality of discourse. As Nicholas Green (1990: 3) says, discourse is 'a coherent pattern of statements across a range of archives and sites'.

In the face of the breadth of source material demanded by discourse analysis, it is useful to begin by thinking about what sources should be selected as the *starting points* for your own research: the sources that are likely to be particularly productive, or particularly interesting. This may mean you draw on sources that others have often used. Or it may mean that you need to locate and access previously unused materials. Or your key sources may already be to hand; perhaps stumbling across them was what started you off on this research in the first place. However, once the more obvious starting points for a discourse analysis have been established, it is important then to *widen* your 'range of archives and sites'. Ways of doing this are diverse. Those initial images and texts may well contain references to other images and texts that you can then track down. Reading what other researchers working on the same or similar topics have said about your area of interest will produce other leads. A discourse analysis may also be able to use verbal material; you may want to conduct interviews yourself, or to record naturally occurring talk (see Potter, 1996; Potter and Wetherell, 1994). You also need to invest time in the kind of browsing research that leads to serendipitous finds. Some of the most interesting discourse analyses are interesting precisely because they bring together, in convincing ways, material that had previously been seen as quite unrelated.

If this sounds potentially time consuming – it can be. Indeed, one of the difficulties of the discourse analytic method is knowing where to stop the data collection process. However, as Tonkiss points out, discourse analysis depends not on the quantity of material analysed, but its quality. 'What matters,' she says, 'is the richness of textual detail, rather than the number of texts analysed' (Tonkiss, 1998: 253). Thus you may quite legitimately select from all possible sources a few that seem particularly interesting to you. As long as you have located some intriguingly complex texts, your discourse analysis can begin.

focus

Suppose you are interested in exploring the ways pregnant women are visualized in contemporary Western culture. What might your initial sources be? Where else might you look for visual images and texts that construct the pregnant female body?

This task raises the question of different, possibly competing discourses that participate in that construction. For example, you may not be familiar with the conventional medical discourse of pregnancy, but this is perhaps the most powerful discourse a pregnant woman encounters as she attends her antenatal appointments. How might you access that particular discourse? And what others might challenge or confirm it? How might you access how some pregnant women construct their sense of bodily self, for example? What about advertising? And are adverts showing pregnant women the only relevant ones? Or is the fact that pregnant women are very rarely visualized in what are called 'women's magazines' also relevant? That is, is the invisibility of pregnant women also an interesting issue to investigate?

3.2 finding your sources: iconography

One method that does offer some clearer guidelines about what sorts of sources are relevant to understanding some kinds of visual images is iconography. Iconography is a method developed by the art historian Erwin Panofsky. Chapter 2 suggested that many art historians rely on having a 'good eye' which focuses almost entirely on how an image looks. Panofsky (1957: 26) distanced himself from this kind of eye by insisting that 'iconography is that branch of the history of art which concerns itself with the subject matter or meaning of works of art, as opposed to their form'. The subject matter or meaning was, for Panofsky, to be established by referring to the understandings of the symbols and signs in a painting that its contemporary audiences would have had. Interpreting those understandings requires a grasp of the historically specific intertextuality on which meaning depends.

Panofsky took care to spell out just how he thought this comparison between different visual images and verbal texts should work. Panofsky (1957) divides visual interpretation into three kinds, which he gives various names to:

1	primary	natural	pre-iconographic
2	secondary	conventional	iconographic
3	intrinsic	symbolic	iconological

The example he uses to explain the differences between these three kinds of images is 'when an acquaintance greets me on the street by lifting his hat' (Panofsky, 1957: 26). He suggests that recognizing that he has encountered a 'gentleman' with a 'hat' requires some interpretation, but of an 'elementary and easily understandable' sort (26). This is therefore interpretation at the primary or pre-iconographic level. (In methodological terms, this level has some parallels to the close observation demanded by compositional interpretation.) However, 'my realization that the lifting of the hat stands for a greeting belongs in an altogether different realm of interpretation' (27). This different realm addresses images which have a specific symbolic resonance; this is the secondary level of interpretation, of a conventional or iconographic image. The third level of interpretation is brought to bear on visual images in order to explore their general cultural significance. Panofsky suggested that, in the case of his acquaintance with the hat, seeing that image in symbolic or iconological terms would mean interpreting the gesture of lifting the hat as a symptom of that man's whole personality and background. The iconological or intrinsic meaning of an image 'is apprehended by ascertaining those underlying principles which reveal the basic attitude of a nation, a period, a class, a religious or philosophical persuasion – qualified by one personality and condensed into one work' (30).

As an example of Panofsky's method (Figure 6.1), we can turn to the portrait painted by Jan van Eyck in 1434 for the marriage of Giovanni Arnolfini, a merchant in Bruges, to Giovanna Cenami (for other accounts of this painting, see Bedaux, 1986; Hall, 1994; Seidel, 1993).

Panofsky (1953: 201–3) offers a detailed iconographic interpretation of this image which depends on his knowledge of the iconography at work in early Netherlandish painting more generally. Thus Panofsky insists that, despite its location in 'a comfortably furnished interior', despite all its signs of worldly wealth (the lamp, mirror, jewellery, clothing), and despite its use of oil paint which, in Berger's (1972) analysis, makes the painting as much of a commodity as the objects it depicts, this is a painting that glorifies the Christian sacrament of marriage. Thus the hand gestures are those of the Catholic marriage ceremony, and the candle, clearly not needed for light since the room is bathed in sunlight from the window, represents the all-seeing Christ. The fruit on the window ledge and chest symbolize the purity of humankind before the Fall. The statue of St Margaret at the top of the tall chairback represents childbirth, and the dog symbolizes marital fidelity. Moreover, the colours used by van Eyck also have symbolic meaning. John Gage (1993: 142–3) notes that the colours in the portrait have significance in relation to the ideas of contemporary alchemists about colours and the essential properties of matter. Deep purple and green – the clothes worn by the couple – symbolize fire and water, as does the jewellery hanging next to the mirror in the painting – amber beads and pearls. The painting thus suggests that this is not only a coupling of two people, but a complementary union of two elemental properties which will be harmonious and fertile. Both Panofsky and Gage rely on the notion of intertextuality in order to interpret the meanings this image would have had for its contemporary audiences, although they relate the portrait to different texts: Gage refers to alchemy books while Panofsky compares the portrait to other marriage portraits.

As an intertextual method, iconography is most often applied to Western figurative images and to architecture, usually from the sixteenth to the eighteenth centuries. During that period, compendia of symbols (in the loose sense of the word) were written for both artists and patrons. These explained the meanings of hundreds of visual motifs, allegories and personifications, and it is these compendia that art historians have consulted to produce iconographic interpretations of specific images. Iconography

Figure 6.1 *Jan van Eyck,* Arnolfini Wedding Portrait, *1434* (National Gallery, London)

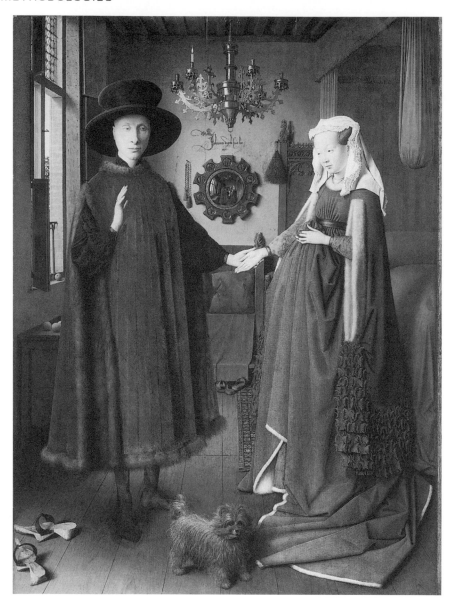

needs a thorough grounding in historical context to be successful, therefore, and Panofsky argued that actually, in order to understand the possible secondary and intrinsic meanings of an image, two things were necessary. One was that deep familiarity with the texts, both visual and written, with which the artist producing a particular piece of work would have been familiar, and this might need to extend beyond those published guides to symbolism just mentioned. The second thing was 'synthetic intuition' (Panofsky, 1957: 38), or what other commentators on this method have called common sense. This second quality was important because, while various texts could provide important information and clues about iconographic and iconological meaning, Panofsky (1957) argued that they could never provide full explanations for a particular image, and their relevance thus had to be judged by the critic on the basis of his or her intuition.

There are some aids available for developing this requisite sense of historical context. Roelof van Straten (1994) provides a guide to the compendia of symbols that were used by artists and patrons. Another very helpful publication is the *Encyclopedia of Comparative Iconography* (Roberts, 1998). This two-volume work consists of a number of long, illustrated essays on themes such as Crucifixion, Death, Arms Raised, Money, Whiteness, Pregnancy and Hair/Haircutting (to list some almost at random). Each entry explores the iconography of its theme and lists relevant works of art from various periods. It also suggests other useful reading which can direct you to original sources.

As defined by Panofsky, iconography is not a Foucauldian method. Panofsky (1957: 41) suggested that iconological analysis could show how the 'essential tendencies of the human mind' were translated into visual themes and concepts, and this reference to the 'essential tendencies of the human mind' is decidedly non-Foucauldian. As we have seen, Foucault insisted that there could be no 'essential tendencies' because human subjectivity is entirely constructed. Iconography has also been seen as close to more structural kinds of semiology, with Panofsky's primary level of interpretation echoed in the notion of denotive signs, and his secondary level in connotive signs. However, in their shared concern with intertextuality, there are some parallels between iconography and the sort of discourse analysis under discussion here, and the term 'iconography' is now often used in a loose sense to refer to the kind of approach to images that I am calling discourse analysis I.

A work that might be described as an 'iconography' in this looser sense is Mary Cowling's (1989) study of 'the representation of type and character in Victorian art'. Cowling's work contributes to an account of the discursive construction of the East End of London in the 1880s too, since she points out that the East Ender was shown by Victorian artists as a particular social type. She argues that Victorian audiences assumed that paintings needed to be read – that their meanings required decoding – and that there were two related bodies of knowledge, both understood as scientifically true, which were used especially frequently for decoding images of social difference: physiognomy and phrenology.

> In the Victorian age, physiognomy, or the indication of character through the facial features and forms of the head and body, was all but universally believed in. The more specific indication of character through the shape of the skull, expounded as a complete system in the form of phrenology, was also widely subscribed to. Whether the human face was looked at with the eyes of the artist, the writer, or even the scientist, belief in physiognomy characterized contemporary attitudes towards it. (Cowling, 1989: 9)

Cowling shows how books like *Physiognomy Made Easy* (c.1880), *Self-Instructor in Phrenology and Physiology* (1886) and *The Study of the Human Face* (1868), among many others, showed faces and heads divided into types that were differentiated in terms of their morality, social position and notions of race. Aspects of heads and faces such as nose profile, forehead slope, chin profile, skull size and lip shape were all presented as clues to the moral standing, social class and race of an individual, and these clues were used too in the work of cartoonists, novelists, scientists and artists. An example of how these shared interpretations of heads and faces were commonplace is given by Cowling (1989: 64–5), and it is also a neat example of her own method. Plate 44 shows a page from the *Self-Instructor in Phrenology and Physiology*. There are two engravings on this page, one of a 'good head' and one of a 'bad head'. Cowling compares these in her plate 45 to a caricature of a 'foreigner' that appeared in the magazine *Punch* in 1862, and in plate 46 to a portrait of J.G. Lockhart, the son-in-law and biographer of Sir Walter Scott, by William Allen in 1876. The 'soaring brow and delicate features' of the latter (Cowling, 1989: 65) are repeated exactly in the *Self-Instructor* as the 'good head', and would have indicated to Victorian audiences that this was a man of high moral probity, high social class and English origin. In contrast, the swarthy and coarse features given to the 'foreigner' by *Punch* recur in the image of the 'bad head'. Cowling argues that Victorian audiences would have made these same connections and interpretations. And it is her method to make them too: to trace the relations between different texts in order to identify the meanings their viewers and readers shared.

Cowling's concern with intertextuality focuses on two particular images, however, one of which is particularly relevant to this discussion since Cowling argues that it contains several images of East Enders. This is a painting by William Powell Frith, exhibited in 1862 and called *The Railway Station* (Cowling, 1989: 185–231). It is a huge canvas showing the crowd accompanying a train about to leave, and Cowling remarks that it was seen by contemporaries as an image of, and a commentary on, the modern London crowd. That is, its theme was social relations and social difference, and Frith and his audience both used physiognomy and phrenology to make sense of this painting. Having consulted books of physiognomy and phrenology herself, Cowling is able to offer her own key to the painting which notes the kind of social type each figure would have represented to its Victorian audiences (Cowling, 1989: 242–3). Her key includes 'gentleman in reduced circumstances', 'his daughter, off to take up her first position' (as a governess) and 'villianous recruit – vicious type'. Cowling suggests that these latter sorts of images, of the various types from the residuum, would have been seen by contemporary audiences as East Enders. The social differences among Londoners were also understood as geographical differences in this period and the residuum, certainly by the end of the 1880s, was always located in the East End of the city. Thus images of members of the residuum were also images of East Enders.

Cowling (1989) uses many sorts of texts to make her case for the importance of facial features and head types for understanding Victorian images of social difference, including magazines, anthropology books, novels, paintings and engravings, as well as those books on physiognomy and phrenology. As I have noted, this range of sources is typical of the kind of discourse analysis to which I am suggesting iconography is related. Cowling's method is to look for the commonalities, both textual and visual, among these sources, and to establish them by citing the words and images they have in common: thus she quotes extensively from her sources and also reproduces their images generously (her book has 370 pages of text and 340 plates). This search for recurring themes is also typical of discourse analysis. However, as the rest of this chapter will show, the proponents of discourse analysis also suggest some further methodological tactics for interpreting intertextual meanings.

4   discourse analysis I: the production and rhetorical organization of discourse

Iconography, then, like discourse analysis, depends on intertextuality for its interpretive power. It also depends, though, on what Panofsky called 'common sense', and many discourse analysts also suggest that successful discourse analysis depends less on rigorous procedures and more on other qualities: craft skill, says Potter (1996: 140), or scholarship, according to Gill (1996: 144). Nonetheless, there have been some efforts to make the procedures of discourse analysis more explicit, especially in the social sciences. This section explores some of those efforts.

In her discussion of discourse analysis, Tonkiss (1998) suggests that those efforts have been directed in two areas. First, there is the analysis of the structure of the discursive statements. Second, there is a concern for the social context of those statements: who is saying them, in what circumstances.

4.1   exploring the rhetorical organization of discourse

One theme of discourse analysis is the organization of discourse itself. How, precisely, is a particular discourse structured, and how then does it produce a particular kind of knowledge? In relation to written or spoken discourses, discourse analysis is interested in, for example, how a particular discourse describes things (although the power of discourse means that it produces those things it purports to be describing), in how it constructs blame and responsibility, in how it constructs stake and accountability, in how it categorizes and particularizes (Potter, 1996). In relation to visual images, many studies have been particularly interested in how social difference is constructed, and the previous section briefly discussed one example of this in relation to the East End: Cowling's (1989) study of the intersection between art, physiognomy and phrenology.

The first step in this interpretive process is, as Tonkiss (1998) and Gill (1996) both emphasize, to try to forget all preconceptions you might have about the materials you are working with. Read them and look at them with fresh eyes. As Foucault (1972: 25) says, pre-existing categories 'must be held in suspense. They must not be rejected definitively, of course, but the tranquillity with which they are accepted must be disturbed; we must show that they do not come about by themselves, but are always the result of a construction the rules of which must be known and the justifications of which must be scrutinized'. In this way, the material may offer you insights and leads that you would otherwise have missed. For visual images, it may be that the tools of detailed description offered by compositional interpretation have a role to play here, in making you look very carefully at every element of an image, and at their interrelation. Allow this process of reading and looking to take its time. Try to immerse yourself in the materials you are dealing with. Read and re-read the texts; look and look again at the images.

Having familiarized yourself with your materials, some slightly more systematic methods might be useful. One is a version of the coding process described in Chapter 3 in connection with content analysis. Familiarity with the sources will allow you to identify *key themes*, which may be key words, or recurring visual images. (Remember, though, that the most important words and images may not be those that occur most often.) Make a list of these words or images and then go through all your sources, coding the material every time that word or image occurs. Then start to think about connections between and among key words and key images. According to Foucault, the task is to examine:

> relations between statements (even if the author is unaware of them; even if the statements do not have the same author; even if the authors were unaware of each other's existence); relations between groups of statements thus established (even if these groups do not concern the same, or

even adjacent fields; even if they do not possess the same formal level; even if they are not the locus of assignable exchanges); relations between statements and groups of statements and events of a quite different kind (technical, economic, political, social). (Foucault, 1972: 29)

How are particular words or images given specific meanings? Are there meaningful clusters of words and images? What associations are established within such clusters? What connections are there between such clusters? Foucault here also suggests the need to consider the broader, non-discursive context of discourse. These sorts of questions address the productivity of discourse in the sense that they focus on its production of meanings and things.

Nead's (1988) discussion of how 'the prostitute' was discursively constructed through recurring images of bodies and places is exemplary here. Nead accumulates a wide range of visual images of this figure, as well as written accounts, and shows how she was understood by pointing to the limited number of key visual terms used to produce her (see also Gilman, 1990; Walkowitz, 1992). The prostitute worked exchanging sex for money. She was therefore constructed as a particular sort of moral problem in bourgeois discourses of femininity, and was placed in the residuum. She could be seen as irredeemable or redeemable; prostitutes were portrayed as both evil women and as victims of an evil society. However, as Nead notes, both arguments worked to place her outside 'normal' femininity. This outsider status was signified visually in the way she dressed (provocatively) and the way she looked, especially how she looked boldly at men. Since she was morally deviant, however, she was also pictured as paying the price of her sin. In visual and written narratives of prostitution, she was frequently visualized as losing her looks and her glamorous clothes, and simultaneously moving from the bright lights of the music hall to the dark streets of the East End, and, eventually, down into the dark and murky depths of the river Thames. This last location was often pictured as her final resting place: disease or pregnancy would take their toll, and her inevitable end, according to this discourse, was her suicide by drowning. The final stage of this visual narrative was the verdict passed on her by society. This was usually pictured by representatives of that society looking at the prostitute's dead body. These representatives might be the rivermen who find her, the policeman who inspects the corpse, the passers-by who see it, or the doctor who dissects it; and these are shown either as pitying or condemning. Nead thus identifies several key visual themes in images of prostitution: dress, bodily condition, location, looks. She shows how these themes could be given different meanings in different images or texts – the looks at her dead body could be compassionate or grimly satisfied, for example, depending on whether the prostitute was being constructed as evil or as a victim – but the basic elements used to represent her were repeated again and again in a wide variety of contexts.

focus

Look at Figures 6.2, 6.3, 6.4, 6.5 and 6.6, all reproduced from Nead's (1988) study.

Figure 6.2 *Gustave Doré, illustration to* The Bridge of Sighs, *1878* (The British Library; Nead, 1988)

Figure 6.3 *W. Gray,* Lost *(W. Hayward, London by Night, c. 1870; Nead, 1988)*

Figure 6.4 *W. Gray,* Found *(W. Hayward, London by Night, c. 1870; Nead, 1988)*

Figure 6.5 *Hablot K. Browne (Phiz),* The River *(Charles Dickens,* David Copperfield, *no. 16, August 1850; Nead, 1988)*

Figure 6.6 *George Frederick Watts,* Found Drowned, *1848–50* (Trustees of the Watts Gallery, Compton, nr Guildford; Nead, 1988)

Consider each one in relation to the key themes identified by Nead: dress, bodily condition, location, looks. In particular, think about how each of those themes can be represented in different ways. Compare this relative flexibility in identifying themes with the coding process demanded by content analysis. Which do you prefer, and why?

Are there other themes that seem to you to be relevant to these images?

As this coding and interpretation process proceeds, other issues may start to become important to your interpretation, perhaps issues that had not initially occurred to you. Unlike content analysis, this does not mean that you have to halt your analytical process and start again with a revised set of categories. Discourse analysis is much more flexible than that. As new questions occur, prompted by one moment of coding, you can return to your materials with different codes in a second – or third or fourth or twentieth – moment of interpretation. While the Foucauldian framework of discourse analysis is giving you a certain approach to your materials, it is also crucial that you let the details of your materials guide your investigations.

An important part of that framework is how a particular discourse works to persuade. How does it produce its *effects of truth*? This is another aspect of discourse that your analysis must address. Often this entails focusing on claims to truth, or to scientific certainty, or to the natural way of things. As well as the visual and textual devices used to claim truth, however, it is useful to look for moments at which dissent from a discourse is acknowledged (even if implicitly) and dealt with. Search for 'the work that is being done to reconcile conflicting ideas, to cope with contradiction or uncertainty, or to counter alternatives' (Tonkiss, 1998: 255), because this work will highlight processes of persuasion that may otherwise be difficult to detect.

An example of an account of the East End of London that claimed to be true because scientific was the map of poverty first published by Charles Booth in 1889 (Figure 6.7).

Booth used 34 school board visitors (the local officials responsible for enforcing attendance at school) to survey the income of every household in the East End. He then calculated how many people were living in poverty, and mapped their location. The survey was seen as scientific in a number of ways. First, its coverage was more or less complete in terms of the East End's population (456,877 people were included, according to Booth's figures). Second, its coverage was seen as complete in terms of its under-standing, and here the visual effect of the map was crucial: the map seemed to lay the East End bare to a scientific gaze that penetrated what others described as its darkest recesses. Third, Booth's survey and the map classi-fied its subjects in ways that were central to contemporary scientific pro-cedures. Booth argued that while over one-third of the residents of the East End were living in poverty, this was mostly due to fecklessness rather than moral depravity; only 2 per cent of the residuum, he argued, fell into that latter category. This sort of moral classification was central to other Victorian sciences, particularly those that constructed racial differences (and it is no coincidence that many journalists compared going into the East End of London with visits to Africa, as did General Booth's *In Darkest England*, published in 1890; see Keating, 1976). Finally, Booth also relied on statistical analyses of his data which gave his arguments scientific authority too; Nead (1988) notes how some arguments about prostitution were also legitimated by statistical claims. Through these

DESCRIPTIVE MAP OF LONDON POVERTY 1889.

Figure 6.7 *Map from Charles Booth's descriptive map of London poverty, 1889 (London Topographical Society)*

various strategies, then, Booth's map was perceived by (most) contemporaries as scientifically true.

focus

Look at the map in Figure 6.8 and compare it to the map reproduced in Figure 6.7.

The *Police Illustrated News* was a popular newspaper offering sensational crime stories. Does the map carry the same claim to accuracy in both cases? If not, why not?

Another emphasis in discourse analysis is the *complexity and contradictions* internal to discourses. Discursive formations have structures but that does not necessarily imply that they are logical or coherent. Indeed, part of the power of a specific discursive formation may rest precisely on

Figure 6.8 Police
Illustrated News,
*17 November
1888* (British
Newspaper
Library; Walkowitz,
1992)

**Interpretative
repertoire**
the multiplicity of different arguments that can be produced in its terms.
Potter (1996) uses the term **interpretative repertoire** to address one aspect
of this complexity.

> Interpretative repertoires are systematically related sets of terms that are
> often used with stylistic and grammatical coherence and often organized
> around one or more central metaphors. They develop historically and
> make up an important part of the 'common sense' of a culture, although
> some are specific to institutional domains. (Potter, 1996: 131)

Potter notes that interpretative repertoires are something like mini-
discourses; they tend to be quite specific to particular social situations. An
example of a visual interpretative repertoire is offered by Nead (1988:

128–32). She discusses a watercolour by the Pre-Raphaelite painter Dante Gabriel Rossetti. Called *The Gate of Memory*, it was painted in 1857 and shows a prostitute standing under an archway staring at a group of children playing. It visualizes one of the final verses of a poem by William Bell Scott called *Maryanne*. But while Scott's poem could describe the degraded body of this woman in some detail, Rossetti's watercolour cannot, says Nead, and this is because 'the prostitute has become the subject of "art" and "art" does not provide space for woman as physically deviant or unpleasurable' (Nead, 1988: 132). That is, the Victorian discourse of femininity entailed a number of interpretative repertoires and the repertoire available to artists could produce only certain kinds of images; hence, in part, the complexity of that discourse.

An example of the contradictions inherent in discursive formations can be given by placing Jones's (1989) account of the 'cockney' next to other discussions of the construction of East Enders. As we have seen, from the 1880s if not before, the East Ender was constructed as marked, physically and visibly, by moral degeneracy. As Jones (1976), Fishman (1988) and Walkowitz (1992) emphasize, this was a construction that could produce considerable fear among the bourgeois readers of the newspapers, novels, pamphlets and poems through which it was articulated. Walkowitz (1992) and Nead (1988) both emphasize the horror of disease that prostitution might spread, for example (which could involve acknowledging, as it did for campaigners against the Contagious Diseases Act of 1860s, that it was actually men who spread disease, and often bourgeois men visiting working class prostitutes at that; a good example of the complexity of discourses). Jones (1976) and Fishman (1988) stress the middle class fear of social unrest that a residuum with no stake in society might create. Hence, through the 1880s and beyond, as a counter to these fears, other images of the East Ender developed. The orderly dock strike of 1889, for example, was seen as evidence that the majority of the poor were decent at heart and not likely to revolt, and Jones (1989) traces the elaboration of the 'cockney' as the acceptable face of the East End. The cockney was constructed as good-hearted, chirpy, with a resigned sense of humour and a particular style of dress, often a bit flash; they look out for their neighbour and, especially, are stoical under conditions of social hardship. Jones argues that the effect of this discourse was to counter imaginatively what was perceived as the threat to society posed by the residuum, by constructing the cockney as different but lovable. Jones (1989) suggests that this vision of the cockney was expressed most unambiguously in music-hall songs at the turn of the century, but he also notes that much of the literature at that period 'veered incoherently' between this cockney and the other vision of the residuum East Ender. Thus Jones's work stresses the contradictions within the discursive construction of the East End, through a careful reading of a wide range of materials.

Finally, discourse analysis also involves reading for what is not seen or said. Absences can be as productive as explicit naming; *invisibility* can have just as powerful effects as visibility. Thus Jones (1989) ends his essay on the construction of the 'cockney' by noting that the cockney was always imagined as white, despite the constant presence of large black communities in the East End. The 'cockney' therefore erased racialized difference by making whiteness the taken-for-granted race of the East Ender. As Jones (1989) also notes, however, this erasure did not last beyond the so-called race riots in Notting Hill in the west end of London in 1958. After that, race could not be made invisible so easily, and the cockney fades as a meaningful cultural category.

Hence discourse analysis depends on reading with great care for detail. It assumes that the efficacy of discourse often resides in the assumptions it makes about what is true, real or natural, in the contradictions that allow it interpretive flexibility, and in what is not said, and none of these are accessible to superficial reading or viewing. Hence Gill's (1996: 144) emphasis on the scholarship entailed in discourse analysis: 'the analysis of discourse and rhetoric requires the careful reading and interpretation of texts, rigorous scholarship rather than adherence to formal procedures'.

To summarize the strategies for the intepretation of the rhetorical organization of discourse outlined in this section, then, they include:

1 looking at your sources with fresh eyes.
2 immersing yourself in your sources.
3 identifying key themes in your sources.
4 examining their effects of truth.
5 paying attention to their complexity and contradictions.
6 looking for the invisible as well as the visible.
7 paying attention to details.

4.2 exploring the social production of discourse

As Gill (1996: 142) notes, 'all discourse is occasioned'. All discourse takes place in specific social circumstances, and the authors discussed in this chapter draw two methodological implications for their sort of discourse analysis from this.

The previous section looked at some rhetorical strategies that could visually or verbally assert the truth of a particular discursive claim. However, this is not the only way that certain discourses can become more dominant than others: the *institutional location* of a discourse is also crucial. Foucault, for all his reluctance to ascribe unidirectional causality, insisted on the need to locate the social site from which particular statements are made, and to position the speaker of a statement in terms of their social authority (Foucault, 1972: 50–2). Thus a statement coming from a source endowed with authority (and just how that authority is established may be an important issue to address) is likely to be more productive than one coming from a marginalized social position. The work of the historians examined in this chapter demonstrates this point in a rather paradoxical way. For they are forced to rely almost entirely on the images and words of the socially and institutionally powerful in their discussions of the discursive construction of the East End, simply because they are the only visions and words that are now available. The powerful had the resources to make their discourses substantial through books and pictures, and these were the materials then put into libraries and archives. It is therefore extraordinarily difficult now to pick up traces of the discourses about the East End articulated by those who lived there in the 1880s, for example, although Fishman (1988) suggests that some contemporary novelists were the faithful recorders of what they heard there. Thus the social location of a discourse's production is important to consider in relation to its effects.

The second way in which the social context of discourse production matters is in terms of the *audience* assumed by images and texts. The explanation given for the same event may be quite different if the audience for that explanation is different. Or the visual images of the same scene or event may be quite different, in terms of their technology or genre or in other ways, for different audiences. The visual images that surrounded the Jack the Ripper murders in the East End in 1888 are a case in point. Popular newspapers, for example, used sketches and maps to show readers the location of the murders and the victims' faces, as Figure 6.8 demonstrates. This was a kind of realism that might be seen as the visual equivalent of the sensationalistic journalism pioneered in the same decade (Walkowitz, 1992). Other images were used for other audiences, though. Sander Gilman (1990), in his essay on the Ripper murders, notes that police photographs of the victims' mutilated bodies were used by the criminologist Alexandre Lacassagne in his 1889 book on sadism. The apparent veracity of photographs was thought necessary for a scientific text; but only an audience of scientists, too, was considered capable of seeing such images in an objective, scientific way. Notions about audience can thus affect the type of image used.

focus

Consider all the figures reproduced in this chapter. How might you go about finding the social locations of their production and reception? What does 'social location' mean in this sense? Does it mean class, gender, 'race', sexuality and so on? How might an institution be ascribed those characteristics?

Thus discourse analysis also entails paying attention to certain aspects of the social context of discourse production. The authors cited in this chapter – Gill, Tonkiss, Potter and Wetherell – tend to focus on the rhetorical organization of a discourse's texts and images and on the impact on those texts and images of the social location of their production. This emphasis neglects to explore the social practices and effects of discourse, however, and indicates the tendency of this sort of discourse analysis to focus more on texts and images than social institutions.

5 reflecting on doing discourse analysis I

Of course, from a Foucauldian perspective the social sciences are just as discursive as any other form of knowledge production, and in producing a piece of research you are participating in their discursive formation. The social sciences are the descendants of those human sciences the truth claims of which Foucault analysed in detail. If you are writing a discourse analysis, then, the arguments about discourse, power and truth/knowledge are just as pertinent to your work as to the materials you are analysing. Doing a discourse analysis demands some sort of critical reflection on your own research practice, then. For, as Tonkiss (1998: 259) says: 'the discourse analyst seeks to open up statements to challenge, interrogate taken-for-granted meanings, and disturb easy claims to objectivity in the texts they are reading. It would therefore be inconsistent to contend that the analyst's own discourse was itself wholly objective, factual or generally true.' Discourse analysts have a number of ways of addressing this issue.

The first is to think carefully about the rhetorical organization of a discourse analysis. How should it be written? Since discourse analyses cannot argue that they are the only, true analysis of the materials discussed, discourse analysis aims to be persuasive rather than truthful, and this entails 'a certain modesty in our analytic claims' (Tonkiss, 1998: 260). This modesty is what discourse analysis substitutes for more conventional notions of reflexivity. Clearly, conventional, autobiographical versions of reflexivity are difficult in Foucauldian accounts, for they depend on a notion of human agency that constructs the author as an autonomous individual who then encounters a part of the world in their research. Just as this autobiographical form of reflexivity is inconsistent with psycho-analytic approaches to visual methods, it is equally incompatible with the Foucauldian notion of a subject constituted through the discourses in which they are saturated. An example of a more modest, Foucauldian approach is Kendall and Wickham's (1999: 101–9) move, in their discussion of reflexivity in relation to Foucauldian methods, towards discussing whether non-human objects or animals should be given the same status as knowledge producers as their human researchers. Their answer is yes. In the visual field, perhaps an equivalent move would be to recognize the power of visual images which in some way limits that of the researcher. W.J.T. Mitchell (1996) has addressed this issue in an essay called 'What do pictures *really* want?'. Although reprimanded by Hal Foster (1996) for a kind of commodity fetishism – and this strategy is also vulnerable to the charge of hiding, under a cloak of respecting pictures, simply the critic's own version of what pictures want – Mitchell is perhaps articulating one form of reflexivity that makes sense for Foucauldian discourse analyses. There must be others, but all would share that mark of modesty mentioned by Tonkiss.

However, a complication to this discursive reflexivity arises when the productive context (rather than the rhetorical organization) of the analysis is considered. For being 'persuasive' or 'modest' depends on the interpretative context in which the discourse analysis is produced. And that context is the social sciences. Thus discourse analysis can end up with a rather conventional list of things to consider when writing up your work. Here are the sorts of things mentioned by Potter (1996: 138–9), Gill (1996: 147) and Tonkiss (1998: 258–60):

1   using detailed textual or visual evidence to support your analysis.
2   using textual or visual details to support your analysis.
3   the coherence the study gives to the discourse examined.
4   the coherence of the analysis itself.
5   the coherence of the study in relation to previous related research.
6   the examination of cases that run counter to the discursive norm established by the analysis, in order to affirm the disruption caused by such deviations.

Clearly, these criteria are unobjectionable in relation to the conventions of the social sciences. However, let us ask a Foucauldian question of them: what are the effects of these criteria? What do they produce? Well, they aim to produce a certain sort of text: one which locates the plausibility of the discourse analysis in the text alone. The effect of this is to erase (again, we might say) the institutional context in which a discourse analysis is produced. So perhaps another, reflexive strategy to mark the modesty of discourse analysis would be to note explicitly that that institution and its audience are the co-authors of the analysis, and to recognize the claims to interpretative authority that such co-authorship entails.

6   discourse analysis I: an assessment

In terms of the critical visual methodology described in Chapter 1, the type of discourse analysis discussed in this chapter has clear strengths. It pays careful attention to images themselves, and to the web of intertextuality in which any individual image is embedded. It is centrally concerned with the production of social difference through visual imagery. It addresses questions of power as they are articulated through visual images themselves. And although reflexivity is a difficult issue for discourse analysis, there are ways in which the authority of the discourse analysis can be both marked (by acknowledging its context of production) and perhaps undermined (by rhetorical strategies of modesty).

There are also some difficulties in the method, however. One of these is knowing where to stop in making intertextual connections, and another related to this is in grounding those connections empirically. Gilman's (1990) essay on Jack the Ripper illustrates the dangers (to me at least) of making so many connections that some start to seem rather tenuous. In order to understand why the murderer was seen by many as Jewish, Gilman cites a huge range of contemporary sources, including London newspapers, Wedekind's play and Berg's opera *Lulu*, Freud and Fliess, Hogarth, medical texts, Bram Stoker's novel *Dracula*, Hood's poetry, paintings, engravings and posters, Hahnemann (the founder of homeopathy), 'Jack's' notes, criminologists Lombroso and Lacassagne, contemporary pornography, *Daniel Deronda*, contemporary tracts, and Proust and Zola. The breadth of scholarship is extraordinary, but I begin to wonder how many of those sources could be said to have produced, even indirectly, the London newspapers' and police description of the Ripper as Jewish? Some, of course, perhaps many. Maybe all. But Gilman's analysis does not attempt to trace such connections in any grounded way; instead, they are related in his work simply through the category of 'discourse'. Discourse as a result seems to become a free-floating web of meanings unconnected to any social practices. The practical problem posed by this sort of discourse analysis, then – where to stop making intertextual connections – can also be an analytical one – how to make the intertextual connections convincingly productive.

Another problem with discourse analysis, for some critics, is its refusal to ascribe causality. As section 1 of this chapter noted, Foucault's project was in some ways descriptive; he wanted to account for how things happened more than why they happened. This means that discourse analysis too is not always very clear about the relation between discourse and its context. Few guidelines are offered about what that context might be, other than the notions addressed in section 4.2 here about the social location of the producers and audiences of specific images or texts. There is also little attempt to outline what the relations between that context and discourse might be, specifically.

Both these problems are connected to the neglected issue in this form of discourse analysis: the social practices of discourse. As this chapter has noted at several points, this kind of discourse analysis is concerned more with images and texts than with the social institutions that produced, archived, displayed or sold them, and the effects of those practices. The next chapter, however, turns to a form of Foucauldian discourse analysis that does address just these issues.

7 summary

- the complex theoretical legacy of Foucault has contributed to diverse methodological practices.
- discourse analysis I uses the notion of discourse to address the rhetorical organization and social production of visual, written and spoken materials.

- discourse analysis I is especially concerned to trace the production of social difference through discursive claims to truth.
- discourse analysis I tends to neglect the social practices and institutions through which discourses are articulated.

further reading

Tonkiss's (1998) chapter is a good general introduction to this form of discourse analysis, while Potter and Wetherell (1994) work through a detailed example of the method in relation to a television programme. As for Foucault, the secondary literature on him is now huge, but he is a much more accessible writer than many students imagine and I suggest trying *Discipline and Punish* (1977) as an introduction to his work.

7

discourse analysis II

institutions and ways of seeing

1 discourse and visual culture: a reprise

The previous chapter began with a brief introduction to the work of Michel Foucault, and suggested that there are two methodologies that have developed from his work. Although these two are related and overlap – most particularly because both share a concern with power/knowledge as it is articulated through discourse – these two methodologies have tended to produce rather different sorts of research. The first type of discourse analysis, discussed in Chapter 6, works with visual images and written or spoken texts. Although it is certainly concerned with the social positions of difference and authority that are articulated through images and texts, it tends to focus on the production and rhetorical organization of visual and textual materials.

In contrast, the second form of discourse analysis, which this chapter will explore, often works with similar sorts of materials, but is much more concerned with their production by, and their reiteration of, particular institutions and their practices, and their production of particular human subjects. This difference can be clarified by looking at how two exponents of these two kinds of discourse analysis use the term 'archive'. In her discussion of the first type of discourse analysis, Tonkiss (1998: 252) describes the material which that sort of analysis works with as an 'archive'. While Tonkiss puts the term in inverted commas, clearly aware that it carries a certain conceptual baggage, she nevertheless uses it to refer to her collection of data, and then moves on to consider what the data shows about certain discursive formations. However, a different kind of discourse analyst, like Alan Sekula (1986, 1989), would spend some time examining the archive itself as an institution, and unpacking the consequences of its particular practices of classification for the meanings of the things placed within it. Referring to archives of photographs in particular, he argues:

> Archives are not neutral; they embody the power inherent in accumu-
> lation, collection and hoarding as well as that power inherent in the
> command of the lexicon and rules of a language . . . any photographic
> archive, no matter how small, appeals indirectly to these institutions for
> its authority. (Sekula, 1986: 155)

No doubt Tonkiss would agree with this comment. However, Sekula is at pains to explore the effects of 'archivalization' on texts and images in a way that Tonkiss is not. Sekula and writers like him make that analytical move because they place their understandings of discourses firmly in relation to the account of institutions given by Foucault. Archives are one sort of institution, in the Foucauldian sense, and this second sort of ana-lysis would not treat them as transparent windows on to source materials in the way that Tonkiss seems to (see also Rose, 2000).

As we have seen, several of Foucault's books examine specific insti-tutions and their disciplines: prisons, hospitals, asylums. For writers con-cerned with visual matters, perhaps the key text is *Discipline and Punish* (Foucault, 1977). Subtitled *The Birth of the Prison*, this is an account of changing penal organization in post-medieval Europe, in which alterations to the organization of visuality (and spatiality) are central. The book begins by quoting a contemporary account of a prolonged torture and execution carried out as a public spectacle in 1757. Foucault then quotes from a prison rulebook written 80 years later which is, as he says, a timetable. Foucault's questions are, how (rather than why) did this change in penal style, from spectacular punishment to institutional routine, take place? And with what effects? Through detailed readings of contemporary texts, *Discipline and Punish* traces this shift. By the mid-nineteenth century:

> The punishment–body relation is not the same as it was in the torture
> during public executions. The body now serves as an instrument or
> intermediary: if one intervenes upon it to imprison it, or to make it work, it
> is in order to deprive the individual of a liberty that is regarded both as a
> right and as a property. The body, according to this penality, is caught up
> in a system of constraints and privations, obligations and prohibitions.
> Physical pain, the pain of the body itself, is no longer the constituent
> element of the penalty. From being an art of unbearable sensation punish-
> ment has become an economy of suspended rights . . . As a result of this
> new restraint, a whole army of technicians took over from the executioner,
> the immediate anatomist of pain: warders, doctors, chaplains, psy-
> chiatrists, psychologists, educationalists. (Foucault, 1977: 11)

The prison was born. As well as a new institution and a new understanding of punishment, in *Discipline and Punish* Foucault describes the emergence of a new set of professions who defined who needed punishment and who could exercise that punishment, and of a new subjectivity produced for those so punished: what he called the 'docile body'. This was the body subjected to these new penal disciplines, the body which had to conform to its 'constraints and privations, obligations and prohibitions'.

A key point of Foucault's argument is that in this new regime of punishment, these docile bodies in a sense disciplined themselves. Foucault argues that this was achieved through a certain visuality (for general discussions of the role of visuality in the work of Foucault, see Jay, 1993 and Rajchman, 1988). Once defined by the new 'expert' knowledges as in some way deviant, these bodies were placed in an institution that was 'a machine for altering minds' (Foucault, 1977: 125). Foucault (1977: 195–228) expands this point, and demonstrates the importance of a visuality to it, by discussing a plan for an institution designed by Jeremy Bentham in **Panopticon** 1791. Bentham called this building a **panopticon**, and suggested it could be used as the plan for all sorts of disciplining institutions: prisons, but also hospitals, workhouses, schools, madhouses. The panopticon was a tall tower, surrounded by an annular building. The latter consisted of cells, one for each inmate, with windows so arranged that the occupant was always visible from the tower. The tower was the location of the supervisor, but because of the arrangement of its windows, blinds, doors and corridors the inmates in their cells could never be certain that they were under observation from the tower at any particular moment. Never certain of invisibility, each inmate therefore had to behave 'properly' all the time: thus they disciplined themselves and were produced as docile bodies. 'Hence the major effect of the Panopticon: to induce in the inmate a state of conscious and permanent visibility that assures the automatic functioning of power' (Foucault, 1977: 210). This sort of visuality, in which one subject is seen without ever seeing, and the other sees without **Surveillance** ever being seen, Foucault called **surveillance**, and he argued that, since it was an efficient means of producing social order, it became a dominant form of visuality throughout modern capitalist societies. Through its operation, says Foucault (1977: 200), in an echo of Lacan, 'visibility is a trap'.

Foucault suggests that institutions work in two ways: through their apparatus and through their technologies. This is a distinction this chapter will use. However, Foucault was rather inconsistent in his use of these terms, and the distinction made here between them is clearer than that **Institutional** found in his work. An **institutional apparatus** is the forms of power/ **apparatus** knowledge which constitute the institutions: for example, architecture, regulations, scientific treatises, philosophical statements, laws, morals, and so on, and the discourse articulated through all these (Hall, 1997b: 47). Hence Foucault described Bentham's panopticon as an apparatus: at once **Institutional** an architectural design and a moral and philosophical treatise. The **institu- technologies** **tional technologies** (sometimes difficult to differentiate from the apparatus) are the practical techniques used to practise that power/knowledge.

Technologies are 'diffuse, rarely formulated in continuous, systematic discourse . . . often made up of bits and pieces . . . a disparate set of tools and methods' (Foucault, 1977: 26). An example might be the design of the windows and blinds in the panopticon.

It has been argued by some historians of photography that it must be understood as a technology in this Foucauldian sense. John Tagg, for example, writes:

> Photography as such has no identity. Its status as technology varies with the power relations that invest it. Its nature as a practice depends on the institutions and agents which define it and set it to work . . . Its history has no unity. It is a flickering across a field of institutional spaces. It is this field we must study, not photography as such. (Tagg, 1988: 63)

For Tagg, photography is diffuse; it is given coherence only by its use in certain institutional apparatuses. He elaborates this claim by studying photographs as they were used in the nineteenth century by police forces, prisons, orphanages, asylums, local government's medical officers of health, and newspaper journalists and publicists. Its uses in these institutions, Tagg argues, give photography its status as a unified something rather than a diffuse no one thing, and that coherent something is, according to Tagg, the belief that photographs picture the real. (Hence he is very critical of Barthes's 1982 assertion, discussed in section 3.2 of Chapter 4, that the *punctum* of a photograph is a trace of an uncoded referent.) The apparatus of these various institutions – the police, prisons, orphanages, asylums, local government, the emergent mass media – asserted the truth of their claims to be able to detect, punish, or cure the criminal, the ill, the orphaned, the mad, the degenerate (in part by relying on the scientific status of the discourses of physiognomy and phrenology, discussed in the previous chapter). Producing a certain regime of truth, these institutions used photography as a crucial technology through which these distinctions were made visible. The related opposite of this, as Sekula (1989) notes, was the detection, celebration and honouring of the moral, the familial and the proper in bourgeois photographic portraiture. Thus the institutional uses of photography make us think photographs are truthful pictures, not photographic techniques themselves. For Tagg, then (and see also Lalvani, 1996; Sekula, 1989), Foucault's emphasis on institutions and power/knowledge is crucial for understanding the belief that photography pictures the real.

This emphasis on institutional apparatus and technologies gives a different inflection to this second kind of discourse analysis. It shifts attention away from the details of individual images – although both Tagg (1988) and Sekula (1989) describe the general characteristics of particular types of photographs – and towards the processes of their production and use. That is, this type of discourse analysis concentrates most on the sites of *production* and *audiencing*, in their *social modality*. In their discussion of nineteenth-century police photography, for example, both Sekula and Tagg pay a good deal of attention to the processes used to classify, file, retrieve and use photographs of those who had been pictured as 'criminal'. Both also argue that photography was only one part of what Sekula (1989: 351) calls 'a bureaucratic-clerical-statistical system of "intelligence"', and he suggests that the filing cabinet was actually a more important piece of institutional technology than the camera. They discuss other technologies – such as phrenology and fingerprinting – that were used alongside photography, and explore other aspects of institutional apparatuses in their studies too. This means that the sources used in their accounts are as eclectic as those of the discourse analysts discussed in Chapter 6. However, certainly in the case of Tagg and Sekula, their work is held together by an insistence on the power relations articulated through these practices and institutions. Visual images and visualities are for them articulations of institutional power.

This is one aspect of their work that has been criticized. For although both take care to distinguish their Foucauldian understanding of power from those who see power simply as repressive, nonetheless there is very little sense in either of their work of the possibility of visualities other than those of dominant institutions. Lindsay Smith (1998), for example, takes them to task for not looking at a wide enough range of nineteenth-century photographic practices, and in particular for neglecting the kinds of domestic photography practised by a number of women in the mid-nineteenth century. These women photographers can be seen as producing images that do not replicate the surveillant gaze of the police mug-shot or the family studio portrait: they thwart that classifying gaze by strategies such as blurred focus, collage and over-exposure. Moreover, like their discourse analyst cousins whose work was discussed in the previous chapter, there is very little reflexivity in this second type of discourse-analytic work. Ironically, considering their critique of truth claims, Tagg and Sekula both make very strong claims themselves about the veracity of their accounts. Tagg (1988: 1–2) in particular is quite scathing about Barthes, implying that Barthes's insistence on the uncoded quality of certain photographs was merely an emotional response to his search for a photograph that would remind him of his mother after she had died. 'I need not point out,' says Tagg (1988: 2) 'that the existence of a photograph is no guarantee of a corresponding pre-photographic existent.' Tagg here counterposes the self-evident ('I need not point out'), which he later expands at great length with the use of much theory, to the emotional need driving Barthes's work. As I read it, Tagg is making an opposition between his masculinized rationality and what he sees as the effeminate emotionality of the grieving Barthes. Hardly a self-reflexive strategy, I think.

This chapter though will not focus on the work of Tagg or Sekula and their interest in photographic archives. Rather, it will turn to work that considers two other kinds of institutions which deal with visual objects – the art gallery and the museum – and which have also been subject to

Foucauldian critique by writers such as Tony Bennett (1995) and Eilean Hooper-Greenhill (1992). (Other important discussions include the essays collected by Barker, 1999; Greenberg et al., 1996; Sherman and Rogoff, 1994; Vergo, 1989.) These accounts explore how visual images and objects are produced in particular ways by institutional apparatuses and technologies (as 'art', for example) and how various subjectivities are also produced, such as the 'curator' and 'the visitor'. However, these are institutions, which while of course not free from the workings of power, are not as obviously coercive as those examined by Tagg and Sekula. Their disciplines are more subtle, and thus they provide a more fruitful ground for exploring the extent to which this second type of discourse analysis can address questions of conflicting discourses and contested ways of seeing. The particular case study will be the American Museum of Natural History in New York (hereafter referred to as the AMNH), as seen by Donna Haraway (1989: 26–58), Ann Reynolds (1995) and Mieke Bal (1996: 13–56) (although Bal's account also incorporates a semiological approach). Their accounts will allow another opportunity to consider the possibility of a reflexive discourse-analytic practice.

The status of the art gallery and museum as institution provides a way of examining the methodology of this second kind of discourse analysis. So, this chapter will:

- examine ways of describing the apparatus of the art gallery and the museum;
- examine ways of describing the technologies of the art gallery and the museum;
- examine how this second kind of discourse analysis argues that these institutions produce and discipline their visitors;
- assess the strengths and weaknesses of this type of discourse analysis of institutions.

2   the sources for discourse analysis II

The kinds of sources used for this type of discourse analysis are as diverse as those deployed by the discourse analysis discussed in Chapter 6. A key Foucauldian account of the emergence of the art gallery and the museum as particular kinds of institutions is Tony Bennett's *The Birth of the Museum* (1995), and he is typical in his use of a wide range of sources. He undertakes a careful reading of the many *written texts* that discussed museums and galleries in the second half of the nineteenth century. These were produced by reformers, philanthropists, civil servants and curators who were all arguing, though often in different ways, for the establishment of galleries and museums that were open to the public. Studies of current discussions about museums and their practices supplement this sort of historical written source with other types of documents available now, such as the annual reports of galleries and museums and their mission statements. *Interviews* with the directors, curators and designers of museums and galleries can also be used in contemporary studies. Both historical and contemporary studies often use photographs or other *visual images* of buildings, rooms and displays too, sometimes simply as illustrations to their written accounts, and both also pay attention to the *architecture* of the institution: its design, decorations, inscriptions, layout and so on. Studies of contemporary museums and galleries also often rely on visits to the institution and *observation* of the way people visit and work in them.

In relation to studies of the AMNH, both Haraway (1989) and Reynolds (1995) are historical accounts of particular halls of that museum, and so they use written texts such as the autobiographies of curators, the minutes of museum committee meetings, scientific texts and the museum's annual reports; Haraway (1989) supplements this with an account of what the hall she is interested in looks like to the visitor now: or, at least, what it looks like to Haraway. Both illustrate their arguments using photographs of museum displays and other images. Bal's (1996) account is a reading of a few halls of the museum based entirely on their layout and the displays on show to the visitor in late 1991. (Her study is also interesting in the way it uses illustrations to make her points, as well as written text.)

---

focus

Visit a gallery or a museum. When we visit a museum or a gallery, it is somehow clear that certain things are 'the objects to be looked at': the paintings, the objects, the items in the shop. This time, spend time looking at other things: the architecture of the building, for example, its floor plan, its warders, its other visitors.

---

3 the apparatus of the gallery and the museum

As Stephen Bann comments, the history of museums can be interpreted:

> *grosso modo* in terms of two conceptually distinct phases. The first, roughly speaking up to the end of the eighteenth century, qualifies as a 'prehistory' in the sense that the collection and display of objects appears to answer no clear principles of ordering by genre, school, and period. The second, which represents an almost irresistible movement towards conformity over the course of the last two centuries, is a history in which the museum has developed and perfected its own principles of ordering by giving spatial distribution to the concepts of school and period, in particular. (Bann, 1998: 231; see also Hooper-Greenhill, 1992)

Bennett's (1995) discussion of museums and galleries focuses on the second of these phases, and draws much theoretical inspiration from Foucault's *Discipline and Punish: The Birth of the Prison* (1977). Bennett points out that both prisons and modern museums were born in broadly the same historical period, and he argues that they deployed a similar disciplining surveillance. In making this claim, Bennett interprets his sources using the kinds of methods discussed in the previous chapter. Thus he too looks for *key themes*, for *truth claims*, for *complexity* and for *absences* (see Chapter 6, section 4.1). He pays attention to the diversity of ways in which public museums and galleries were justified by nineteenth-century commentators, noting, for example, that they were defended as an antidote to working-class men's drunkenness, as an alternative to working-class disaffection and riot, and as a means to civilize manners and morals. But his overall emphasis is very much on the way this discursive formation produced the museum as a disciplining machine:

> The museum, in providing a new setting for works of culture, also functioned as a technological environment which allowed cultural arte-facts to be refashioned in ways that would facilitate their deployment for new purposes as part of governmental programmes aimed at reshaping general norms of social behaviour. (Bennett, 1995: 6)

His concern, then, is with the power that saturated the museum and gallery, and he explores that power in terms of those institutions' appara-tuses. In particular, he focuses on particular discourses of culture and science that shaped their design and practice, and also produced certain subject positions. Hooper-Greenhill (1992: 176) too is interested in the way 'new technologies and new subject positions were constituted through the adminstration of [a museum's] newly acquired material'.

Bennett argues that there was a specific discourse of 'culture' which saturated the births of the museum and gallery. Using the sources men-tioned in section 2, he argues that the power of museums and galleries had the same aim: both use 'culture' as a tool of social management. He notes that the definition of 'culture' used in the two sorts of institutions is somewhat different and that does produce some differences between them, especially in the sorts of objects they display. In the museum, 'culture' tends to refer to that later nineteenth-century understanding of culture as 'a whole way of life', and museums often collect objects that are meant to exemplify the way of life of particular social groups. In the nineteenth century, this meant that museums collected and displayed the artefacts of colonized peoples, but these peoples were also seen as less cultured and more natural than those of the West. (Annie Coombes, 1994 discusses nineteenth-century displays of African artefacts in European and North American museums in her book *Reinventing Africa* and Cathine Lutz and Jane Collins (1993) in their study of *National Geographic* magazine demonstrate the persistence of this notion.) Bal's (1996) account of her

1991 visit to the AMNH emphasizes its continued articulation of imperialist, white discourse, noting that halls showing the way of life of certain third world peoples are entered directly after halls displaying stuffed mammals and birds, thus implying that certain cultural groups are closer to nature than others. Galleries, on the other hand, work with an older definition of 'culture' as that which can ennoble the human spirit, and the objects they display are those defined as Art (see the focus in Chapter 2 section 3.5 for more on this notion of Art). Such objects – usually paintings and sculpture from Western traditions – are then also constituted as 'Art', and as noble and uplifting, by being on display.

Bennett also discusses, more briefly, a specific discourse of science that was part of the museum's apparatus of power. In museums, he notes, objects are always classified according to what are claimed to be 'scientific' or 'objective' principles, whether they be drawn from notions of historical progress, scientific rationality or anthropological analysis.

Bal (1996) remarks that differentiations made by the complex discourse of culture are expressed in the gallery and museum that flank either side of Central Park in New York; on the one side, the AMNH, on the other, the Metropolitan Museum of Art:

> By this very division of the city map, the universal concept of 'humanity' is filled with specific meaning. The division of 'culture' and 'nature' between the East Side and the West Side of Manhattan relegates the large majority of the world's population to the status of static being, assigning to a small portion only the higher status of art producers in history. Where 'nature', in the [AMNH] dioramas, is a backdrop, transfixed in stasis, 'art', presented in the Met as an ineluctable evolution, is endowed with a story. (Bal, 1996: 15–16)

Bennett (1995) also pays much attention to the way the *architecture* of museums and galleries articulated these various discourses of culture, art and science. As well as the distinction between two sorts of building – the museum and the gallery – there are the imposing *façades* and *entrance halls* of many nineteenth-century galleries and museums, for example, which were designed to be as inspiring and uplifting as the understanding of culture and science articulated within. Haraway looks at the façade of the Theodore Roosevelt Memorial – the main building of the AMNH – and considers the effects of its design:

> The facade of the memorial . . . is classical, with four Ionic columns 54 feet high topped by statues of the great explorers Boone, Audubon, Lewis and Clark. The coin-like, bas-relief seals of the United States and of the Liberty Bell are stamped on the front panels. Inscribed across the top are the words TRUTH, KNOWLEDGE, VISION and the dedication to Roosevelt as 'a great leader of the youth of America, in energy and

fortitude in the faith of our fathers, in defense of the rights of the people, in the love and conservation of nature and of the best in life and in man'. Youth, paternal solicitude, virile defense of democracy, and intense emotional connection to nature are the unmistakable themes. (Haraway, 1989: 27)

The *internal layout* also echoes the discourses of science and culture. In the case of galleries, for example, paintings are hung in groups in separate rooms according to periods and (often national) schools, and this works to naturalize these periods, schools and nations, and also to produce a narrative of development from medieval painting to the present day (Bal's art production in history; see also Bann, 1998).

As well as these architectural articulations, Bennett (1995) is especially concerned to examine the *social subjectivities* produced through these discursive apparatuses. The strong emphasis he places on how discourse produces social positions, and the consequences for how museums were designed and policed, distinguishes his study from many of those that rely on the type of discourse analysis examined in Chapter 6. He identifies three subject positions produced by the museum and gallery. First, there were the patrons of these new institutions. Thus he is clear that the emergent 'experts' on museum and gallery policy and patronage were white middle-class men, their social position produced through their claims to 'expertness' as well as through the larger discourses of capitalism, patriarchy and racism. Similarly, Haraway (1989: 54–8), in her discussion of the AMNH as 'institution' in the early twentieth century, carefully explores the intersecting discourses of eugenics, exhibition and conservation that were mobilized to justify the founding of the museum, and also notes those three discursive themes were all 'prescriptions against decadence, the dread disease of imperialist, capitalist, white culture' (Haraway, 1989: 55). The museum's funders were precisely representatives of 'imperialist, capitalist, white culture', and thus she too is clear on the coincidence between the discourses of the museum and the wider power relations of society. Richard Bolton (1989) offers a more recent example of the effects of exhibition patronage in his discussion of the sponsorship of an exhibition of Richard Avedon photographs at the Institute of Contemporary Art in Boston by a local department store.

Second, there were the scientists and curators: the technical experts, if you like, who operationalize those discourses of culture and science in their classifying and displaying practices (section 4.5 will return to these latter practices; Bennett pays them little attention). Third, there are the visitors. The visitor with whom the nineteenth-century patrons of museums and galleries were most concerned was produced as the morally weak, probably drunk, working-class man. The contemplation of art and the appreciation of museums' knowledge was constructed discursively by these patrons as involving particular ways of visiting museums and galleries, and Bennett (1995) argues that these ways involved orderly appreciation rather than unruly entertainment. In ways he less than convincingly demonstrates, he argues that both sorts of institutions disciplined their visitors into what were seen as civilized ways of behaving. Bennett again pays some attention to the visual and spatial aspects of museums and galleries when making this argument, examining architectural plans and noting the way that surveillance of other visitors was often built into the designs of these institutions; he also reproduces some contemporary photographs of museums and exhibitions taken from positions which he claims again articulate the surveillant quality of these spaces. He thus suggests that museums and galleries worked to regulate social behaviour by producing docile bodies. Reynolds (1995) discusses a hall of the AMNH in the 1950s, and notes how it too assumed, addressed and produced a very specific audience, again one in apparent need of education: city dwellers.

Bennett (1995) also makes a distinction between the construction of the gallery visitor and the museum visitor, though. Galleries, he argues, rely on a notion of Art that always remains implicit:

> In art galleries [Art] theory, understood as a particular set of explanatory and evaluative categories and principles of classification, mediates the relations between the visitor and the art on display in such a way that, for some but not for others, seeing the art exhibited serves as a means of *seeing through* those artefacts to see an invisible order of significance that they have been arranged to represent. (Bennett, 1995: 165)

Following the work of Bourdieu and Darbel (1991), who found that the visitors to art galleries were overwhelmingly bourgeois, he argues that this particular sort of Art theory is understood only by middle-class gallery-goers because only they have been allowed access to the sort of education that considers Art. This is a problematic claim and Bennett himself worries that it is too crude in the class categories it uses; nevertheless, Bennett concludes that art galleries remain obscure places to some social groups, and that this is a contradiction at the heart of their institutional apparatus. In contrast, museums often do make their classification systems as explicit; Henrietta Lidchi (1997), for example, in her account of an exhibition that opened at the Museum of Mankind in London in 1993 which sought to portray the way of life of the Wahgi people on Papua New Guinea, shows the way the exhibition admitted to its own practices of collection and reconstruction. This admission produced a visitor capable of critique, a possibility Bennett suggests is not available in galleries. However, the question of how visitors actually do look in museums and galleries is one that none of these writers address; indeed, Bennett (1995: 11) notes explicitly that he is less interested in the visitors to museums and galleries than in their institutional apparatuses. No reason is given for this absence, and it is an absence that occurs in all the studies of the AMNH. Section 4 of this chapter will return to it.

This section's discussion of the discourses that were part of the institutional apparatus of the museum and gallery has been partial. Bennett (1995) ranges more widely in his book; for example, he explores the role of national government in funding public museums and galleries, and notes that this makes the visitors to museums and galleries citizens instead of, or perhaps as well as, docile bodies, and was therefore a potentially democratizing move. Similarly, writers on the AMNH draw on a range of institutions, practices and sites in order to describe the multiplicity of meanings residing in that institution. Haraway (1989), for example, suggests that in order to understand the dioramas in the Akeley African Hall, it is necessary to understand not only the practices of diorama and taxidermy, but of early twentieth-century safaris too, the role played in them by photography, and the wider discourses of nature, culture, patriarchal masculinity, eugenics, conservation and so on that were articulated through them. However, the broad aims of these discussions of the institutional apparatus are I hope clear. In their explorations of institutional apparatuses, these discourse analysts of institutional power/ knowledge focus not only on discourses about museums and galleries, but also on how those discourses are materialized in the forms of architecture and subject positions. Their concern is always with the intersection of power/knowledge and with the production of differentiated subject positions.

4   the technologies of the gallery and museum

Section 1 of this chapter defined institutional technologies as the practical techniques used to articulate particular forms of power/knowledge: 'the techniques of effecting meanings' (Haraway, 1989: 35). Foucault described them as diffuse and disparate sets of bits and pieces, and this section will enumerate some of these bits and pieces as they work in museums and galleries. The question posed by this second type of discourse analysis is, again, what the effects of certain technologies are in terms of what they produce; and Bann (1998) insists that this question demands carefully detailed and historically sensitive empirical answers. All the studies of museum and gallery technologies discussed here focus on the public display areas of the institution in question.

4.1   technologies of display

Section 3 has already touched on some aspects of how images and objects are displayed in museums and galleries, but on the large scale: how buildings are differentiated into museums or galleries, how whole rooms are labelled and how this then classifies objects and paintings in particular ways. This section will focus instead on more small-scale techniques of display. These are usually accessed by researchers through visits to museums or galleries, or through historical documentation. In museums, several technologies of display are available (Lidchi, 1997: 172):

1 *display cases*, mounted either on walls or on tables.
2 *open display*, with no protective cover.
3 *reconstructions*, which are supposedly life-like scenes. The dioramas discussed by Haraway (1989) in the AMNH are a particular sort of reconstruction.
4 *simulacra*: objects made by the museum in order to fill a gap in their collection.

Each of these different display techniques can have rather different effects, and their precise effects very often depend on their intersection with other technologies, especially written text. For example, Lidchi (1997: 173) suggests that reconstructions in museums usually consist of everyday objects put together with some kind of reference to their everyday use. Reconstructions thus depend on the presence of 'real' artefacts in an 'accurate' combination, and this makes their display seem truthful; although, as Lidchi also points out, this effect also depends on the visitor's prior faith in the accuracy of the anthropological knowledge used to make the display. Glass display cases, on the other hand, produce a truth not in relation to the apparent representational accuracy of what is on display, but in relation to the classification system of the museum. When placed in a case, an object is dislocated from the everyday context that reconstructions attempt to evoke, and is instead placed in the classificatory schema of the museum. Again though, given the truth regime of the museum as an institution, the effect on the visitor is of a truth: an analytic one this time rather than a representational one.

All the discussions of the AMNH pay a good deal of attention to the social meanings produced through the 'truthful' display of exhibits in their cases or dioramas. These discussions often focus on the effects of the *spatial organization* of displays: how different objects are placed in relation to one another. Haraway (1989: 30), for example, says that in the dioramas showing stuffed large African mammals against painted back-drops of their natural habitat, 'most groups are made up of only a few animals, usually a large and vigilant male, a female or two, and one baby . . . The groups are peaceful, composed, illuminated . . . Each group forms a community structured by a natural division of function . . . these habitat groups . . . tell of communities and families, peacefully and hierarchically ordered. Sexual specialization of function – the organic bodily and social sexual division of labour – is unobtrusively ubiquitous, unquestionable, right.' Thus patriarchy is naturalized, she says. Similarly, Bal (1996: 40–2) looks at a glass display case in the AMNH's Hall of African Peoples which, according to its caption, contains objects that show the hybridization of Christianity with indigenous African religions. However, Bal notes that the display is dominated by a large carving in the centre of the case of a Madonna and child: thus 'my overall impression of this exhibit is its emphasis on Christianity' (Bal, 1996: 42).

Reynolds's (1995) discussion of the Felix Warburg Man and Nature Hall in the AMNH, which opened in 1951, is an especially detailed exploration of the way of seeing invited by a particular group of displays. The displays in this hall refuse the apparent reality of the dioramas that Haraway (1989) discusses. Instead, Reynolds shows how they offer a visually and spatially fragmented, and clearly illusionistic, series of views of a landscape that draw the visitor closer in for a detailed look at each of the component parts. The effect, 'through foregrounding the very devices of illusionism', says Reynolds (1995: 99), is to transform 'the visitors' eyes into magnifying glasses, microscopes, or scalpels, which could reveal the invisible workings of a previously familiar but superficially understood natural world'. Hence the spatial organization of these displays still produces a reality effect, but it is a rather different one from those that Haraway (1989) and Bal (1996) explore.

In the case of the gallery, consider how the images are *framed* and *hung*. Paintings are now very often hung in a single row around the walls of a room, inviting you to follow them round, looking at each one in turn. That is, they are hung as individual images. This is a twentieth-century practice (Celant, 1996; Waterfield, 1991); in the nineteenth century, it was very common instead for the walls of galleries to be packed almost from floor to ceiling with paintings. This change is associated with increasingly detailed modes of classification and changing notions of Art. The discourse of Art as something to be contemplated for universal truths, which section 3 of this chapter described (see also section 3.5 of Chapter 2), became widespread in the twentieth century, and it changed hanging practices. If paintings are hung side by side, it is possible to contemplate each of them individually as pieces of Art. This also has an effect on the viewer: to encourage that contemplative way of viewing (Duncan, 1995). The combination of this kind of hanging with the layout of galleries often heightens this effect. As Jean-François Lyotard says of the spectator at an exhibition:

> – the visitor is an eye. The way he looks, not only at the works exhibited but also at the place where the exhibition takes place, is supposedly governed by the principles of 'legitimate construction' established in the *quattrocento*: the geometry of the domination over perceptual space. (Lyotard, 1996: 167)

Thus it could be argued that both the image and the viewer are individualized through this technology of hanging, and that viewers are produced as contemplative eyes and paintings as objects to be contemplated.

focus

What technologies of display are used in the gallery or museum you visited? Is the list of possibilities provided in this section adequate to their description? Or are there technologies of display that you want to consider?

4.2 textual and visual technologies of interpretation

These sorts of display effects always work in conjunction with other technologies, especially written and visual ones. There are a number of textual technologies to consider, and they can be interpreted using the tools of the first kind of discourse analysis, described in Chapter 6.

1 *labels and captions*. These are a key way in which objects and images are produced in particular ways. For example, in a gallery, a painting will always have a caption with the name of the artist; it will almost always have the date of the painting and its title, and very often the materials it was made with. These apparently innocuous pieces of information nonetheless work to prioritize certain sorts of information about paintings over others. In particular, it makes the artist the most important aspect of the painting, in accordance with the notions of Art and genius examined in section 3.5 of Chapter 2; whereas Chapter 1 was at pains to suggest that there are many other aspects of an image which are much more important than who made it. In a museum, labels have similar effects; they make some aspects of the objects on display more important than others. Bal (1991: 32) notes that labels and captions at the AMNH almost always deploy a rhetoric of realism – 'realism, the description of a world so lifelike that omissions are unnoticed, elisions sustained, and repressions invisible' – which makes it difficult for visitors to question the kinds of knowledge they offer.
2 *panels*. Both galleries and museums often have large display panels of text in their display rooms. These often provide some sort of wider context for the objects or images on display. In the case of the exhibition discussed by Lidchi (1997), the panels were where the exhibition's practices of representation were made explicit. Panels are often more explicitly interpretive than labels and captions.
3 *catalogues*. Most larger exhibitions, and many galleries and museums, produce catalogues for sale. These too are part of their technologies of interpretation. Like labels, captions and display panels, though, they convey very particular kinds of knowledge.

focus

Look at the labels and captions in the museum or gallery you're visiting. What might be the effect of taking all the labels and captions away? Take two or three images or objects and invent some new labels for them. What kind of effects are you aiming for in your new text? Bal (1996) also suggests some strategies for undermining the realism of museum labels and captions.

Visual technologies can also shape the effects of a museum or gallery. Museums often use photographs as part of display panels or catalogues to show what the use of an object 'really' was, or to assert the authenticity of an object on display by showing a picture of it, or one like it, in its original context of use. Galleries use photographs in display panels much less often, but their catalogues often have them, again usually as apparently documentary images.

All of these visual and textual technologies can be examined using the method of discourse analysis described in Chapter 6. Read them for their key themes, their claims to truth, their complexities and their silences.

4.3 technologies of layout

Section 3 has already touched on aspects of the overall layout of museum and gallery space. Here some of its smaller-scale spatial and visual effects will be explored.

First, there is the *layout* of an individual room. As Kevin Hetherington (1997: 215) says, 'as classifying machines, museums have to deal with heterogeneity through the distribution of effects in space'. Hence the importance of the spatial organization of displays and buildings, but also of rooms. Haraway's (1989) discussion of the Akeley African Hall in the AMNH describes the effect of its spatial organization by means of an analogy:

> The Hall is darkened, lit only from the display cases which line the sides of the spacious room. In the center of the Hall is a group of elephants so lifelike that a moment's fantasy suffices for awakening a premonition of their movement, perhaps an angry charge at one's personal intrusion. The elephants stand like a high altar in the nave of a great cathedral. The impression is strengthened by one's growing consciousness of the dioramas that line both sides of the main Hall and the spacious gallery above. Lit from within, the dioramas contain detailed and lifelike groups of large African mammals – game for the wealthy New York hunters who financed this experience . . . each diorama presents itself as a side altar, a stage, an unspoiled garden in nature, a hearth for home and

family . . . Above all, inviting the visitor to share its revelation, each tells the truth. Each offers a vision. Each is a window into knowledge. (Haraway, 1989: 29)

Here, Haraway considers the relation established between elements in the room, and writes to convey the effect of their combination. She emphasizes the coherence of this hall, both in its spatial organization and in its effects. Hetherington (1997), on the other hand, reminds us that museum and gallery spaces can also be incoherent. Particular objects can disrupt the symmetry or the clarity of the museum or gallery layout, for example.

Rooms can also be *decorated* in particular ways, with particular effects. In galleries of modern art, and also in galleries showing photography as art, the walls are often painted white and any seating is modern and minimal. This practice of display became common after World War II, and Duncan (1993) argues that it was encouraged by the insistence of the Museum of Modern Art in New York that that was how its big touring exhibition of post-war abstract expressionist American art should be shown. Duncan places this exhibition in the context of US attempts to assert its cultural dominance in the Cold War. The effects of this mode of display are suggested by Brian O'Doherty (1996: 321–2): 'the new god, extensive, homogeneous space, flowed easily into every part of the gallery. All impediments except "art" were removed . . . the empty gallery [is] now full of that elastic space we call Mind.' O'Doherty is suggesting that the minimality of the white gallery space again produces the Art work as something to be contemplated separately from any other distractions; and again, it produces the visitor to such galleries as simply an eye unencumbered by considerations other than looking (see also Grunenberg, 1999).

focus

By no means all galleries have white walls, and few museums do. In the museum or gallery you visited, what other elements of decoration were important? What about coloured wall coverings, lighting, carpet, screens, other objects? What effects did they produce? If you visited a gallery that had white walls in some of its rooms and not in others, what was the difference between the white and non-white rooms, in terms of their objects on display and the effects created?

4.4 tactile technologies

One of the most important disciplines of museum and gallery spaces for visitors is the almost universal rule that you cannot touch the exhibits. This is enforced in a number of ways: objects are placed in glass cases, ropes are placed in front of paintings, warders watch visitors. Again, the Foucauldian question must be, what kind of subjectivities does this produce? Obviously, it produces a visitor who looks rather than touches (again).

focus

So far, this section has listed a number of 'bits and pieces' that are used in museums and galleries. It has focused on their possible effects in terms of the productivity of their power/knowledge; that is, on how they produce certain knowledges about paintings and objects, and certain subjectivities of visiting and curating.

Does the gallery or museum you have visited use any other technologies to produce particular interpretations of its contents or visitors?

4.5   spaces behind the displays

The rooms in which objects are displayed are of course only some of the spaces through which a museum's or a gallery's power/knowledge works. There are also the *stores* and the *archives*, the *laboratories* and the *libraries*, the *offices* and *service areas*. As Hooper-Greenhill (1992: 7) notes, these spaces are not open to the public (although researchers can often gain access) because they are the spaces in which the museums and galleries produce their knowledges. They are the spaces in which the museum professionals such as curators, restorers, designers and managers work; the spaces in which the classification schemes that structure the public display areas are put into practice:

> A division [is] drawn . . . between knowing subjects, between the producers and consumers of knowledge, between expert and layman . . . In the public museum, the producing subject 'works' in the hidden spaces of the museum, while the consuming subject 'works' in the public spaces. Relations within the institution are skewed to privilege the hidden, productive 'work' of the museum, the production of knowledge through the compilation of catalogues, inventories and installations. (Hooper-Greenhill, 1992: 190)

Yet very little attention is paid by Foucauldian studies of museums and galleries to these spaces and their particular technologies. Indeed Bal (1996: 16) argues that the curators and other museum staff who work in these spaces are 'only a tiny connection in a long chain of subjects' and are therefore not worth studying in any detail. Bann (1998) however demurs, and I too find this rather an odd omission. While writers like Bal (1996) and Hetherington (1997) are happy to explore the discursive contradictions of museums' and galleries' display spaces, they seem uninterested in the possibly more subversive contradictions at work in the behind-the-scenes practices that operationalize those institutions' regimes of truth. If, as Bann (1998: 239) argues, there are 'internal contradictions built into the development of the modern museum', they too require investigation and might perhaps be best seen in these hidden spaces.

focus

Few of these accounts of museums and galleries deal in any detail with what are now surely two more key spaces which visitors to these institutions encounter: the *shop* and the *café*. Visit the shop and café of your museum or gallery. What sorts of discourses are at work here? What sorts of practices? Are they connected to those of the display spaces? If so, how? If not, how not? Could you use the methods used by the discourse analysts in this chapter to examine the productivities of these spaces?

5 the visitor

Sections 3 and 4 have both noted that, according to these Foucauldian accounts of museums and galleries, as well as producing the images and objects in their possession in particular ways, these institutions also produce a certain sort of visitor. This visitor is perhaps above all constituted as an 'eye': someone who sees and, through seeing, understands. Museums do this explicitly, precisely offering their objects to their visitors as a kind of educational spectacle. According to Bennett (1995), things are slightly more complicated in the case of galleries, where the knowledge that produces the 'good eye' is kept invisible in order to maintain the gallery as a space where the middle class can distinguish itself from other social groups by displaying apparently innate 'taste'.

There are though more prosaic ways in which visitors to galleries and museums are disciplined. Section 4.4 noted some of these in relation to the prohibition on touching objects and images. There are many other *rules* about what visitors can and cannot do in galleries and museums, and these are enforced by warders. Picnicking and playing music, for example, are forbidden: the effect of this prohibition is to reiterate the 'higher', contemplative or pedagogic, aims of the institution. Other forms of discipline include the *spatial routeing* of visitors. Often galleries and museums invite visitors to follow a particular route, either through the layout of rooms or through the provision of floor plans marked with suggested walks (this is common for very large galleries which expect visitors with little time: routes are suggested which ensure that sort of visitor will see (what are constructed as) the highlights of the collection). Some galleries also give you a clue as to which paintings are especially deserving of this kind of viewing by providing *seating* in front of them. As section 3 of this chapter noted, Bal (1996) pays a lot of attention to the effects of this sort of spatial routeing of visitors at the AMNH.

Bennett (1995) argues that there are other, less overt forms of disciplining behaviour in museums and galleries, though. From his historical work, he argues that the contemplation of art and the appreciation of museums' knowledge were expected to involve particular ways of visiting these places, and that these ways were policed not only by rules and warders but also by other visitors. That is, he reworks Foucault's discussion of the way surveillance makes the operation of power 'automatic' by suggesting that the regulation of social behaviour in these museums is conducted as much by the visitors' knowledge that they are being watched by other visitors, as it is by more obvious forms of discipline.

This emphasis on the productivity of the museum or gallery as institution in relation to its visitors raises a key question though. Just how effective are these disciplining technologies? Chapter 6 noted that Foucault insisted that wherever there was power, there were counter-struggles. But a common criticism of Foucauldian methods is that they concentrate too much on the disciplining effects of institutions and not enough on the way these disciplines may fail or be disrupted. This is a criticism which can be made of nearly all the accounts of museums and galleries cited in this chapter. The previous section remarked on their frequent uninterest in exploring the working practices behind the scenes in museums and galleries, for example. It seems to be assumed that in those spaces, classifying systems and rhetorics of realism are successfully coherent, even by those writers who question its success in the more public spaces of these institutions. Similarly, few of these studies consider the possibility that visitors may be bringing knowledges and practices to the museum or gallery that are very different from those institutions' knowledges and practices. Bennett (1995: 11) is quite clear that this is not an issue his book is concerned to address:

> My concern in this book is largely with museums, fairs and exhibitions as envisaged in the plans and projections of their advocates, designers, directors and managers. The degree to which such plans and projections were successful in organizing and framing the experience of the visitor or, to the contrary, the degree to which such planned effects are evaded, sidestepped or simply not noticed raises different questions which, important though they are, I have not addressed here. (Bennett, 1995: 11)

Hooper-Greenhill's (1994) book on *Museums and their Visitors* focuses on recent attempts by museums and galleries to attract more visitors by increasing the relevance of their displays to potential visitors' lives (and suggests in passing that this involves the decentring of curatorial power), but says little about how visitors respond to their efforts. This neglect parallels the critique made by Smith (1998) of the Foucauldian histories of photography offered by Tagg (1988) and Sekula (1986, 1989). There too, the diversity of engagements with particular fields of power/knowledge is underestimated.

There are a few exceptions to this neglect of visitors as subjects constituted through discourses other than those of the museum or gallery. There are a number of case studies that have focused on exhibitions which have been especially controversial (see, for example, Lidchi, 1997). Several recent exhibitions displaying the artefacts of native peoples, for example, have been heavily criticized for their continued naturalization or exoticization of those peoples, and Elsbeth Court (1999) discusses both this accusation and some artistic and curatorial responses to it in a case study of displays of art by Africans. However, much less attention has been paid to less organized forms of resistance to the museum and gallery's disciplines. One exception to this general neglect is the study by Gordon Fyfe and Max Ross (1996); they interviewed a range of people who visited museums in Stoke-on-Trent, England, in order to explore the particularities of their ways of seeing. Their study invites more general questions about the visitors to museums and galleries. Do they critique the particularity of the sort of knowledge about Art offered by a gallery, for example? If so, how? Through their own experience? Through boredom? Through more formalized kinds of understanding, wondering why almost all the artists produced by galleries as great were men, or white? Do visitors touch objects on display surreptitiously? Do they find routes around museums they shouldn't, or sneak a sandwich while a warder looks the other way? And what are the effects of these possible strategies on the visuality and spatiality of the museum and gallery, and on their paintings and objects? These sorts of questions are not made impossible by this second type of discourse analysis, but they have been pursued only very rarely. Hence none of these studies offer any methodological clues as to how such questions might be answered.

focus

This section has noted the consequence of the emphasis in this second kind of discourse analysis on the institution rather than the visitors. What did your visit to a gallery or museum suggest about the power of the institution over its visitors? Did all the visitors you saw behave 'properly'? If not, how not? Were there certain groups allowed to behave differently – children, for example? How were any deviations policed, if at all?

6   discourse analysis II: its own productivity

This second type of discourse analysis follows Foucault in understanding visual images as embedded in the practices of institutions and their exercise of power. It thus pays less attention to visual images and objects themselves than to the institutional apparatus and technologies that surround them and which, according to this approach, produce them as particular kinds of images and objects. This approach is thus centrally concerned with the social production and effects of visual images, and to that extent conforms to one of the criteria set out in Chapter 1 of this book for a critical visual methodology. It offers a methodology that allows detailed consideration of how the effects of dominant power relations work through the details of an institution's practice.

However, this type of discourse analysis pays little attention to the specific ways of seeing invited by an image itself. Nor, as sections 4.5 and 5 have noted, has it paid much attention to the way that 'power is exercised from innumerable points, in the interplay of nonegalitarian and mobile relations' (Foucault, 1979: 94). Foucault's own arguments do not rule out this latter as a topic of research, but it has not so far been developed by these Foucauldian analysts.

Finally, there is the question of reflexivity. The kind of discourse analysis discussed in this chapter does not spend time on reflexive contemplation. This is no doubt for the same reasons as section 5 of the previous chapter outlined: many of the assumptions underlying the conventional forms of reflexivity in the social sciences are not tenable within a Foucauldian framework. However, unlike the 'certain modesty in our analytic claims' nonetheless advocated by Tonkiss (1998: 260) in her discussion of the first type of discourse analysis, discussed in section 5 of the previous chapter, this second type of discourse analysis tends, if anything, to the immodest. The introduction to this chapter noted as an example of this analytical self-confidence the stinging critique of Barthes made by Tagg (1988). But all the writers on museums and galleries cited in this chapter appear equally confident that the claims they make about the effects of these institutions are correct. Haraway's (1989) essay, for example, makes some highly coloured assertions about the effects of the AMNH's Akeley Hall that give me pause. Here's a taster of her style:

> Scene after scene draws the visitor into itself through the eyes of the animals in the tableaux. Each diorama has at least one animal that catches the viewer's gaze and holds it in communion. The animal is vigilant . . . but ready also to hold forever the gaze of meeting, the moment of truth, the original encounter. The moment seems fragile, the animals about to disappear, the communion about to break; the Hall threatens to dissolve into the chaos of the Age of Man. But it does not. The gaze holds, and the wary animal heals those who will look. (Haraway, 1989: 30)

While Haraway here may be attempting, in the Foucauldian manner advocated by Kendall and Wickham (1999: 101–9), to give co-authorship of her encounter with the Akeley Hall to its inanimate objects, she might also be read as offering an account of the effects of the hall that is somewhat ungrounded in the details of its apparatus or technologies.

Moreover, I suspect that this sort of writing makes the AMNH a lot more exciting – and powerful – than it is to the vast majority of its visitors.

Hence, this second form of discourse analysis focuses very clearly on the power relations at work in institutions of visual display. However, this focus produces some absences in its methodology too: an uninterest in images themselves, a lack of concern for conflicts and disruptions within institutional practices, a neglect of the practices of viewing brought by visitors to those institutions, and a lack of any form of reflexivity.

7   summary

- discourse analysis II focuses on the articulation of discourses through institutional apparatuses and institutional technologies.
- in doing this, it utilizes similar methods to discourse analysis I.
- discourse analysis II pays much attention to the powerful discourses that saturate institutions and apparatuses to produce their subjects.
- discourse analysis II is less interested in the site of the image itself, and in practice seems uninterested in the complexities and contradictions of discourse.
- discourse analysis II is not concerned with reflexive strategies.

further reading

Henrietta Lidchi (1997) provides a detailed study of a particular museum exhibition that is carefully grounded in the details of the exhibition's apparatus and technologies, and also makes some connections with other methods of looking at museum and gallery spaces, while Mary Anne Staniszewski (1998) discusses the effects of different display practices at the Museum of Modern Art in New York from 1921 to 1970.

other methods, mixing methods

1 introduction

This chapter ends the book by both rehearsing its central themes and by
introducing some new considerations. Each chapter has explored a
particular method for interpreting a particular kind of visual imagery, and
the first section of this chapter will compare the methods a little more
systematically than previous chapters have done. For each of these methods
has its strengths and weaknesses not only in relation to the criteria for a
critical visual methodology laid out in Chapter 1, but also in terms of what
it is most effective in exploring empirically. These empirical focuses do not
concern the kinds of visual images on which each method can be deployed.
Although most chapters have concentrated on only one sort of visual
image, every method discussed here can be applied to images other than
the sort discussed in that method's chapter. Rather, the specificity of the
empirical orientations of these methods concerns the sites and modalities
of visual meaning-making, and this specificity leads to the two other
considerations of this chapter: the possibility of mixing methods, in order
to broaden the empirical scope of a study; and of using other methods in
order to access issues otherwise neglected by the methods so far discussed.
Of these neglected issues, perhaps the most obvious is the site of audiencing. Although several of the methods discussed in previous chapters
make certain assumptions and claims about the effects of images on
audiences, none of them are directed exclusively at the site of audiencing
and none of them aim to explore the ways in which audiences make sense
of images. This final chapter will therefore also examine ways of exploring
this site. Thus this chapter will:

- briefly rehearse the arguments of Chapter 1 concerning the sites and
  modalities of the meanings of visual images, and place the methods so
  far discussed in relation to them.

- examine other methods that have been used in relation to visual images, especially those used to explore the site of audiencing.
- discuss the merits of mixing methods.

2 sites, modalities and methods

Chapter 1 commented that the large body of work exploring the meanings of visual images suggests that there are three sites at which the meanings of images are made: the site of *production*, the site of the *image itself*, and the site of its *audiencing*. That is, how an image is made, what it looks like, and how it is seen are the three crucial ways in which a visual image becomes culturally meaningful. Chapter 1 also suggested that each of those three sites could be understood in terms of three modalities, which it termed the *technological*, the *compositional* and the *social*. The technological concerns the tools and equipment used to make, structure and display an image; the compositional concerns the visual construction, qualities and reception of an image; and the social concerns the social, economic, political and institutional practices and relations that produce, saturate and interpret an image.

Clearly, these three sites and modalities are in practice often difficult to distinguish neatly one from another. Because of that, Figure 1.4 is a visual image that draws boundaries between things that are rarely so neatly divided one from another. Its lines are misleading solid; and by this point in the book you may feel that a list of questions like the one that follows is a more appropriate way of approaching the complexity and richness of meaning in a visual image than the demarcated fields offered in Figure 1.4.

some questions about the production of an image

- when was it made?
- where was it made?
- who made it?
- was it made for someone else?
- what technologies does its production depend on?
- what were the social identities of the maker, the owner and the subject of the image?
- what were the relations between the maker, the owner and the subject?
- does the genre of the image address these identities and relations of its production?
- does the form of the image reconstitute those identities and relations?

some questions about the image

- what is being shown? what are the components of the image? how are they arranged?
- is it one of series?
- where is the viewer's eye drawn to in the image, and why?
- what is the vantage point of the image?
- what relationships are established between the components of the image visually?
- what use is made of colour?
- how has its technology affected the text?
- what is, or are, the genre(s) of the image? Is it documentary, soap opera, or melodrama, for example?
- to what extent does this image draw on the characteristics of its genre?
- does this image comment critically on the characteristics of its genre?
- what do the different components of an image signify?
- what knowledges are being deployed?
- whose knowledges are excluded from this representation?
- does this image's particular look at its subject disempower its subject?
- are the relations between the components of this image unstable?
- Is this a contradictory image?

some questions about audiencing

- who were the original audience(s) for this image?
- where and how would the text have been displayed originally?
- how is it circulated?
- how is it stored?
- how is it redisplayed?
- who are the more recent audiences for this text?
- where is the spectator positioned in relation to the components of the image?
- what relation does this produce between the image and its viewers?
- is the image one of a series, and how do the preceding and subsequent images affect its meanings?
- would the image have had a written text to guide its interpretation in its initial moment of display, for example, a caption or a catalogue entry?
- is the image represented elsewhere in a way which invites a particular relation to it, in publicity materials, for example, or in reviews?
- have the technologies of circulation and display affected the audiences' interpretation of this image?

- what are the conventions for viewing this technology?
- is more than one interpretation of the image possible?
- how actively does a particular audience engage with the image?
- is there any evidence that a particular audience produced a meaning for an image that differed from the meanings made at the site of its production or by the image itself?
- how do different audiences interpret this image?
- how are these audiences different from each other, in terms of class, gender, race, sexuality and so on?
- how do these axes of social identity structure different interpretations?

Such a long list of questions addressed to a particular visual image may be a useful starting point for your study. It may prompt new ideas because the questions ask about something you haven't thought about before; or your image may suggest other questions to you that become more interesting by their absence from this list.

However, this list of questions is very eclectic. It doesn't suggest that any one series of questions is any more important than another. The usefulness of Figure 1.4 was precisely to suggest that the theoretical debates in which many of the methods discussed in this book are embedded are important because they do claim that certain sites or certain modalities are more fundamental for understanding the meaning of an image than others. That is, they suggest that some questions in that list are more important than others. So, as Chapter 1 also insisted, you need to engage with these more theoretical debates about how to interpret images before deploying any of the methods discussed in this book.

Since many of the methods examined here are related to specific arguments about how images become significant, it is not surprising that many of them produce quite specific empirical focuses when they are used, as well as implying their own conceptual understanding of imagery. Figure 1.4 suggests what these empirical focuses are – although it should be noted that in some cases, these focuses are more a matter of what has been done so far by those researchers interested in visual matters than what the method itself might allow. This is the case, I think, in relation to the neglect of audiencing by the second type of discourse analysis discussed in Chapter 7. There doesn't seem to be anything in the founding arguments of that kind of discourse analysis that precludes exploring the site of audiencing, but very few of its proponents have carried out that kind of research. Instead, those sorts of discourse analysts have focused on the institutional sites of image production, use and display, and on particular genres of images. On the other hand, semiology (particularly its earlier manifestations) and much psychoanalysis also neglect to explore the processes of audiencing, but this is because both claim that it is the image itself that produces its audiences' positions. Since both these theories conceptualize the image as productive of spectatorship, both have developed complex and elaborate ways of interpreting what their proponents argue are the effects of those images by looking only at the images in question. The notion that different audiences might react differently to the same image is so rarely acknowledged conceptually, that the methodologies that flow from that conceptualization therefore also neglect the processes of audiencing. Hence it would be very difficult, using either of those methods, to explore how audiences make sense of images.

Indeed, Figure 1.4 suggests that none of the methods discussed so far in this book offer any means to examine the site of audiencing. Compositional interpretation concentrates almost entirely on the compositional modality of the image itself and, because it relies implicitly on the idea that Art and genius are universally recognized, it is uninterested in how different viewers might see the same image differently. Content analysis, on the other hand, in its faith in the possibility of replicable research results, assumes that audience variability is a problem to be overcome rather than an issue to be explored. And, as I have just noted, both semiology and psychoanalysis tend to assume that the image produces the audience rather than vice versa. Discourse analysis, meanwhile, though it does not preclude exploring the discourses audiences bring to bear on an image, does not so far seem to have pursued this possibility.

These sorts of considerations suggest the issues that the next two sections of this chapter address. The first is the question of whether there are any other methods that have been developed to explore how particular audiences react to specific images. The second is whether mixing one method with another is a useful strategy for widening the empirical focus of a research project.

3 other methods: exploring audiencing

This book has already implied that there are ways of interpreting visual images other than those to which chapters have been devoted. For example, section 4.1 of Chapter 1 said very little about the methods used by those authors who argue that economic processes and relations determine the meaning of visual images. And the discussions of the different kinds of discourse analysis in Chapters 6 and 7 both suggested that interviews might be useful ways of accessing the discursive production of visualities. There is, of course, a huge literature on doing and interpreting interviews, and this chapter cannot hope to do justice to the details of that particular research method. Nonetheless, this section will examine one particular use of interviews as a method for exploring the meanings of visual images, since it is the method most often used to explore how audiences make sense of images. This section will also look at one other method used for the same ends: ethnography.

3.1 the site of audiencing

Before discussing the various interviewing – and other – strategies used by researchers interested in the site of audiencing, it is worth spending a little time considering how that site is understood by those researchers, and hence what their use of interviews is trying to achieve.

As Shaun Moores (1993) notes in his useful discussion of research into audiences, the first studies to explore how audiences reacted to specific visual images emerged in the late 1970s and depended on a critique of those approaches to visual images that had been dominant in critical social theory through the 1970s: semiology and psychoanalysis. In a key text, David Morley (1980) argued that these forms of analysis were overly **Formalist** formalist: that is, they paid too much attention to the formal qualities of the visual image and not enough attention to the ways actual audiences made sense of it. (For example, recall here the way Judith Williamson (1978) suggests we are constituted in specific ways by advertising, or Laura Mulvey's (1989) claim that everyone is masculinized when they view Hollywood narrative cinema.) In opposition to this formalism, Morley (1980) argued that audiences actively responded to an image's meaning, bringing their own experiences and knowledges to bear on it. To make this argument he drew on a number of authors, but especially important was Stuart Hall's (1980) discussion of the reception of preferred meanings (see section 4 of Chapter 4). Hall (1980) argued that although visual images (and indeed all cultural texts) were encoded in their production with a preferred meaning – by which Hall meant the imprint of the ideology of **Decoded** the dominant cultural order – this meaning could be **decoded** in quite different terms by a specific audience. As Moores (1993: 16) says, 'while recognizing the text's construction of subject positions, [this argument] pointed to readers as the possessors of cultural knowledges and competences that have been acquired in previous social experiences and which are drawn on in the act of interpretation'. Thus, as the next section will show, Morley's early work demonstrated the acceptance but also the ambivalence and outright hostility that specific audiences showed towards the preferred meanings of a particular tv programme.

It was in order to explore these 'cultural knowledges and competences' that the early studies of audiencing turned to interviews with audience members. Interviews are not used in this body of work to discover what people 'actually watch'; other methods are available for that, for example, asking people to keep a diary of their viewing. Instead, interviews are used to explore the sense people make of television. Morley (1992: 181) advocates the interview method, for example, 'not simply for the access it gives the research to the respondents' conscious opinions and statements but also for the access that it gives to the linguistic terms and categories . . . through which respondents construct their words and their own understandings of their activities'. This sort of interview can take different forms, as section 3.2 will describe. However, it should also be noted that other researchers have used other methods to gain access to audience interpretations. In her study of how viewers of the American soap opera *Dallas* understood the programme, for example, Ien Ang placed a small ad in a women's magazine asking people to write to her about why they liked or disliked watching it, saying that she would use their responses in her dissertation. She received 42 replies and used these in her book *Watching Dallas* (Ang, 1985).

Much of this work on audiencing has concentrated on television, and it is on these studies that this section will focus. Morley's early study looked at audience reactions to an early evening news magazine broadcast by the British Broadcasting Corporation called *Nationwide*; there is Ang's (1985) discussion of *Dallas*; and David Buckingham (1987) explored how children watched the BBC soap *EastEnders*, for example. Thus this work was looking at popular cultural forms. No one interested in audiences' reactions to visual images went to art galleries, cinemas or museums to explore qualitatively the sorts of questions raised by Bourdieu and Darbel's (1991) large-scale quantitative survey of their visitors (although John Ellis, 1992 raises some interesting questions about how we watch a movie differently depending on whether we see it at a cinema or watch it on television). The emphasis on television has continued in more recent studies so that, as Moores (1993: 2) comments, 'audience' in this kind of work has become equivalent to 'the consumers of electronically mediated messages'. This interest in television audiences was caused by a development in cultural studies that paralleled its anti-formalist stand. As well as objecting to the formalism of semiology and psychoanalysis, writers like Morley also objected to the kinds of images they tended to study, which were those associated with what have been constructed as the 'higher' art forms. Even Mulvey's (1989) polemic against Hollywood cinema was directed at its classics rather than at its more pedestrian productions that had not stood the test of time. Much of this work on audiences instead wanted to recover and often to celebrate the complex cultural work that surrounded more mundane cultural productions; and much of it wanted to argue that in fact these sorts of productions did indeed deal with complex issues and debates. Some writers – Ang (1985) for example – even declared themselves to be avid fans of supposedly trashy cultural forms like *Dallas*. Ang (1985) actually argued that *Dallas* was less trivial than it seemed to many cultural critics; on the basis of the letters she received, she argued that fans of the series loved it for its emotional realism. They were quite aware that its storylines were improbably melodramatic and on occasion absurd; but they loved it because it showed that relationships were difficult and that happiness was very hard to find. For all its schlock, then, Ang suggested *Dallas* did nonetheless address some important emotional issues; and that, most importantly, it was necessary to listen to the views of its audiences to understand that.

Audiencing, then, is an important site for two reasons. First, how audiences react to a visual image can be used, as Ang (1985) did, to produce a particular understanding of that image. Second, exploring how different audiences react to the same image, as Morley (1980) did, can demonstrate the complexity of the decoding process. The next section explores interviewing as a method for listening to audiences.

3.2 interviewing audiences

There have been three sorts of interviews used by researchers interested in how audiences interpret television programmes. All are usually unstructured and open-ended discussions of watching television (and, more recently, its associated technologies like videos).

The first sort of interview is the *one-to-one interview*, conducted by the researcher with one interviewee. This is the sort of interview used by Ann Gray (1992) in her study of how women used video cassette recorders in their homes. The second sort of interview is the *group interview*. This has usually involved working with groups that are already constituted. Morley (1980), for example, found his groups by going into classes that were already established at various institutions of higher education, and Buckingham (1987) found his by working with groups of friends established at schools and youth clubs. The third type of interview that has been used is also a kind of group interview: the *family interview*, in which most or all the members of a family are interviewed together in their home. Clearly these three types do not exhaust the possibilities of interviewing. Group interviews can be carried out with groups brought together especially for the research project, for example, though this is often time consuming to organize and it can be difficult to find an appropriate venue. Another possibility, implied by Morley's (1986: 174) comment that the young children in a family often get bored in family interviews, is to interview the younger and older members of a family separately. Finally, it would also be feasible, given the resources, to combine different interview methods, for example, interviewing each family member separately either before or after the family interview. Again, Morley (1986: 174) implies this might be useful in his comment on the impact of family dynamics on what a researcher is told in an interview. A dominant family member may impose his or her views in a group interview in ways that one-to-one interviews with other family members would reveal.

These sorts of interviews are tape recorded, transcribed and then analysed. Recording a group interview requires a high-quality tape recorder; transcribing group interviews is also notoriously even more time consuming than transcribing one-to-one interviews. The analysis of the interviews is also complex and time consuming. It is possible to use the procedures of discourse analysis I discussed in Chapter 6. There are also more formalized methods for interpreting interview transcripts, for example, the grounded theory approach of Strauss and Corbin (1999), or the rigorous coding procedures advocated by writers like Miles and Hubermann (1994) or Dey

(1993). There is no space here to detail these different possibilities, and they are discussed at length in many textbooks on qualitative methods; instead, the following discussion will concentrate on some other methodological issues.

First, more needs to be said about interview methods and especially about the logics underlying the recruitment of interviewees. The early work in cultural studies that was concerned with audiences made some assumptions – later to be problematized – about why it was that different audiences decoded television programmes in different ways. The argument was that it was the socio-economic position of the audience members which shaped their reaction to the preferred meaning of a tv show. Morley (1980) was clear that this position did not determine the decoding process, and he stated explicitly that other things might affect it, in particular the audience members' involvement in different cultural frameworks such as a particular youth culture or membership of 'racial minorities' (Morley, 1980: 23). However, Morley did argue that these sorts of social positionings could explain why certain groups reacted in certain ways to the same programme. He recruited his groups accordingly. While he was happy to mix the gendered and racialized composition of his groups, he never mixed the class composition, and thus he found his groups through different higher education institutions with different student bodies. There were groups of mainly white working-class young men found through an apprenticeship course at Birmingham Polytechnic, for example, and groups of mainly white middle-class men found at a bank's training college; he also found mainly black groups through further education classes, and a group of shop stewards through a Trades Union Congress training college. He screened two *Nationwide* programmes for these groups in their established group setting, and then held the group interview. Similarly, in her study of VCR use Gray (1992) assumed that gender was an important analytical category which might well explain video use and therefore chose only to interview women; she did though try also to interview both working-class and middle-class women. Thus theoretical arguments about what structures the diversity of audience reactions are used to inform the choice of interviewees.

One difference between Gray (1992) and Morley (1980) though, is that Gray chose to use one-to-one interviews while Morley preferred group interviews. Morley (1980: 33) explains his preference for group interviews by suggesting that one-to-one interviews imply that people are 'social atoms', while group interviews allow for the dynamics of social interaction to become evident. Two points could be made here. One is that Gray's (1992) study is very far from assuming that the women she spoke to are social atoms; indeed the whole point of her interviews was to understand the women's video use as a consequence of their role in their family. Although she does not state it explicitly, I imagine she chose to interview women on their own in part because she wanted to access the specificity of individual women's experiences. However, her desire to examine women's views might also have led her to choose one-to-one interviews instead of family interviews in order to avoid the difficulty that Morley does not mention in his 1980 study, which is the issue of family dynamics. Much feminist research on domestic labour has found that in households where men and women cohabit, men tend to overestimate their contribution to that labour and, moreover, that their version of events often prevails in interviews in which both the man and the woman are present. Gray's own work on VCRs (confirmed by Morley's 1986 own later work on television use in families) suggests that, generally, it is the adult man of the household who controls its use when he is present. This may have been a difficult issue to explore in depth in family interviews – men may have underestimated their control in order not to appear selfish – and thus Gray's choice of one-to-one interviews seems justified as a way of accessing women's views. Indeed, although Morley argues that one of the strengths of group interviews is to make the dynamics of social interaction evident, he does not acknowledge what an extraordinarily complex process making sense of those dynamics is. Nor does he mention the potential difficulties an interviewer might have in facilitating an open discussion in a group with complex dynamics. Buckingham (1991) gives some examples of complicated group interactions in his account of group interviewing children about television. Group interviews are very challenging, both to do and to understand.

Once the interviews have been completed, the interpretation begins. Moores (1993: 18) describes this process as finding 'significant clusters' of meaning and then 'charting the lines that join these clusters with the social and discursive positionings of readers'. For Morley (1980: 34), these significant clusters emerged from a close study of the working vocabulary and speech forms of his interviewees. He established from these what he called their 'lexical repertoires', then looked for patterns of argument and evidence, and finally tried to ascertain the ideologies underlying all of them. His conclusion identified two sorts of decodings of the *Nationwide* programmes, which he did relate to two socio-economic groups. The first was a decoding that broadly accepted the preferred meanings of *Nationwide*, and this was produced by the middle-class members of Morley's groups (as well as many of the young apprentices). The second was an oppositional reading, produced by working-class members of his groups, but with important differences among them. Thus the shop stewards produced a politically informed 'radical rank-and-file perspective' while the black further education students offered an 'alienated "critique of silence"' (Morley, 1980: 137). Thus Morley could insist that class position alone did not determine the processes of decoding: so too did the cultural constitution of racialized and politicized identities, for example.

In presenting his work, Morley (1980, 1986), like Gray (1992), uses large amounts of transcript in order to allow his readers to make their own assessments of his interpretations. Indeed, in his 1980 study Morley (1980: 163) admitted that he was unhappy with aspects of his methodology and felt that it needed further development. His later study of *Family*

Television (1986) did take his work in new directions. In that work he chose to use family interviews. This was because he was increasingly interested in two issues that his earlier research methodology had made difficult to access. The first of these was the ways in which the actual practices of watching television at home were difficult to access through groups that were not constituted through shared domestic spaces. The second of these was the question of what people chose to watch in the first place. His 1980 study had assumed that all his groups would be familiar with *Nationwide*; but what if the blacks students' 'alienated "critique of silence"' was a consequence of their total uninterest in the programme? Thus in *Family Television*, Morley (1986) interviewed 18 white nuclear families living in south London. All were working class or lower middle class, as defined by Morley using notions of cultural capital rather than income (Morley, 1986: 52–3); all had two adults and at least two kids less than 18 years old, and all owned at least one television and one VCR. He used the unstructured interviews (which took place in the family's home and which lasted one or two hours each) to explore how the use of television was embedded in the wider family dynamics. How were tvs and videos used? What was watched and with what reaction? How were decisions about what to watch made? Most of his results (again with lots of transcripts reproduced) are recorded family by family, but there is one thematic chapter on television and gendered relations which argues that, in these households, the adult men tend to plan the viewing, control the remote control, watch in silence, watch more tv than anyone else, prefer more factual programmes, work the video and not to like admitting to talking about tv.

Morley's move to considering the social practices through which watching tv occurs is a shift that many others interested in audiencing have also advocated. As John Fiske (1994: 198) notes, 'audiencing is a variety of practices, an activity', and exploring that activity is of increasing interest to many researchers. However, many of these other writers have also advocated the use of other methods to access those practices. Chief among them is ethnography.

3.3 ethnographies of audiencing

Like interviewing, ethnography is a method long established and much discussed in the social sciences and, again, there are excellent discussions of it elsewhere. It usually entails, first, extended periods of observation 'in the field' and, second, unstructured, conversational interviews with those active in that field (however, for other possible ways of gaining ethnographic data, see Silverstone et al., 1991). If the aim is to explore 'the immediate physical and interpersonal contexts of daily media reception' (Moores, 1993: 7), then an ethnographic approach would involve the researcher observing an audience in their homes over an extended period of time, and talking with them about their viewing but probably also about many other things.

Not surprisingly perhaps, examples of this sort of ethnography are rare, because it is difficult to get access to people's houses for the length of time that an ethnographic study requires. However, there are one or two examples of ethnographic study that offer some pointers to other researchers. The first is reported by James Lull (1990: 174-85). Lull (1990: 183) defines ethnographic audiencing research as 'an interpretive enterprise whereby the investigator uses observation and in-depth interviewing to grasp the meaning of communication by analysing the perceptions, shared assumptions, and activities of the social actors under scrutiny'. He suggests that there are four things to consider when planning an ethnographic study of audiencing:

1   *access to the audience*. Lull (1990: 175) notes that this is very difficult. He suggests going through the committee or board that runs a local institution such as a school or a church. (He notes that this may involve gaining access only to a specific social group.) Explain what you want to do to them (and Lull suggests keeping this as vague as possible), ask them to give you access to their membership list and then contact the names on that list. He suggests that 25 to 30 per cent of families thus contacted will agree to participate in the study.
2   *observation techniques*. Lull (1990: 177) advocates the usual ethnographic means of recording what you see and hear: unobtrusive note-taking.
3   *data collection*. Lull (1990: 178–80) suggests that spending between three and seven days with a family is enough to give the researcher access to their usual behaviour, and that during this period there are different stages of data collection. The first one or two days he suggests spending in collecting the more obvious kinds of data: what the house looks like, family history, biographical sketches. The next couple of days should focus on recording the dynamics of the family, especially by participating in its important routines. The final stage is to interview each family member separately.
4   *analysing data*. As Lull (1990: 180) comments, ethnographic work generates lots of data. He rather briefly recommends interpreting it by organizing it into internally coherent topics which can be used to illustrate conceptual points. Judith Okely (1994) in her discussion of interpreting ethnographic data is more detailed about difficulty of dealing with observational notes and interview material.

Lull (1990) puts these precepts to work in large-scale studies, the aim of which is the objective study of family viewing habits. According to him, 'the observer must create and sustain rapport with family members while maintaining the disinterested eye and ear of the objective observer-reporter' (Lull, 1990: 179), and he recommends that the researcher does not reveal at any stage in the process what their real object of interest is: tv viewing. This raises an issue concerning the ethics of research. Ang (1989) has commented that qualitative methods do not necessarily guarantee a critical research methodology, and Lull's discussion of ethnography seems to bear this claim out. In his advocacy of deceiving research subjects in the name of objective research, he shows no concern for the power relations between the researcher and researched. Thus there is no reflexive consideration of how those relations might affect his research findings either.

Another example of ethnographic research – and one that Lull (1990: 16–17) dismisses for being too personal – is Valerie Walkerdine's (1990) account of watching a family watch a video of *Rocky II*. Walkerdine is certainly very personal in this essay, but she is so in order to explore just those issues that Lull's methodological orientation evades: her own complicity in the power dynamics between an academic researcher and, in this case, a working-class man who cheers as he watches the boxer Rocky smashes his opponent into pulp. Walkerdine watched him do this when she was in the family living-room, ethnographically observing their activities, and she describes her own revulsion at this scene and also her revulsion at the man's pleasure in it. Later though, she describes how she watched the video herself in the privacy of her office and found herself breaking down in tears as she watched the same scene in another way; this time as a woman herself from a working-class background absolutely at one with Rocky's brutal determination to succeed, to get out, to fight his way free. What her own changed audiencing suggests to Walkerdine is her complicity with the ways in which the academy so often denigrates working-class understandings. In that living-room, she says, she was acting as a feminist academic horrified at male violence, and in that position she could not see any other way; in particular, the class dynamics of the situation were invisible to her.

Walkerdine (1990) and Lull (1990) offer very different models for ethnographic research into audiencing. Walkerdine's account is certainly less methodologically explicit than Lull's, but its contribution to a critical visual methodology may nonetheless be greater. For her account is one of the very few sustained reflexive discussions of viewing in the large literature cited in this book.

focus

The previous chapter suggested that very few studies of museums and galleries had paid attention to their visitors.

Consider the museum or gallery you visited for the last chapter, or think about a museum or gallery you are familiar with. In the light of the debates about researching audiencing just discussed, how would you go about exploring what sense various visitors made of that museum or gallery?

3.4   assessing analysing audiencing

The difference between Walkerdine (1990) and Lull (1990) leads to this section's more general assessment of methods for accessing audiencing.

The work cited here explores an issue mentioned frequently in the preceding chapters of this book but not so far addressed directly. This work takes the site of audiencing as its main focus, and offers a number of theoretical and methodological resources for understanding its dynamics. Clearly, 'audience' is not a simple category: how it is defined (see also Ang, 1991), how its social position relates to its interpretive practices and how best to access that relation are all debated. More recently too, a number of questions have been raised about how this work relates to other aspects of the critical visual methodology that this book has been advocating.

One of these questions concerns that very focus on the site of audiencing alone, and the way in which that site is approached almost exclusively in its social modality. Mark Jancovich (1992) remarks that as a consequence of the attention it pays to audiencing, this body of work neglects the image itself and its production. That is, 'the textual processes through which television establishes social, cultural and political agendas' are ignored (Jancovich, 1992: 136). This is taken to an extreme in some work which takes for granted that audiences will produce viewings subversive of both those textual processes and those agendas. Fiske (1994: 192), for example, watches a group of teenagers watch a sitcom and decides that they 'produced a cultural experience within which the show, the behaviour of watching it, and the place where it was watched were all mobilized to produce social identities and social relations that were within their control as opposed to, and in emancipation from, those institutionalized for them in the officially approved family'. Maybe for that particular audience that was the case; but to assume it will always be the case neglects the power of visual imagery to exert its own effects, and the effects of its meanings. Other modalities are also neglected in much of this work; if there is little on the compositional modality of television itself, nor is there much on its technological modality (although this absence is beginning to be rectified; see Gray, 1992; Silverstone et al., 1991). Indeed, the emphasis on the social modality of tv watching is so strong that Moores (1993: 54) wonders whether studies like Morley's (1986), that aim to embed tv watching firmly in the dynamics of classed and gendered family relations, end up being more about domestic interaction and household leisure and labour than about television. Jancovich (1992: 136) pursues this worry when he says that it is not clear in Morley's (1986) study of family television precisely how those dynamics of family interaction affect the decoding of tv programmes. Clearly they do affect crucial aspects of television use, such as who decides to watch what and when; but their effect on who interprets what and how is much less clear.

Another set of concerns clusters around the reflexivity of this work on audiencing. Ang (1989) argues that much of the early work on audiencing assumed the authoritative researcher who knew more, or better, about tv programmes than the people they were interviewing. Moores (1993: 65) responds that some of her critique is misplaced, since authors like Morley (1980) explicitly invited their readers to make their own sense of their interview material by including large amounts of interview transcripts in their accounts. In this way, Morley is somewhat more modest in his interpretive claims than Ang allows, since his readers can reach their own conclusions on the basis of the materials provided by Morley. However, on one point Ang's (1989) critique does seem fair. She says that there is a tendency for researchers to assume there is a preferred meaning contained in a visual image, that only the researcher can access it, and that it can act as a kind of baseline from which other audience interpretations can be assessed. Morley (1980: 22) actually deploys a number of ideas from semiology to describe the preferred meanings of *Nationwide* or, as he puts it, 'to establish provisional readings of their main communicative and ideological structures'. But as Moores (1993: 28) asks of these 'communicative and ideological structures', 'can we be sure we didn't put it there ourselves while we were looking?' Thus the notion of a preferred meaning is vulnerable to the same kind of questioning as all non-reflexive semiological claims to access the hidden meanings in images (see section 5 of Chapter 4).

Another concern about the methods used to access audiencing processes also focuses on the role of the researcher. This time, the issue concerns the impact of the researcher on their research subjects when they are interviewing them. As Buckingham (1991: 229) notes, all talk is done in a specific context, and that context affects what sort of talk is done. This is true of all social interactions, as those discourse analysts discussed in Chapter 6 here insist. However, Buckingham (1991) suggests that those researching audiencing should pay a little more attention to the effects of the interview context on what is said in the interview. I have already suggested that Gray (1992) might have considered this issue when making her decision to interview women VCR users on a one-to-one basis rather than in family groups. Obviously one-to-one interviews have their own specificities, which Gray (1992: 34) does explore, but it is rare to find any consideration of the way the researcher might have affected group or family interviews. The example Buckingham (1991: 229–32) uses is from his own work with school-age children. He notes that he interviewed these children at school and was introduced to them by their teacher, so that the children in those groups most likely associated him with teachers. In the group interviews, the kids were very critical of tv advertising, and also discussed the racism and sexism of some kids' cartoon series; but the question Buckingham asks is, were these children employing an 'interpretative repertoire' that they thought was appropriate to the situation (see Chapter 6, section 3.1), a situation in which an adult was listening to them and when they know many adults, especially teachers, disapprove of television? Buckingham (1991) is not suggesting that the children were not saying what they thought, still less that they were lying; he is simply considering what effect the interview situation itself might have had on the material he gathered there. Again, this is a reflexive strategy rarely deployed in studies of audiencing.

In sum, this body of work on audiencing strongly emphasizes the importance of the social modality of the audiencing site. However, in terms of a critical visual methodology, it pays little attention to the power of images themselves, and nor is it especially reflexive about its own practices.

4 mixing methods

Each of the methods discussed in this book, then, has been applied, either necessarily or contingently, on only one of the sites at which the meanings of images are made (see Figure 1.4 again). This raises the question of mixing different methods to explore more fully the range of meanings invested in an image at its different sites.

This book has already mentioned some studies which choose to use more than one method in order precisely to explore the diverse meanings that particular images carry at their various sites of production, image and reception. Catherine Lutz and Jane Collins (1993), for example, used several methods to access each of these three sites in their study of the photographs in the *National Geographic* magazine. At the site of the photographs' production, they studied the archives of the magazine and interviewed editors, journalists and photographers. At the site of the photographs themselves, they used content analysis, as Chapter 3 examined. At the audiencing site, they were typical in their use of group interviews, showing different groups the same few key photographs and examining their reactions. Similarly, in her study of an exhibition in a museum, Henrietta Lidchi (1997) suggests using discourse analysis II to interpret the institutional processes that produced the exhibition's effects, and semiology for interpreting the effects of the technologies of display.

Using more than one method in this manner clearly has benefits. It allows a richly detailed picture of images' significance to be developed, and in particular it can shed interesting light on the contradictory meanings an image may articulate. The visualities articulated by producers, images and audiences may not coincide, and this may in itself be an important issue to address. However, simply discovering that different sites produce different meanings may also be a rather obvious finding. And that kind of argument can easily shift into a claim that 'everyone sees things in their own way', a claim that obscures the very real power relations in which visual images – and all social life – participate. As Ang (1989: 107) argues in the context of audience studies, the critical task is to assess what the significance of diverse audience interpretations might be, not simply to mark their existence.

My assessments of methods in this book have depended on this argument about the power relations articulated through visual images. Hence the critique of compositional interpretation, mentioned in section 3.5 of Chapter 2, which in its turn to universalized notions of Art and genius ignores the social modality of art entirely. Hence the critique, mentioned in section 2.4 of this chapter, that studies of creative audiences often neglect the powerful effects of images' ways of seeing. And hence too the problems with Lutz and Collins's (1993) use of content analysis (discussed in section 3 of Chapter 3), where their advocacy of that method as the most 'objective' means of avoiding the unconscious interpretation of images implies that researchers are more analytically powerful than other sorts of audiences. These criticisms all depend for their force on an abiding concern for the power relations which saturate all ways of seeing: producers', images', and audiences', including researchers like us. This is important to bear in mind when mixing methods, then. Be methodologically eclectic or, even better, methodologically innovative; but do so bearing in mind the power relations that structure the connections between the different sites and modalities you want to bring together.

Finally then, I would like to reiterate the criteria for a critical visual methodology outlined in Chapter 1. Precisely because images matter, because they are powerful and seductive, it is necessary to consider them critically. Whatever method you choose to use, make sure that your account acknowledges the differentiated effects of both an image's way of seeing and your own.

5   summary

- Each of the methods examined in this book tends to focus on a limited number of sites and modalities.
- These selective focuses are a consequence of theoretical arguments, so care must be taken when combining different methods to ensure theoretical consistency.
- The two methods most often used to explore audiences' interpretations of images are interviews of various kinds and ethnography.
- Studies of audiences tend to neglect the site of the image itself.
- Given that the researcher is also an audience, there is a lack of reflexivity in much work on audiencing.

further reading

Shaun Moores's (1993) book on *Interpreting Audiences* is a very useful account of the whys and hows of audience research.

useful reading on various visual media

a useful guide to picture archives and libraries

Evans, H. and M. (1996) *Picture Researcher's Handbook: An International Guide to Picture Sources and How to Use Them*, 6th edition. London: Routledge.

fine art

Carr, D.W. and Leonard, M. (1992) *Looking at Paintings: A Guide to Technical Terms*. London: J. Paul Getty Museum in association with the British Museum Press.
Pollard, E.B. (1986) *Visual Arts Research: A Handbook*. London: Greenwood Press.
Turner, J. (ed.) (1996) *The Dictionary of Art*. 34 vols. London: Macmillan.
Roberts, H.E. (ed.) (1998) *Encyclopedia of Comparative Iconography: Themes Depicted in Works of Art*. 2 vols. London: Fitzroy Dearborn.
Straten, van R. (1994) *An Introduction to Iconography*. Translated by P. de Man. Reading: Gordon and Breach.

photography

Barthes, R. (1982) *Camera Lucida: Reflections on Photography*. Translated by R. Howard. London: Jonathan Cape.
Wells, L. (ed.) *Photography: A Critical Introduction*. London: Routledge.
Wright, T. (1999) *The Photography Handbook*. London: Routledge.

film

Bordwell, D., Staiger, J. and Thompson, K. (1988) *The Classical Hollywood Cinema: Film Style and Mode of Production to 1960*. London: Routledge.

Ellis, J. (1992) *Visible Fictions: Cinema, Television, Video*. London: Routledge.
Monaco, J. (2000) *How to Read a Film: Movies, Media, Multimedia*, 3rd edition. London: Oxford University Press.
Neale, S. and Smith, M. (eds) (1998) *Contemporary Hollywood Cinema*. London: Routledge.

television

Ellis, J. (1992) *Visible Fictions: Cinema, Television, Video*. London: Routledge.
Silverstone, R. (1994) *Television and Everyday Life*. London: Routledge.
Williams, R. (1989) *Raymond Williams on Television: Selected Writings*. Edited by A. O'Connor. London: Routledge.

video

Ellis, J. (1992) *Visible Fictions: Cinema, Television, Video*. London: Routledge.
Monaco, J. (2000) *How to Read a Film: Movies, Media, Multimedia*, 3rd edition. London: Oxford University Press.

maps

Cosgrove, D. (ed.) (1998) *Mappings*. London: Reaktion Books.
Dorling, D. and Fairbairn, D. (1997) *Mapping: Ways of Representing the World*. Harlow: Longman.
Harley, J.B. (1992) 'Reconstructing the map', in T.J. Barnes and J.S. Duncan (eds), *Writing Worlds: Discourse, Text and Metaphor in the Representation of Landscape*. London: Routledge, pp. 231–47.

references

Acton, M. (1997) *Learning to Look at Paintings*. London: Routledge.

Adler, J. (1989) 'Origins of sightseeing', *Annals of Tourism Research* 16: 7–29.

Alpers, S. (1983) *The Art of Describing: Dutch Art in the Seventeenth Century*. London: John Murray.

Andrews, S. (1995) *Story and Space in Renaissance Art*. Cambridge: Cambridge University Press.

Ang, I. (1985) *Watching Dallas*. London: Methuen.

Ang, I. (1989) 'Wanted: Audiences. On the politics of empirical audience studies', in E. Seiter, H. Borchers, G. Kreutzner and E.-M. Warth (eds), *Remote Control: Television, Audiences, and Cultural Power*. London: Routledge, pp. 96–105.

Ang, I. (1991) *Desperately Seeking the Audience*. London: Routledge.

Armstrong, C. (1996) 'Visual culture questionnaire', *October* 77: 26–8.

Armstrong, C. (1998) *Scenes in a Library: Reading the Photograph in the Book*. London: MIT Press.

Back, L. and Quaade, V. (1993) 'Dream utopias, nightmare realities: imagining race and culture within the world of Benetton', *Third Text* 22: 65–80.

Bal, M. (1991) *Reading Rembrandt: Beyond the Word–Image Opposition*. Cambridge: Cambridge University Press.

Bal, M. (1996) *Double Exposures: The Subject of Cultural Analysis*. London: Routledge.

Bal, M. and Bryson, N. (1991) 'Semiotics and art history', *Art Bulletin* 73: 174–208.

Ball M.S. and Smith, G.W.H. (1992) *Analyzing Visual Data*. London: Sage.

Bann, S. (1998) 'Art history and museums', in M.A. Cheetham, M.A. Holly and K. Moxey (eds), *The Subjects of Art History: Historical Objects in Contemporary Perspective*. Cambridge: Cambridge University Press, pp. 230–49.

Barker, E. (ed.) (1999) *Contemporary Cultures of Display*. London: Yale University Press in association with The Open University.

Barrett, M. (1991) *The Politics of Truth: From Marx to Foucault*. Cambridge: Polity Press.

Barthes, R. (1973) *Mythologies*. Translated by A. Lavers. London: Paladin.

Barthes, R. (1977) *Image–Music–Text*. Edited and translated by S. Heath. London: Fontana.

Barthes, R. (1982) *Camera Lucida: Reflections on Photography*. Translated by R. Howard. London: Jonathan Cape.

Battersby, C. (1994) *Gender and Genius: Towards a Feminist Aesthetics*. London: Women's Press.

Baudrillard, J. (1988) *Selected Writings*. Edited by M. Poster. Cambridge: Polity Press.

Baxandall, M. (1972) *Painting and Experience in Fifteenth Century Italy: A Primer in the Social History of Pictorial Style*. Oxford: Oxford University Press.

Becker, H.S. (1982) *Art Worlds*. Berkeley: University of California Press.

Bedaux, J.B. (1986) 'The reality of symbols', *Semiolus* 16: 5–28.

Bennett, T. (1995) *The Birth of the Museum: History, Theory, Politics*. London: Routledge.

Berger, J. (1972) *Ways of Seeing*. London: British Broadcasting Association and Penguin.

Bird, J. et al. (eds) (1996) *The BLOCK Reader in Visual Culture*. London: Routledge.

Bolton, R. (1989) 'In the American West: Richard Avedon Incorporated', in R. Bolton (ed.), *The Contest of Meaning: Critical Histories of Photography*. London: MIT Press, pp. 261–82.

Bordo, S. (1993) *Unbearable Weight: Feminism, Western Culture, and the Body*. Berkeley: California University Press.

Bourdieu, P. (1984) *Distinction: A Social Critique of the Judgement of Taste*. Translated by R. Nice. London: Routledge and Kegan Paul.

Bourdieu, P. and Darbel, A. with Schnapper, D. (1991) *The Love of Art: European Art Museums and Their Public*. Cambridge: Polity Press.

Bowie, M. (1991) *Lacan*. London: Fontana.

Brennan, T. and Jay, M. (eds) (1996) *Vision in Context: Historical and Contemporary Perspectives on Sight*. London: Routledge.

Bronfen, E. (1992) 'Castration complex', in E. Wright (ed.), *Feminism and Psychoanalysis: A Critical Dictionary*. Oxford: Basil Blackwell, pp. 41–5.

Bryson, N. (1988) 'The gaze in the expanded field', in H. Foster (ed.), *Vision and Visuality*. Seattle: Bay Press, pp. 87–108.

Bryson, N. (1991) 'Semiology and visual interpretation', in N. Bryson, M.A. Holly and K. Moxey (eds), *Visual Theory: Painting and Interpretation*. Cambridge: Polity Press, pp. 61–73.

Bryson, N., Holly, M.A. and Moxey, K. (1994) 'Introduction', in N. Bryson, M.A. Holly and K. Moxey (eds), *Visual Culture: Images and Intepretations*. London: Wesleyan University Press of New England, pp. xv–xxix.

Buckingham, D. (1987) *Public Secrets: EastEnders and Its Audience*. London: British Film Institute.

Buckingham, D. (1991) 'What are words worth? Interpreting children's talk about television', *Cultural Studies* 5: 228–45.

Burgin, V. (1986) *The End of Art Theory: Criticism and Postmodernity*. Basingstoke: Macmillan.

Burgin, V. (1992) 'Fantasy', in E. Wright (ed.), *Feminism and Psychoanalysis: A Critical Dictionary*. Oxford: Basil Blackwell, pp. 84–8.

Butler, J. (1990) *Gender Trouble: Feminism and the Subversion of Identity*. London: Routledge.

Celant, G. (1996) 'A visual machine: art installation and its modern archetypes', in R. Greenberg, B.W. Ferguson and S. Nairne (eds), *Thinking About Exhibitions*. London: Routledge, pp. 371–86.

Cohan, S. and Hark, I.R. (eds) (1993) *Screening the Male: Exploring Masculinities in Hollywood Cinema*. London: Routledge.

Condee, N. (1995) 'Introduction', in N. Condee (ed.), *Soviet Hieroglyphics: Visual*

Culture in Late Twentieth-Century Russia. Bloomington and London: Indiana University Press and British Film Institute, pp. vii–xxiii.

Coombes, A. (1994) *Reinventing Africa: Museums, Material Culture and Popular Imagination in Late Victorian and Edwardian England.* London: Yale University Press.

Copjec, J. (1989) 'The orthopsychic subject: film theory and the reception of Lacan', *October* 49: 53–72.

Court, E. (1999) 'Africa on display: exhibiting art by Africans', in E. Barker (ed.), *Contemporary Cultures of Display.* London: Yale University Press in association with The Open University, pp. 147–73.

Cowie, E. (1990) 'Fantasia', in P. Adams and E. Cowie (eds), *The Woman in Question: m/f.* London: Verso, pp. 149–96.

Cowling, M. (1989) *The Artist as Anthropologist: The Representation of Type and Character in Victorian Art.* Cambridge: Cambridge University Press.

Crary, J. (1992) *Techniques of the Observer: Vision and Modernity in the Nineteenth Century.* London: MIT Press.

De Lauretis, T. (1994) *The Practice of Love: Lesbian Sexuality and Perverse Desire.* Bloomington: Indiana University Press.

De Lauretis, T. (1995) 'On the subject of fantasy', in L. Pietropaulo and A. Testaferri (eds), *Feminisms in the Cinema.* Bloomington: Indiana University Press, pp. 63–5.

Debord, G. (1983) *Society of the Spectacle.* Detroit: Black and Red.

Deutsche, R. (1991) 'Boys town', *Environment and Planning D: Society and Space* 9: 5–30.

Dey, I. (1993) *Qualitative Data Analysis: A User-Friendly Guide for Social Scientists.* London: Routledge.

Doane, M.A. (1982) 'Film and the masquerade: theorising the female spectator', *Screen* 3: 74–87.

Doane, M.A. (1987) *The Desire to Desire: The Woman's Film of the 1940s.* Bloomington: Indiana University Press.

Doane, M.A. (1991) *Femmes Fatales: Feminism, Film Theory, Psychoanalysis.* London: Routledge.

Doisneau, R. (1990) *Renault: In the Thirties.* Edited by M. Koetzle. London: Dirk Nishen.

Doisneau, R. (1991) *Robert Doisneau: Interview with Robert Doisneau by Sylvain Roumette.* London: Thames and Hudson.

Duncan, C. (1993) *The Aesthetics of Power: Essays in Critical Art History.* Cambridge: Cambridge University Press.

Duncan, C. (1995) *Civilising Rituals: Inside Public Art Museums.* London: Routledge.

Dyer, G. (1982) *Advertising as Communication.* London: Methuen.

Dyer, R. (1982) 'Don't look now: the male pin-up', *Screen* 23: 61–73.

Dyer, R. (1990) *Now You See It: Historical Studies on Lesbian and Gay Film.* London: Routledge.

Dyer, R. (1997) *White.* London: Routledge.

Eakins, R. and Loving, E. (1985) *Picture Sources UK.* London: MacDonald.

Edgerton, S.Y. (1975) *The Renaissance Rediscovery of Perspective.* New York: Harper and Row.

Edwards, E. (ed.) (1992) *Anthropology and Photography 1860–1920.* London: Yale University Press and the Royal Anthropological Institute.

Elkins, J. (1991) 'On the *Arnolfini Portrait* and the *Luca Madonna*: did Jan van Eyck have a perspectival system?' *Art Bulletin* LXXIII: 53–62.

Elkins, J. (1994) *The Poetics of Perspective*. Ithaca: Cornell University Press.

Ellis, J. (1992) *Visible Fictions: Cinema, Television, Video*. London: Routledge.

Evans, H. and M. (1996) *Picture Researcher's Handbook: An International Guide to Picture Sources and How to Use Them*, 6th edition. London: Routledge.

Evans, J. and Hall, S. (1999) *Visual Culture: The Reader*. London: Sage in association with The Open University.

Fanon, F. (1986) *Black Skin, White Masks*. New York: Grove Press.

Fernie, E. (1995) *Art History and Its Methods: A Critical Anthology*. London: Phaidon.

Fishman, W.J. (1988) *East End 1888*. London: Duckworth.

Fiske, J. (1994) 'Audiencing', in N.K. Denzin and Y.S. Lincoln (eds), *Handbook of Qualitative Methods*. London: Sage.

Foster, H. (1988a) 'Preface', in H. Foster (ed.), *Vision and Visuality*. Seattle: Bay Press, pp. ix–xiv.

Foster, H. (ed.) (1988b) *Vision and Visuality*. Seattle: Bay Press.

Foster, H. (1996) 'The archive without museums', *October* 77: 97–119.

Foucault, M. (1972) *The Archeology of Knowledge*. Translated by A.M. Sheridan Smith. London: Tavistock Publications.

Foucault, M. (1977) *Discipline and Punish: The Birth of the Prison*. Translated by A. Sheridan. London: Allen Lane.

Foucault, M. (1979) *The History of Sexuality, Volume I: An Introduction*. Translated by R. Hurley. London: Allen Lane.

Fyfe, G. and Law. J. (1988) 'Introduction: on the invisibility of the visible', in G. Fyfe and J. Law (eds), *Picturing Power: Visual Depiction and Social Relations*. London: Routledge, pp. 1–14.

Fyfe, G. and Ross, M. (1996) 'Decoding the visitor's gaze: rethinking museum visiting', in S. MacDonald and G. Fyfe (eds), *Theorizing Museums*. Oxford: Basil Blackwell, pp. 127–50.

Gage, J. (1993) *Colour and Culture: Practice and Meaning from Antiquity to Abstraction*. London: Thames and Hudson.

Gaines, J. (1988) 'White privilege and looking relations: race and gender in feminist film theory', *Screen* 29: 12–27.

Gilbert, R. (1995) *Living With Art*, 4th edition. London: McGraw Hill.

Gill, R. (1996) 'Discourse analysis: practical implementation', in J.T.E. Richardson (ed.), *Handbook of Qualitative Methods for Psychology and the Social Sciences*. Leicester: British Psychological Society, pp. 141–56.

Gilman, S. (1985) *Difference and Pathology: Stereotypes of Sexuality, Race and Madness*. Ithaca: Cornell University Press.

Gilman, S. (1990) '"I'm down on whores": race and gender in Victorian London', in D. Goldberg (ed.), *The Anatomy of Racism*. Minneapolis: Minnesota University Press, pp. 146–70.

Gilroy, P. (1987) *There Ain't No Black in the Union Jack: The Cultural Politics of Race and Nation*. London: Hutchinson.

Goldman, R. (1992) *Reading Ads Socially*. London: Routledge.

Graham-Brown, S. (1988) *Images of Women: The Portrayal of Women in Photography of the Middle East, 1860–1950*. London: Quartet.

Gray, A. (1992) *Video Playtime: The Gendering of a Leisure Technology*. London: Routledge.

Green, N. (1990) *The Spectacle of Nature: Landscape and Bourgeois Nature in Nineteenth-Century France*. Manchester: Manchester University Press.

Greenberg, R., Ferguson, B.W. and Nairne, S. (eds) (1996) *Thinking About Exhibitions*. London: Routledge.

Grunenberg, C. (1999) 'The modern art museum', in E. Barker (ed.), *Contemporary Cultures of Display*. London: Yale University Press in association with The Open University, pp. 26–49.

Hall, E. (1994) *The Arnolfini Betrothal*. Berkeley: California University Press.

Hall, S. (1980) 'Encoding/decoding', in Centre for Contemporary Cultural Studies Culture, *Media, Language: Working Papers in Cultural Studies*. London: Hutchinson, pp. 128–38.

Hall, S. (1996) 'Introduction: who needs identity?', in S. Hall and P. du Gay (eds), *Questions of Cultural Identity*. London: Sage, pp. 1–17.

Hall, S. (1997a) 'Introduction', in S. Hall (ed.), *Representation: Cultural Representations and Signifying Practices*. London: Sage, pp. 1–12.

Hall, S. (1997b) 'The work of representation', in S. Hall (ed.), *Representation: Cultural Representations and Signifying Practices*. London: Sage, pp. 13–74.

Hall, S. (1999) 'Introduction: looking and subjectivity', in J. Evans and S. Hall (eds), *Visual Culture. The Reader*. London: Sage, pp. 309–14.

Hamburger, J.F. (1997) *Nuns as Artists: The Visual Culture of a Medieval Convent*. Berkeley: California University Press.

Hamilton, P. (1997) 'Representing the social: France and Frenchness in post-war humanist photography', in S. Hall (ed.), *Representation: Cultural Representations and Signifying Practices*. London: Sage, pp. 75–150.

Haraway, D. (1989) *Primate Visions: Gender, Race, and Nature in the World of Modern Science*. London: Routledge.

Haraway, D. (1991) *Simians, Cyborgs, and Women: The Reinvention of Nature*. London: Free Association Books.

Harvey, D. (1989) *The Condition of Postmodernity*. Oxford: Basil Blackwell.

Hetherington, K. (1997) 'Museum topology and the will to connect', *Journal of Material Culture* 2: 199–218.

Heywood, I. and Sandywell, B. (1999) 'Introduction: explorations in the hermeneutics of vision', in I. Heywood and B. Sandywell (eds), *Interpreting Visual Culture: Explorations in the Hermeneutics of the Visual*. London: Routledge, pp. ix–xviii.

Hodge, R. and Kress, G. (1988) *Social Semiotics*. Cambridge: Polity Press.

Holly, M.A. (1996) *Past Looking: Historical Imagination and the Rhetoric of the Image*. Ithaca: Cornell University Press.

Hooper-Greenhill, E. (1992) *Museums and the Shaping of Knowledge*. London: Routledge.

Hooper-Greenhill, E. (1994) *Museums and Their Visitors*. London: Routledge.

Iginla, B. (1992) 'Black feminist critique of psychoanalysis', in E. Wright (ed.), *Feminism and Psychoanalysis: A Critical Dictionary*. Oxford: Basil Blackwell, pp. 31–33.

Irigaray, L. (1985) *This Sex Which is Not One*. Translated by C. Porter. Ithaca: Cornell University Press.

Iversen, M. (1986) 'Saussure v. Pierce: models for a semiotics of visual art', in A.L. Rees and F. Borzello (eds), *The New Art History*. London: Camden Press, pp. 82–94.

Jameson, F. (1984) 'Postmodernism, or the cultural logic of late capitalism', *New Left Review* 146: 53–92.

Jancovich, M. (1992) 'David Morley, The *Nationwide* studies', in M. Barker and A. Beezer (eds), *Reading into Cultural Studies*. London: Routledge, pp. 134–47.

Jay, M. (1993) *Downcast Eyes: The Denigration of Vision in Twentieth-Century French Thought*. Berkeley: California University Press.

Jenks, C. (1995) 'The centrality of the eye in Western culture', in C. Jenks (ed.), *Visual Culture*. London: Routledge, pp. 1–12.

Jones, G.S. (1976) *Outcast London: A Study in the Relationship between Classes in Victorian Society*. London: Peregrine Books.

Jones, G.S. (1989) 'The "cockney" and the nation, 1780–1988', in D. Feldman and G.S. Jones (eds), *Metropolis London: Histories and Representations since 1800*. London: Routledge, pp. 272–324.

Keating, P. (1976) 'Introduction', in P. Keating (ed.), *Into Unknown England 1866–1913: Selections from the Social Explorers*. London: Fontana, pp. 11–32.

Kendall, G. and Wickham, G. (1999) *Using Foucault's Methods*. London: Sage.

Kress, G. and van Leeuwen, T. (1996) *Reading Images: The Grammar of Visual Design*. London: Routledge.

Krippendorf, K. (1980) *Content Analysis: An Introduction to its Methodologies*. London: Sage.

Lacan, J. (1977) *The Four Fundamental Concepts of Psychoanalysis*. Translated by A. Sheridan. London: Hogarth Press.

Lalvani, S. (1996) *Photography, Vision and the Production of Modern Bodies*. Albany: SUNY Press.

Leiss, W., Kline, S. and Jhally, S. (1986) *Social Communication in Advertising: Persons, Products and Images of Well-Being*. London: Methuen.

Lidchi, H. (1997) 'The poetics and the politics of exhibiting other cultures', in S. Hall (ed.), *Representation: Cultural Representations and Signifying Practices*. London: Sage, pp. 151–222.

Lull, J. (1990) *Inside Family Viewing: Ethnographic Research on Television's Audiences*. London: Routledge.

Lutz, C.A. and Collins, J.L. (1993) *Reading National Geographic*. Chicago: University of Chicago Press.

Lyman, C.M. (1982) *The Vanishing Race and Other Illusions: Photographs of Indians by Edward S. Curtis*. Washington, DC: Smithsonian Institute.

Lyotard, J.-F. (1996) 'Les immatérieux', in R. Greenberg, B.W. Ferguson and S. Nairne (eds), *Thinking About Exhibitions*. London: Routledge, pp. 113–31.

Marling, K.A. (1994) *As Seen on TV: The Visual Culture of Everyday Life in the 1950s*. Cambridge, MA: Harvard University Press.

Mayne, J. (1993) *Cinema and Spectatorship*. London: Routledge.

Miles, M.B. and Hubermann A.M. (1994) *Qualitative Data Analysis: An Expanded Source Book*, 2nd edition. London: Sage.

Mirzoeff, N. (1998) 'What is visual culture?', in N. Mirzoeff (ed.), *The Visual Culture Reader*. London: Routledge, pp. 3–13.

Mirzoeff, N. (1999) *An Introduction to Visual Culture*. London: Routledge.

Mitchell, J. (1974) *Psychoanalysis and Feminism*. London: Allen Lane.

Mitchell, T. (1988) *Colonising Egypt*. Cambridge: Cambridge University Press.

Mitchell, W.J.T. (1994) *Picture Theory: Essays on Verbal and Visual Representation*. Chicago: Chicago University Press.

Mitchell, W.J.T. (1996) 'What do pictures *really* want?' *October* 77: 71–82.

Modleski, T. (1986) 'Feminism and the power of interpretation', in T. de Lauretis (ed.), *Feminist Studies/Critical Studies*. Basingstoke: Macmillan.

Modleski, T. (1988) *The Women Who Knew Too Much: Hitchcock and Feminist Theory*. London: Methuen.

Monaco, J. (2000) *How to Read a Film: Movies, Media, Multimedia*, 3rd edition. London: Oxford University Press.

Moores, S. (1993) *Interpreting Audiences: The Ethnography of Media Consumption*. London: Sage.

Morley, D. (1980) *The Nationwide Audience: Structure and Decoding*. London: British Film Institute.

Morley, D. (1986) *Family Television*. London: Routledge.

Morley, D. (1992) *Television, Audiences and Cultural Studies*. London: Routledge.

Morley, D. and Robins, K. (1995) *Spaces of Identity: Global Media, Electronic Landscapes and Cultural Boundaries*. London: Routledge.

Mulvey, L. (1989) *Visual and Other Pleasures*. London: Macmillan.

Myers, K. (1983) 'Understanding advertisers', in H. Davis and P. Walton (eds), *Language, Image, Media*. Oxford: Basil Blackwell, pp. 205–23.

Nead, L. (1988) *Myths of Sexuality: Representations of Women in Victorian Britain*. Oxford: Basil Blackwell.

Neale, S. (1983) 'Masculinity as spectacle', *Screen* 24.

Nochlin, L. (1989) *Women, Art and Power and Other Essays*. London: Thames and Hudson.

O'Doherty, B. (1996) 'The gallery as gesture', in R. Greenberg, B.W. Ferguson and S. Nairne (eds), *Thinking About Exhibitions*. London: Routledge, pp. 321–40.

O'Toole, M. (1994) *The Language of Displayed Art*. Leicester: Leicester University Press.

Okely, J. (1994) 'Thinking through fieldwork', in A. Bryman and A. Burgess (eds), *Analyzing Qualitative Data*. London: Routledge, pp. 18–34.

Panofsky, E. (1953) *Early Netherlandish Painting: Its Origin and Character, Volume I*. Cambridge, MA: Harvard University Press.

Panofsky, E. (1957) *Meaning in the Visual Arts*. New York: Doubleday Anchor.

Pollock, G. (1988) *Vision and Difference: Femininity, Feminism and the Histories of Art*. London: Routledge.

Pollock, G. (1992) 'Art', in E. Wright (ed.), *Feminism and Psychoanalysis: A Critical Dictionary*. Oxford: Basil Blackwell, pp. 9–16.

Pollock, G. (1994) '"With my own eyes": fetishism, the labouring body and the colour of its sex', *Art History* 17: 342–82.

Potter, J. (1996) 'Discourse analysis and constructionist approaches: theoretical background', in J.T.E. Richardson (ed.), *Handbook of Qualitative Methods for Psychology and the Social Sciences*. Leicester: British Psychological Society, pp. 125–40.

Potter, J. and Wetherell, M. (1987) *Discourse and Social Psychology*. London: Sage.

Potter, J. and Wetherell, M. (1994) 'Analyzing discourse', in A. Bryman and R.G. Burgess (eds), *Analyzing Qualitative Data*. London: Routledge, pp. 47–66.

Pratt, M.L. (1992) *Imperial Eyes: Travel Writing and Transculturation*. London: Routledge.

Preziosi, D. (1989) *Rethinking Art History: Meditations on a Coy Science*. London: Yale University Press.

Pryce, D. (1997) 'Surveyors and surveyed: photography out and about', in L. Wells (ed.), *Photography: A Critical Introduction*. London: Routledge, pp. 55–102.

Rajchman, J. (1988) 'Foucault's art of seeing', *October* 44: 89–117.

Ramamurthy, A. (1997) 'Constructions of illusion: photography and commodity culture', in L. Wells (ed.), *Photography: A Critical Introduction*. London: Routledge, pp. 151–98.

Reynolds, A. (1995) 'Visual stories', in L. Cooke and P. Wollen (eds), *Visual Display: Culture Beyond Appearances*. Seattle: Bay Press, pp. 82–108.

Riviere, J. (1986) 'Womanliness as masquerade', in V. Burgin, J. Donald and C. Kaplan (eds), *Formations of Fantasy*. London: Methuen, pp. 35–44.

Roberts, H.E. (ed.) (1998) *Encyclopedia of Comparative Iconography: Themes Depicted in Works of Art*. 2 vols. London: Fitzroy Dearborn.

Rogoff, I. (1998) 'Studying visual culture', in N. Mirzoeff (ed.), *The Visual Culture Reader*. London: Routledge, pp. 14–26.

Rorty, R. (1980) *Philosophy and the Mirror of Nature*. Oxford: Basil Blackwell.

Rose, G. (1997) 'Situating knowledges: positionality, reflexivities and other tactics', *Progress in Human Geography* 21: 305–20.

Rose, G. (2000) 'Practising photography: an archive, a study, some photographs and a researcher', *Journal of Historical Geography* 26.

Rose, J. (1986) *Sexuality in the Field of Vision*. London: Verso.

Seidel, L. (1993) *Jan van Eyck's Arnolfini Portrait: Stories of an Icon*. Cambridge: Cambridge University Press.

Sekula, A. (1986) 'Reading an archive: photography between labour and capital', in P. Holland, J. Spence and S. Watney (eds), *Photography/Politics: 2*. London: Comedia, pp. 153–61.

Sekula, A. (1989) 'The body and the archive', in R. Bolton (ed.), *The Contest of Meaning: Critical Histories of Photography*. London: MIT Press, pp. 342–88.

Sherman, D.J. and Rogoff, I. (1994) *Museum Culture: Histories, Discourses, Spectacles*. London: Routledge.

Shohat, E. and Stam, R. (1998) 'Narrativizing visual culture: towards a polycentric aesthetic', in N. Mirzoeff (ed.), *The Visual Culture Reader*. London: Routledge, pp. 27–49.

Silverman, K. (1988) *The Acoustic Mirror: The Female Voice in Psychoanalysis and Cinema*. Bloomington: Indiana University Press.

Silverman, K. (1992) *Male Subjectivity at the Margins*. London: Routledge.

Silverman, K. (1996) *The Threshold of the Visible World*. London: Routledge.

Silverstone, R., Hirsch, E. and Morley, D. (1991) 'Listening to a long coversation: an ethnographic approach to the study of information and communication technologies in the home', *Cultural Studies* 5: 204–27.

Slater, D. (1983) 'Marketing mass photography', in H. Davis and P. Walton (eds), *Language, Image, Media*. Oxford: Basil Blackwell, pp. 245–63.

Slater, D. (1995) 'Photography and modern vision: the spectacle of "natural magic"', in C. Jenks (ed.), *Visual Culture*. London: Routledge, pp. 218–37.

Slater, D. (1998) 'Analysing cultural objects: content analysis and semiotics', in C. Seale (ed.), *Researching Society and Culture*. London: Sage, pp. 233–44.

Smith, L. (1998) *The Politics of Focus: Women, Children and Nineteenth-Century Photography*. Manchester: Manchester University Press.

Stafford, B.M. (1984) *Voyage into Substance: Art, Science, Nature and the Illustrated Travel Account, 1760–1840*. Cambridge, MA: MIT Press.

Stafford, B.M. (1991) *Body Criticism: Imaging the Unseen in Enlightenment Art and Science*. London: MIT Press.

Stafford, B.M. (1996) *Good Looking: Essays on the Virtue of Images*. London: MIT Press.

Staniszewski, M.A. (1998) *The Power of Display: A History of Exhibition Installation at the Museum of Modern Art*. London: MIT Press.

Strauss, A. and Corbin, J. (1999) *Basics of Qualitative Research: Techniques and Procedures for Developing Grounded Theory*, 2nd edition. London: Sage.

Swan-Jones, L. (1999) *Art Information and the Internet: How to Find it, How to Use it*. London: Fitzroy Dearborn.

Tagg, J. (1988) *The Burden of Representation: Essays on Photographies and Histories*. London: Macmillan.

Taylor, J.C. (1957) *Learning to Look: A Handbook for the Visual Arts*. Chicago: Chicago University Press.

Thornham, S. (1997) *Passionate Detachments: An Introduction to Feminist Film Theory*. London: Arnold.

Tonkiss, F. (1998) 'Analysing discourse', in C. Seale (ed.), *Researching Society and Culture*. London: Sage, pp. 245–60.

Tufte, E.R. (1983) *The Visual Display of Quantitative Information*. Cheshire, CT: Graphics Press.

Turner, J. (ed.) (1996) *The Dictionary of Art*. 34 vols. London: Macmillan.

Urry, J. (1990) *The Tourist Gaze: Leisure and Travel in Contemporary Societies*. London: Sage.

van Straten, R. (1994) *An Introduction to Iconography*. Translated by P. de Man. Reading: Gordon and Breach.

Vergo, P. (ed.) (1989) *The New Museology*. London: Reaktion Books.

Virilio, P. (1994) *The Vision Machine*. London: British Film Institute.

Walker, J.A. and Chaplin, S. (1997) *Visual Culture: An Introduction*. Manchester: Manchester University Press.

Walkerdine, V. (1990) *Schoolgirl Fictions*. London: Verso.

Walkowitz, J. (1992) *City of Dreadful Delight: Narratives of Sexual Danger in Late-Victorian London*. London: Virago.

Waterfield, G. (1991) *Palaces of Art: Art Galleries in Britain 1790–1990*. London: Dulwich Picture Gallery.

Weber, R.P. (1990) *Basic Content Analysis*. London: Sage.

Wells, L. (1992) 'Judith Williamson, *Decoding Advertisements*' in M. Barker and A. Beezer (eds), *Reading into Cultural Studies*. London: Routledge, pp. 165–80.

Westerbeck, C. and Meyerowitz, J. (1994) *Bystander: A History of Street Photography*. London: Thames and Hudson.

White, P. (1995) 'Governing lesbian desire: *Nocturne*'s Oedipal fantasy', in L. Pietropaulo and A. Testaferri (eds), *Feminisms in the Cinema*. Bloomington: Indiana University Press, pp. 86–105.

Whitely, N. (1999) 'Readers of the lost art: visuality and particularity in art criticism', in I. Heywood and B. Sandywell (eds), *Interpreting Visual Culture: Explorations in the Hermeneutics of the Visual*. London: Routledge, pp. 99–122.

Williams, R. (1976) *Keywords: A Vocabulary of Culture and Society*. London: Croom Helm.

Williamson, J.E. (1978) *Decoding Advertisements: Ideology and Meaning in Advertising*. London: Marion Boyars.

Wollen, P. (1970) *Signs and Meaning in Cinema*. London: British Film Institute and Thames and Hudson.

Young, L. (1996) *Fear of the Dark: 'Race', Gender and Sexuality in the Cinema*. London: Routledge.

list of key terms

This index is designed to be used in conjunction with the **list of key terms** on pages 216–17.